Also by Martin Blumenson

Breakout and Pursuit

The Duel for France: 1944

Anzio: The Gamble That Failed

Kasserine Pass

Sicily: Whose Victory?

Salerno to Cassino

Bloody River: The Tragedy of the Rapido
Eisenhower ·

The Patton Paper: 1885–1940

The Patton Papers: 1940–1945

Masters of the Art of Command
(with James L. Stokesbury)

The Vildé Affair:
Beginnings of the French Resistance

Liberation
(with the editors of Time–Life Books)

Mark Clark

George Smith Patton, Jr. 1885–1945

PHOTOGRAPH BY MARGARET BOURKE-WHITE, © TIME INC.

NETHERLANDS

GERMANY

Elbe River

Arnhem

Rhine River

Weser River

Buchenwald

The Siegfried Line
(West Wall)

Liege

Remagen
Koblenz

Hammelburg

The Bulge
Dec. 16, 1944–
Jan. 16, 1945

Frankfurt

TO PILSEN

Bastogne

Worms
Mannheim
Heidelberg

Nurnberg

Arlon

Trier

Meuse

LUXEMBOURG

Luxembourg
Verdun

Metz

Moselle River

Saverne

Commercy

River

Nancy
Strasbourg

Muihouse

Belfort

AUSTRIA

SWITZERLAND

ITALY

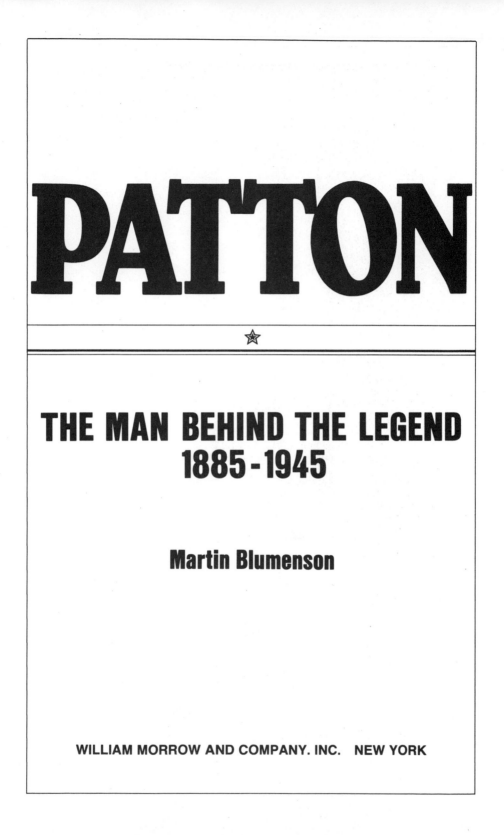

PATTON

☆

THE MAN BEHIND THE LEGEND
1885-1945

Martin Blumenson

WILLIAM MORROW AND COMPANY. INC.   NEW YORK

To Ruth Ellen

Library of Congress Cataloging-in-Publication Data

Blumenson, Martin.
Patton, the man behind the legend, 1885-1945.

Bibliography: p.
Includes index.
1. Patton, George S. (George Smith), 1885-1945.
2. Generals—United States—Biography.   3. United
States. Army—Biography.   I. Title.
E745.P293B553   1985   355'.0092'4 [B]   85-15301
ISBN 0-688-06082-X

A Thomas Congdon Book

Printed in the United States of America

First Edition

1 2 3 4 5 6 7 8 9 10

BOOK DESIGN BY RICHARD ORIOLO

CONTENTS

AUTHOR'S NOTE

I joined General George S. Patton, Jr.'s Third Army head-quarters in Luxembourg early in 1945. I never knew my commanding general, never talked with him; I gazed at him in wonder from afar. His exploits were already legendary.

He was an imposing figure. Whether riding in a jeep, standing at attention, or listening to a briefing, he dominated the scene. His polished exterior glistened. He was always on display, his energy coiled like a cat's. He bent his head to pray and also, in the ample courtyard of the old people's home, to let a French general, who was decorating him, kiss his cheeks. He inspired excitement and awe, as well as loyalty and trust.

Duty there was like nowhere else. The customary helmet with rank painted on the front was not good enough; an ordnance shop welded on a gold bar for me. The food was standard fare, but the cooks were required to show imagination. A slice of bologna would be skewered by a toothpick and served on a piece of toast. In the mess hall, the grand dining room of the Hotel Brasseur, elderly civilian waiters wearing tails served us in exquisite style. We had special treatment, we were made to realize, because we were special persons, superior to the troops in the other armies, and so we acted accordingly. Despite our travels through the mud of the springtime thaws, we were neat and clean, on the qui vive. I recall no griping. I was, and still am, proud to have been a member, no matter how insignificant, of the Patton team. Like thousands of men who still say with quiet satisfaction, "I rolled with Patton," I have glad recollections. His death was a personal loss, and the news of it brought me close to tears.

Since then, I have spent much of my life studying Patton, the soldier and the man. My first effort to describe him was in *Breakout and Pursuit,* published in 1961, which was devoted in large part to his battlefield exploits in Normandy. Additional endeavors followed. In the two volumes entitled *The Patton Papers,* appearing in 1972 and 1974, I tried to let him speak for himself in his own words. Continuing inquiry and reflection have led me to revise and, I hope, to clarify his portrait. This account is a new and different look at the officer and his record.

Many friends have helped me, and I express my gratitude and thanks to them, in particular to Ruth Ellen Patton Totten, Waverly Lowell, and my editor, Thomas Congdon; also to Theodore Antonelli, Allerton Cushman, Margaret Eley, Sieglinde Friedman, Blanche Gregory, Ann Lancer, John Lindon, Charles B. MacDonald, Millicent Neusner, George S. Patton, Ginger Pinchot, Christine Shirley, Michael Slackman, Richard Sommers, George Watson, Hannah Zeidlik, and my wife, who is always my collaborator.

I am, of course, solely responsible for errors.

M. B.

PREFACE

George S. Patton, Jr., gained fame as a battlefield leader. Ranking with the world's great army commanders, he has been called the greatest combat general of modern times and the most inspiring. Troop proficiency, discipline, and determination were his trademarks. No strategist or theorist, Patton had few equals in preparing, then directing men and units to fight in war.

His lifetime, from 1885 to 1945, coincided with enormous transformations in society, politics, and technology. The United States moved into the industrial age and emerged an international power, and the U.S. Army grew from a small and dispersed frontier force into a huge mechanized establishment. During this evolution, the transition from the horse and the saber to the tank, Patton played an important role.

In the course of his career, he mastered the changing conditions and circumstances of warfare in the twentieth century.

Serving in sequence as a cavalryman, the foremost American tank expert, and the leading exponent of armored action, he participated in three armed conflicts: the relatively primitive campaign in Mexico, the massive confrontation on the Western Front, and the challenging variety of operations on the European side of World War II. He occupied every grade from second lieutenant to full general and commanded units of every size from platoon to field army.

He was thoroughly professional. Even as a boy he showed an interest in military matters and a natural understanding of tactics and maneuver. His school papers displayed his admiration for Epaminondas' battle formations; Julius Caesar's system of intelligence, which gave him knowledge of enemy movements; and, above all, Alexander the Great, who, Patton wrote, "always aspired to perfection in everything." The Athenians failed in their expedition to Sicily (where Patton would later succeed) because, according to Patton, Nicias' procrastination "proved fatal." Young Patton appreciated the value of the cavalry charge as well as the use of concentrated forces. Most important, he recognized what he called "the undefinable difference which makes a good or a great general."

Seeking to emulate the masters of the art of war, Patton strove continually to discover that "undefinable difference" between the merely good and the sublime great so that he himself could bridge the gap. His constant reading in history and military affairs presented him with a thorough understanding of past warfare; he alluded with authority to the fighting skills of warriors as various as Cossacks, Poles, Turks, Arabs, Moors, and Moros. He gave rapt attention to the martial skills deemed necessary for each time and place.

But what set him apart from those who were similarly schooled and obsessed was his ability to transmit to his soldiers a driving will to win. It was the essence of his leadership.

This extra dimension derived from his unique character and personality. They were his own invention and creation and arose out of feelings of inadequacy. Shy and withdrawn by temperament, tending easily to tears of emotion, unsure of himself, sensitive to natural and artistic beauty, he scorned these characteristics. "A man of diffident manner," he once wrote, speaking of himself, "will never inspire confidence. A cold reserve cannot beget enthusiasm" in combat. Thus, "the leader," he continued, referring to himself, "must be an actor," have "the fixed determination to acquire the warrior soul," and "is unconvincing unless he lives his part."

Seeing himself to be unfit because he lacked what he considered to be the military virtues, he struggled with single-minded devotion to remake himself, to alter his inner nature into his image of the fighting man. He consciously shaped the talents he had inherited, modified his strengths and outlook, stifled the qualities he regarded as unworthy, cultivated the traits he believed to be desirable, and periodically tested himself to see whether he measured up to his standards.

No wonder he loved masquerade parties where he could dress as King Arthur or Ivanhoe and in an instant assume a new and faultless identity. No wonder his behavior was unpredictable and sometimes contradictory, flamboyant on one occasion, introspective on another. Hot-tempered, sentimental, profane, humble before God, he was an exhibitionist who played to the gallery, with his pistols and polished appearance his props. Through the exterior of this exaggerated man, who was larger than life to his children and colleagues, peeped a barely controlled hysteria. His extraordinary fluency with language, his saucy wit, his unexpected turns of phrase covered his troubled interior, where opposing inclinations battled for supremacy. Toward the end of his life, even he could barely distinguish his real self from the portrait he had deliberately faked.

Sallie Flint, widow of Colonel Harry Flint, a close friend of Patton's who was killed while leading his regiment in Normandy, said it best. "Few people outside of his family," she wrote, "knew the gentleness, the true courtesy, the almost puritanical uprightness and devotion to his religious convictions that were the real George Patton. . . . Underneath the seemingly rough and tough exterior was the thoughtful, sympathetic, almost boyish man. . . . The 'Blood and Guts' manner, the tough talking, was really a sort of whistling in the dark which he had from the very first contrived to serve as a kind of apparatus to build himself into the person he wanted to be as a soldier . . . strong, physically, mentally, morally (and he was all these) . . . unmoved by fear and suffering, the sight of death, blood, any horrible or vile thing. . . . This . . . was the motivation back of all the rough, profane, and at times vulgar manner and speech. . . . Underneath the rough-spoken, cold-blooded exterior he was a gentle and kindly person who had to make himself tough to do the job he had. He wasn't born that way."

An extraordinary individual both exuberant and meditative, Patton carried with him a vision of his own fulfillment, a Holy Grail he pursued with all his might. He worked hard, avoided relaxation, feared complacency. Every activity he chose to engage in contributed to his mastery of warfare. He had the good fortune to receive the opportunity to perform on the field of battle and, thereby, to achieve his ambition. His victories in World War II turned him into a folk hero, half man, half god, a mythic figure who, four decades after his death, dazzles still the public imagination.

The following interpretation seeks to penetrate the several mysteries attaching to George Patton—among others, the sources of his insecurity, the substance and shadow of his being, the tissue of his motivation, the influences operating on him, his method of exercising leadership, and the results of his genius in war.

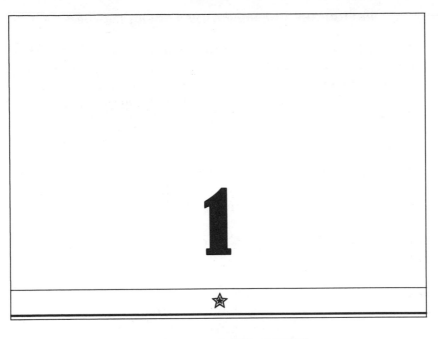

THE GHOSTS

Papa was from Virginia, a handsome slim young man of twenty-nine, with elegant manners and fastidious dress. Extremely proud of his lineage, he thought of himself as a Southern gentleman. He maintained an air of reserve and cultivated a pose of aloofness, although he was articulate and a good speaker. A lawyer, a member of the Democratic party, the elected district attorney of Los Angeles County, he aspired to a political or judicial career. He wore a floppy mustache, perhaps to cover his sensitive mouth.

Mama was born in southern California, the daughter of a pioneer settler named Wilson. In those parts the Wilson name meant something. She possessed the social graces and played the piano, a sign of the family's affluence. At twenty-four she was dignified, though capable of the unexpected jest, and sure and firm in her actions. She radiated strength and no nonsense.

Married a year, the young couple lived in the Wilson home, a modest yet spacious ranch house overlooking Lake Vineyard and called by that name. Above them towered the San Gabriel Mountains. Below them on a gently sloping plain could be seen in the distance the Episcopal Church of Our Savior, where they worshiped, and, farther away, the old Spanish mission.

In this setting, at Lake Vineyard, Mama and Papa had a son on November 11, 1885. They named him George Smith Patton, Jr., after his father and grandfather. A sickly infant whose nurse, Mary Scally, feared he would die in the first few months, he grew into a strong and healthy, exuberant child.

Soon after his birth, the Pattons moved to Los Angeles, twelve miles to the southwest, so that Papa could be closer to his work. Two years later, they had a daughter, whom they christened Anne and who came to be known as Nita or Anita. Although they lived in town, they spent much time at Lake Vineyard, and Georgie and Nita had the impression of growing up there in the country.

The Patton children adored Papa. He was with them, it seemed, all the time. He took them fishing and sailing, taught them how to ride a horse and to shoot a rifle. They liked to play soldier, and Nita "was a major while I claimed to be a private which I thought was superior." Every morning Papa saluted them "and asked how the private and the major were." Later Georgie called himself under his breath "Georgie S. Patton, Jr., Lieutenant General," and Papa made him a wooden sword and showed him how to build a fort. The bond between Papa and his towheaded son was unusually strong and close. When Georgie said goodnight to his parents, he showered Papa with kisses, was more restrained with Mama. He recognized his father's distaste for the exertions of outdoor life and loved him more because of his efforts for Georgie's sake. Georgie always needed to be active and to exercise vigorously.

In the evenings, he and Nita spent hours in Papa's lap or by his side, listening as he read aloud to them. This too was mainly for Georgie's benefit. For although he was bright and intelligent and bursting with energy, he was unable to read and to write. To him, the letters on the printed page appeared upside down or reversed.

Half a century later, physicians and educators recognized this sort of abnormality and gave it the name "dyslexia"; still later they identified a similar neurological-chemical condition they called "attention deficit disorder." Symptoms of both include feelings of inadequacy, a frustration with books and studies, a limited span of concentration, an impairment of the learning process, and the need to compensate for the deficiency by accomplishment in other areas.

Georgie had all of these. His parents hardly comprehended his strange affliction, but they were extremely patient with him and enveloped him in affection. They kept him out of school, where the taunts of classmates and their cruel laughter at apparently stupid mistakes of pronunciation and penmanship might have seared his soul. They hired tutors and coaches to help him overcome his disability. They let him express his high spirits however he could and encouraged him to vent his frustrations in physical activity.

These two facts, his dyslexic flaw, which gave him an enduring sense of insecurity, and the unbounded love of Mama and Papa, which provided him with self-assurance, were the basic elements of Patton's ambition and achievement. The clash of these tendencies shaped him. Without them, he would never have aspired with so much might, with so much determination to gain distinction, glory, and fame.

Several sets of ghosts haunted Patton throughout his lifetime and exerted a powerful influence on him. He felt their presence close to him and regarded them with wonder and awe. They set him a code of conduct and inspired him to live up to their deeds. What he feared above all was to disgrace himself in their eyes by falling short of their ideals.

The most important group consisted of his Patton forefathers. He idolized them as an exalted coterie of military men. Virginia gentlemen, they represented the aristocratic notion, feudal in origin, that birth alone qualified one for leadership. It was social station that determined who had the right and the duty to lead others. Persons of higher status had the innate responsibility to direct lesser men.

In a time of general familiarity with animal husbandry, people were quick to think in terms of breeding—genetic engineering—as the means to special qualities. A thoroughbred horse was superior in terms of power, beauty, form, and heart, and the same applied to human beings. Care was required to match partners, to preserve bloodlines, and to pass along desirable traits. Then came the indoctrination of chil-

Patton's birthplace, Old Lake Vineyard, twelve miles northeast of Los Angeles. This photo, taken in 1889, shows four-year-old Georgie, second from left, and his sister Anne (called Nita), on a nursemaid's lap.

dren to practice the accepted virtues and manners and to strive to fulfill the group's expectations.

Thus, families were sacred, for they produced and transmitted certain strengths. In Patton's case, he believed himself heir to his ancestors' ardor, energy, and endurance, together with their rage to lead. Yet he feared certain other kinships.

The first American forebear was a person of unknown antecedents. He was said to have been a smallish man who was hot-tempered and something of a dandy. He had departed Scotland in mysterious circumstances, whether to escape criminal prosecution, political arrest, or parental discipline. He assumed a new name in the new world, Robert Patton, and never revealed his original identity except to hint on occasion of a father who was a substantial landowner, a laird, even a noble. Perhaps because of this uncertain pedigree, Patton men of the following generations always made a point of marrying well.

Robert Patton marked his initial presence in the country by signing a deed of land in Fredericksburg, Virginia, in 1771. Twenty years later he was sufficiently well placed in society to wed Anne Gordon Mercer. She was the daughter of the highly esteemed Hugh Mercer. Born in Scotland in 1725 and educated as a physician at Aberdeen University, he fought during the Jacobite rebellion at Culloden. In 1747 he emigrated to America. A friend of George Washington, he was a member of Braddock's expedition and rose to the rank of brigadier general in the patriot forces during the war for independence. He was wounded in the battle of Princeton and perished as a hero. He personified the solemn words of his family credo: "Then, Mercer, bear ye bravely, do no shame, Nor blot the scutcheon of our ancient name." On Hugh Mercer, Patton fastened his boyish admiration. He heeded seriously the Mercer abjuration.

Robert Patton and his wife had seven children. Among them was John Mercer Patton, born in 1797, a lawyer and a governor of Virginia. His wife was Margaret French Williams, descended from the Slaughter family of Culpeper County.

Their progeny numbered twelve, and their seven sons, among them Patton's grandfather, fought with distinction as Confederate officers in the Civil War. Three Patton brothers were graduates of the Virginia Military Institute and students of Thomas J. Jackson, later known as "Stonewall."

John Mercer Patton, Jr., VMI 1846, commanded the 21st

Virginia Infantry until sickness forced his return to civilian life. Isaac William Patton, who had moved to New Orleans, headed the 21st and 22d Louisiana regiments, fighting in the Mississippi Valley. Waller Tazewell Patton, VMI 1855, led the 7th Virginia and was killed at Gettysburg in 1863 during Pickett's charge. James French Patton and Hugh Mercer Patton were teenaged lieutenants wounded at Second Manasses and Cold Harbor. The youngest, William Macfarland Patton, marched with the VMI cadets to the glorious battle at Newmarket. All these brothers, his great-uncles, inspired Patton, but the seventh, his grandfather, was a more direct source of pride.

George Smith Patton, the first to bear this name, was born in 1833 and graduated from VMI in 1852. He read and practiced law in Charleston, now the capital of West Virginia. In 1859, after John Brown's insurrection, Patton organized a volunteer military formation called, after the river in town, the Kanawha Rifles. When Virginia seceded from the Union and prepared for war, the unit, under Patton's command, entered Confederate service as Company H, 22d Virginia Infantry.

An exemplary commander, Patton rose in rank, was wounded and captured in the Shenandoah Valley, then exchanged, and eventually led the 22d Regiment as a colonel. Serving under Lieutenant General Jubal Early in the raid on Washington, D.C., he was with the advance guard that entered the outskirts of the city near the present Soldiers' Home. At the third battle of Winchester, sometimes called the battle of Opequon or Cedar Creek, in September 1864, Patton was mortally wounded at the head of his troops.

In addition to these warriors, many cousins held senior rank in the war—at least three Slaughters, one Mercer, and three Pattons. The bloodlines were running pure, rich, and true.

All these progenitors, and particularly his grandfather, Patton regarded romantically as aristocratic fighters who had displayed bravery, the highest manly quality. They had been virtuous and honorable, as well as dashing and handsome. They became beacons for the future general. His kinsmen, he believed literally, watched from above, and, jealous of their tradition and ready to praise or condemn, judged the actions of their descendants. Patton resolved to measure up, to earn their approval. He would, he promised himself, be like them—that is, if he could overcome his weaknesses. To this end he pledged a constant effort, and he tested himself often

George Smith Patton with his namesake in 1895. Right,
Georgie and Nita with Ruth Wilson Patton, their beloved
Mama.

★

to see whether he was worthy of his Patton heritage. "Men of my blood," he wrote, ". . . have ever inspired me." What terrified him: "Should I falter, I will have disgraced my blood."

His chance of being a Virginian by birth vanished when his widowed grandmother, Susan Thornton Glassell Patton, left the devastated postwar South. With her four small children, she traveled to California and joined her brother Andrew Glassell, a prominent attorney in Los Angeles. She taught school and lived in straitened means until 1871, when she married her former husband's first cousin, George Hugh Smith, whose mother was a sister of Margaret French Williams Patton.

Smith had graduated from VMI in 1853 and had commanded the 62d Virginia Infantry as a colonel during the war. Unwilling to take the oath of allegiance to the Union required of Confederate officers, Smith went to Mexico to grow cotton before coming to California. He joined the law firm of Glassell and Chapman and eventually became a partner.

In honor of his stepfather, Susan's son George William Patton, born in 1856, changed his name to George Smith Patton, the second to be so called. He was to be Patton's Papa. He remembered with distaste the destitution of the South during the war and the financial difficulties of his early existence in California, and according to his son, "he developed an intense aversion to poverty." He achieved public mention at age thirteen, when a local newspaper reported him to be a high school debater of "great force and polish." He returned to Virginia to attend VMI, and in his senior year, as the top-ranked first captain, led the cadets to Philadelphia, where they paraded at the national centennial celebration, the first Southern military formation to appear in the north after the war. In 1878, after graduation and a year as an instructor of French, he came back to Los Angeles.

Twenty-two years old, the young man read law with Glassell, Smith, and Chapman, eventually becoming a member of the firm. In 1884 he was elected district attorney of Los Angeles County. With his future thus apparently assured, he married Ruth Wilson, the younger of two sisters who were both smitten with him.

Their son Georgie revered the ancestors on his father's side but paid little attention to the Wilsons. He denied his debt to Benjamin Davis Wilson, his maternal grandfather, who seemed to have transmitted to him his physical hardihood, mental perseverance, personal charisma, and driving willpower. Patton never wished to hear of his resemblance to Wilson, for Wilson was a self-made man and quite unlike the Patton aristocrats. Yet he was a ghost too, and Patton feared him.

Wilson's father, David Wilson, a major in the American war for independence, became a pioneer in Tennessee. He was a member of the territorial assembly and speaker of the house before his death in 1826. B. D. Wilson, who was then fifteen years old, set out for the West. In what later became Mississippi and again in New Mexico, he worked as a trapper, Indian trader, and storekeeper for fifteen years, then moved on to southern California. In 1841, at age thirty, he arrived at the San Gabriel mission. He became a member of the gentry when for $1,000 he purchased 2,200 acres near present-day San Bernardino and Riverside. He stocked his property for the profitable hide and tallow trade.

In that sparsely populated country, most settlers were Catholic Mexicans of Spanish descent, and in 1844 he married Ramona, the sixteen-year-old daughter of Bernardo Yorba, whose vast ranch, later most of Orange County, adjoined his own. Their union produced two children, Maria de Jesus Wilson, Sue to Americans, and John Bernardo Wilson, Juan to the Spanish.

A man of respectability and standing, Wilson inevitably became involved in the politics and minor rebellions of the area, essentially as a pacifier. After subduing and punishing marauding Mojave Indians, he was appointed *alcalde*, or justice of the peace, of the San Bernardino district. He held court at his home, was known for his justice and generosity, and was affectionately addressed as Don Benito. During the war with Mexico, Wilson found himself in the middle of the tangled disputes of John C. Frémont, Stephen Kearny, and Robert P. Stockton. From the latter he accepted a temporary commission as an Army captain and helped conciliate the population during the transition to American jurisdiction.

Selling his stock, Wilson moved to the center of Los Angeles. At the corner of Alameda and Macy streets, the present site of the Union Station, he bought ten acres of vineyard and orchard, made wine, and sold citrus fruit. He opened a general merchandising business, acquired a hotel and bar, purchased lots at auction, and became prosperous.

When his wife Ramona died in 1849 at the age of twenty-one, leaving two small children, Wilson hired a housekeeper,

Margaret Hereford. She and her husband and their young son Edward, known as Eddy, had traveled from St. Louis to California in search of health and fortune. Both eluded Hereford, who died in 1852. In the following year Wilson married his widow. They had two surviving children, Anne, born in 1858, and Ruth, born in 1861. It was Ruth who would become the mother of George S. Patton, Jr.

B. D. Wilson was elected county clerk, city councilman, and first mayor of Los Angeles in swift succession. On more than 4,000 acres of ground he owned—now the University of California, Los Angeles campus—he raised cattle and sheep. With a partner, he bought 2,400 acres in Wilmington. In 1854 he acquired the Hugo Reid ranch of 128 acres at Lake Vineyard, now Lacy Park in San Marino, then gradually extended his holdings to the boundaries of the original Spanish mission, about 14,000 acres of a vast plain spreading from the San Gabriel Mountains foothills, including what is now Pasadena, South Pasadena, San Marino, Alhambra, and San Gabriel. Two years later he sold his Los Angeles property and made his home at Lake Vineyard.

During the Civil War, despite his Southern sympathies, he and his partner donated land in Wilmington to the federal government for a military post. He participated in the short-lived oil boom in 1865, but his principal work was at Lake Vineyard, where he had 2,000 acres of orchard and grapes in cultivation. By 1871, he was the biggest manufacturer of wine and brandy in the state. In quest of timber for his casks, he cut a mule trail up what is now called Mount Wilson, where the observatory stands.

By this time Wilson was relying heavily on his son-in-law, James de Barth Shorb, born of a prominent Catholic family in Emmitsburg, Maryland. After marrying Sue Wilson in 1867, Shorb increasingly managed the winery, the land sales, and a growing system of piped irrigation works.

When B. D. Wilson died in 1878—leaving a considerable reputation as one of the respected Yankee dons of southern California and having helped transform Los Angeles from a village to a small city about to explode into a metropolis— Shorb took over the Wilson enterprise. He was soon worth $2,000,000. He and Sue built a large Victorian mansion for themselves and their nine surviving children. They lived in extravagant and ostentatious fashion, with a private railroad car luxuriously fitted for their travels. Unfortunately, droughts and freezing weather killed fruits, a disease temporarily destroyed vineyards, and increasing competition from other winemakers and citrus growers cut into profits. At his death in 1896, Shorb was heavily in debt. The winery and his property of about 500 acres were mortgaged to the Farmers and Merchants Bank of Los Angeles.

Shorb's brother-in-law, Papa Patton, nobly came to the rescue. Putting aside his law practice, abandoning his hopes for a career in politics, he, together with his wife Ruth, their son Georgie, who was then eleven years old, and their daughter Nita, moved from Los Angeles to Lake Vineyard.

Papa assumed two separate functions formerly carried out by Shorb. He administered the Wilson interests, sold lots, and carefully disbursed funds to the three Wilson sisters—Sue, Anne, and his wife Ruth—as well as to Mrs. Wilson until she died toward the end of the century. He built roads, water works, and trolley lines, and provided utilities to Pasadena and San Gabriel, sometimes in association with Henry E. Huntington, nephew and heir of Collis P. Huntington, the railroad magnate. He maintained the family in an affluence well suited to their image of respectability. In 1913, he became the first mayor of San Marino, an exclusive residential community for well-off Christian Caucasians.

In addition, Papa was manager of the San Gabriel Winery, successor, according to the business letterhead, of B. D. Wilson Company and J. de Barth Shorb. Trying to pay off the debt, Papa kept the winery producing. His employer was the Farmers and Merchants Bank of Los Angeles, founded by Isaias W. Hellman, a friend of B. D. Wilson's and a model of integrity and financial wizardry, and controlled by the Hellman family. Though conscientious and devoted, Papa failed to save the Shorb estate. The mortgage was foreclosed in 1899, and the bank obtained the property by sheriff's sale. Papa continued as manager of the winery until 1903, when the bank deeded the land to Henry Huntington, who dismantled the winery, demolished the Shorb house, and began to build the library, museum, and gardens that stand there today. Papa became general manager of the Huntington Land and Improvement Company.

Did Papa's experience with the Hellmans—Hebrews, as they were called in those days—reinforce his inherent snobbery? If so, was this the seed of a similar sentiment in his son? What would have been unthinkable to Wilson—who had married first a Catholic, then a Protestant, and who had watched with sympathy as the Hellmans and others established the first synagogue in Los Angeles—had become fashionable in a later time. The rough and egalitarian society of southern California, which had offered immense opportunities to newcomers with acumen, energy, and luck, had turned into a stratified structure in which the advantages of wealth produced certain other distinctions.

A child of the South, a world destroyed, Papa Patton had as his foremost aim the recovery of social position, which required the acquisition of money.

His son cherished him because he was a Patton, a descendant of the handsome and aristocratic Virginians who were members of the professions of law, the ministry, and the military. When Papa assumed the management of the Wilson and Shorb affairs, he became heavily immersed in business. Traveling to San Francisco almost every month, he had less time to spend with his children and was frequently absent from home. For all this, his son blamed the Shorbs.

The Shorb style of living contrasted with the more sober Patton ways, and Georgie always felt that Shorb had mismanaged the Wilson estate, perhaps had diverted to his own pockets money rightfully belonging to the Pattons. Shorb had left his wife Sue and their children virtually destitute, an unpardonable lapse. By his death Shorb had compelled Papa to give up his lofty practice of law and politics for the lesser world of business and profits.

Another subtle prejudice, probably emanating from his father, perhaps also from Grandmother Wilson, warped his view of the Shorbs, who were Catholic and had too many children. Sue Wilson Shorb was, in addition, half Mexican. Her brother John's alcoholism and suicide made evident the weakness in the Wilson heritage. Even Georgie's maternal grandmother suffered in his eyes, for her son Eddy drank heavily and never amounted to much. To what extent was Georgie's own mother blemished?

The frontiersman who had become the Honorable B. D. Wilson had been less than careful and had soiled his heritage, Patton believed. What he overlooked was Wilson's relentless drive tempered by character, a force of will that descended to Patton.

THE GHOSTS

*   *   *

Among the ghosts influencing young George were the military greats of history and literature, a panoply of heroes he learned about from Papa's reading aloud. The books were carefully chosen. Sir Walter Scott was a favorite, and his epics of Scottish life and lore, the clans, the tartans, the bagpipes, the chivalry, reinforced the boy's sense of heritage. Homer's *Iliad* and *Odyssey* led young Patton to perceive human struggles against the implacable destiny imposed by the gods, men who worked out their fates in heroic or mean fashion and received their just and deserved rewards. Xenophon's thrilling adventure of the Ten Thousand and their leader Clearchus provided a wish for imitation. Shakespeare, particularly in the tragedies, produced insights into human conflict. The Old Testament brought visions of wrath and righteousness. Kipling was fun.

The stories had a strong impact. They induced in him a strain of mysticism, a sense of déjà vu, an acceptance of telepathy, and a belief in reincarnation, the feeling that he had lived before in other historical periods, always as a soldier—a Greek hoplite, a Roman legionnaire, a cavalryman with Belisarius, a highlander with the House of Stuart, a trooper with Napoleon and Murat. But some of this descended as well from his Grandmother Patton, who knew instantly, before the news came, each time her husband was wounded in the Civil War. Some came from Papa, too, who studied the science of prediction and used the measurements of the Great Pyramid of Cheops for his prophecies. His son turned to history as a means of understanding the present and foretelling the future.

Like many persons who are denied the pleasure of reading early in life, like those who are brought up in an oral tradition, Patton memorized lengthy passages of poetry and prose, from the Bible, Kipling, Shakespeare. Throughout his lifetime he recited lines of passionate meaning to him.

At age eleven, when Patton, stocky and athletic, entered Stephen Cutter Clark's School for Boys in Pasadena, he began to study the lives of the great leaders of antiquity. They imbued in him the importance of character. Those who made moral choices succeeded, he learned, while those who sacrificed honor for expediency failed and merited disgrace.

Historical figures instructed him in the military profession. Scipio and Hannibal in North Africa showed a thorough grasp of soldiering, along with personal courage and the intuition to be at the critical place at the crucial moment. Caesar to his Tenth Legion in Gaul, Joan of Arc at Orleans, Napoleon to his Army of Italy provided personal and dynamic leadership, together with direct inspiration that touched every man under arms. Stonewall Jackson gave his followers the willingness to go beyond the limits of endurance and to accept risks and the prospect of disfigurement and death. These commanders who exhibited self-confidence, enthusiasm, and bravery became his models, and he absorbed their genius.

A third set of ghosts consisted of those wondrous individuals who peopled his early years and promoted admiration and imitation. Probably the most important was his step-grandfather George Hugh Smith, Civil War veteran, cultivated jurist and judge in the California court system, and military historian. A model of rectitude and, more important to Patton, a man who had been a close friend of his grandfather's, he sometimes reminisced about combat and campaigns and the conditions of armed strife.

Visiting Smith and the Pattons from time to time was Colonel John Singleton Mosby, the legendary Confederate cavalry leader known as the "Gray Ghost," who had become a lawyer for the Southern Pacific Railroad. His wartime recollections made a strong impression on the youngster. So did the words of another occasional guest, Captain Arthur Hutchinson, a retired British army officer who had fought in India and had married a Patton girl.

Others schooled the boy in flamboyance. The sons of B. D. Wilson's friend and business associate Phineas Banning were altogether exciting, particularly the time one of them arrived at Lake Vineyard driving a stagecoach at great speed, handling the six horses, and, with style and aplomb, pulling up in front of the house in a cloud of dust. All the Banning boys were more or less eccentric. One painted zebra stripes on his school headmaster's horse. Another once filled an empty house with fireworks, then set fire to the structure for a spectacular pyrotechnical display.

In a society of worldly position, where money and ease derived from good breeding and dedicated application, harmless eccentricity in speech or manner or temperament was permitted and even encouraged. So long as persons of this milieu maintained genealogical purity and family tradition, so long as they exhibited the proper virtues of loyalty, bravery, and self-discipline, they could affect any behavior they chose. That too was an inheritance of Patton's. His profanity, never obscene nor truly blasphemous, was an indulgence he cultivated in order to be different.

His family had participated in three lost romantic causes, the struggles in Scotland and the Confederate South, and on another level, his father's high-minded attempt to save the Shorb estate. Instead of producing rue and melancholy, these failures inculcated in Patton a drive to succeed the next time. The figures remained heroic despite the setbacks. When Papa talked of Robert E. Lee, Patton was thrilled and excited.

In a house of Irish and Mexican servants, surrounded by horses, dogs, and cats, warmed by the love of his parents, his younger sister Nita, his doting Aunt Nannie (Anne), Patton, he later said, was "the happiest boy in the world." He knew absolutely his place: at the top of respectable society, among those amply endowed with material and spiritual goods. Although his dyslexic flaw tormented him, he never doubted his station. His position was a fact of life, and it brought a sense of superiority and, its perversion, a tinge of snobbery and racism. Planted securely, Patton could strive for the stars. Whatever rewards he earned by excellence would be normal, even expected, never surprising, received with equanimity as his due.

Resolved at an early age to be a soldier-officer like his Virginia ancestors and a captain like the great warriors of antiquity, Patton was determined to realize his exalted, royal, kingly heritage. He pushed for recognition of his blood, which required praiseworthy performance, and to this end he developed a superb sense of theater and a flair for the dramatic. Believing that military traits must never be concealed but rather displayed, he worked on himself to appear the military leader he wished to be. All his life he honed his image, developing what he felt were the appropriate mannerisms—profanity in language, aristocratic bearing, the fierce scowl, ruthlessness. And in the process he killed much of his sensitivity and warmth and thereby turned a sweet-tempered and affectionate child into a seemingly hard-eyed and choleric adult.

THE WARRIOR MOLD

In the dozen years between 1897 and 1909, when Patton received his schooling, he established his basic characteristics, both personal and military. He also found a young lady who provided the strength, stability, and love he needed for his development.

Perhaps because Papa was too busy taking over the business affairs after Shorb's death to spend as much time with his son as he wished, perhaps because George was starting to cope with his dyslexia and beginning to read and write, his parents sent him to Stephen Clark's private academy, a one-story redwood building at the end of the Pasadena mule-car trolley line. He was two months short of his twelfth birthday, strong, willful, yet quiet like Mama, when he entered. With about twenty-five students from the best families in southern California, young Patton attended classes for six years. He gained a good high school education.

He struggled constantly to deal with his reading and writing disability, which hindered his learning. Acquiring knowledge demanded intense concentration and diligence. The deficiency led to occasional humiliation, for his schoolmates mocked his errors at the blackboard and his reading aloud. His parents' love, their warm support, sustained his spirits and fueled his determination to succeed. He had to win, not only for himself but also for them. Although in large part he overcame his handicap, his spelling was always individualistic. For example, he characterized the detested Athenian leader Cleon as "a great baster."

History was his best subject. He saw human affairs as turning on the personal qualities of the great figures. Men displayed patriotism and self-sacrifice to advance the course of progress, or weakness and expediency to betray the interests of nations. Themistocles, he wrote, "was eggotistical . . . unscrupiolos in attaining his ends," while Cimon's "ideals were greater . . . but he was not."

Individual struggles to attain high rank and its attendant power were hardly lost on Patton. All the great leaders, good and bad, he understood, climbed to their positions of eminence by demonstrating a mastery of the circumstances. In order to wield influence on public events, a man had to be prominent. Not only must he excel in his career, but his excellence had to be recognized. Proficiency and character led to advancement, but promotion alone was no guarantee of widespread approbation. One's superior qualifications had to be perceived and appreciated, even acclaimed. Only then could a leader perform on the stage of history.

This was Patton's ambition. His consuming desire was to prepare for a high place in his profession and to ensure that all who mattered were impressed with his qualities of leadership. More competent than most, he could then exercise his gifts in the service of his country. Glory and fame would inevitably follow.

His written school papers showed a concern with earning credit and obtaining recognition. They also demonstrated high spirits and a gift for an original turn of phrase, and perhaps unintended humor. "The common people of ancient times," he set down, "were very ignorant, as is the case with many in modern tim[e]s also."

During the summer vacations, George and his sister Nita, usually accompanied by Aunt Nannie, sometimes by their parents, spent several weeks on Santa Catalina Island, an hour and a half or so by steamboat from the San Pedro dock. Virtually pristine, the place had lovely beaches for swimming, a pier for boating, as well as mountains in the interior where wild goats roamed. Young Patton swam, sailed, fished for the huge sea bass, hunted goats, and enjoyed himself thoroughly.

The sons of B. D. Wilson's partner Phineas Banning were handling much of the shipping to and from the island when they purchased Catalina in 1892 and set about to turn it into a vacation resort for the well-to-do. Besides operating the ferry, they managed the Hotel Metropole in the village of Avalon. They sold some land and cottages to their friends, among them Papa Patton. There, in the middle of 1902, when George was not yet seventeen, he met and became acquainted with Beatrice Banning Ayer, who was two months younger than he. The fateful encounter occurred as the result of family connections.

B. D. Wilson had been associated in various ventures with Phineas Banning, and the friendship of the Wilsons, Pattons, and Bannings was strengthened by marriage. Hancock Banning, Phineas's youngest son, wed Anne Ophelia Smith, Papa Patton's half sister, the daughter of George Hugh Smith and the former Susan Thornton Glassell Patton.

The Bannings had originally settled in Delaware, and the town in California founded by Phineas a few miles inland from San Pedro he nostalgically named Wilmington. His brother, who had since moved to Minnesota, had three daughters. One of them, Ellen Barrows Banning, a beautiful and charming lady who had studied dramatics in London and appeared briefly on the stage in New York, was the second wife of Frederick Ayer, a wealthy Massachusetts industrialist much older than she.

Ayer was a self-made man who had started working in a store as a lad and amassed an enormous fortune in textiles, drugs, the soft drink sarsaparilla, printing, real estate, and banking. After the disastrous Chicago fire, he made available a large amount of cash to rebuild the city, asking in return for ownership of a downtown block. Ayer had four children from his deceased wife. With Ellen Banning Ayer, he had three, Beatrice, Katharine, and Frederick, Jr. They lived in a mansion on Commonwealth Avenue in Boston.

In 1902, when Ayer was eighty years old, he, his wife, and their children traveled to California and visited the Bannings.

☆

At the family preserve on Catalina Island, 1902: Patton is sitting on the grass at far right. The woman farthest to the left is Beatrice Banning Ayer, later Patton's wife; next to her is Patton's sister Nita. Seated at center are Beatrice's parents, Ellen and Frederick Ayer (white beard). *Courtesy of the Gen. Phineas Banning Residence Museum*

☆

They spent part of their time on Catalina. A highlight that summer was a play performed by a cast consisting of the Ayer, Banning, and Patton children, who called themselves the Eight Cousins. Beatrice Ayer was polished in the principal role. George Patton was overdramatic in his. After the performance and the presentation of flowers, there were music and dancing under Japanese lanterns on the veranda, and punch and cookies. The youngsters, well dressed and well behaved, were in high spirits. The genteel adults had a general feeling of satisfaction and well-being.

Although George was barely interested in girls, he found Beatrice attractive. Small, trim, and elegant, she had no doubt that he was someone special.

They were quite different. He was inclined to be abrupt and rough in his movements, while she had taken elocution lessons and was graceful. He had never been away from home, but she had traveled in Europe and attended schools in France and Switzerland and spoke fluent French. He was virtually tone-deaf, while she was an accomplished pianist who read music and also played by ear, in any key, any song she had heard. If he represented the Wild West, she was on her way to becoming a finished product of the Eastern Seaboard establishment.

She was young for her sixteen years and still played with dolls. At home in the salon, she was also an avid and excellent sailor. With a decided will of her own, she was fearless. Although her nearsightedness made it dangerous for her to ride to the hounds, she would later participate in hunts and show no apprehension at the jumps as she followed the color of her husband's bright scarlet jacket.

After the Ayers departed for home and George returned for what would be his last year at the Clark school, he and Beatrice exchanged several self-conscious letters. She sent him a tiepin for Christmas, and he wrote to thank her for "the very thing I most wanted" and report that "when I first wore it and looked into a glass to see if it was in straight, I involuntarily raised my hat." She was enchanted.

That fall, George, with the approval of his parents, decided definitely to become an Army officer. The best way to do this was to complete the four-year course at the Military Academy at West Point, New York. West Point was then a small institution with a student body of about 500 cadets. The President of the United States was entitled to have thirty young men of his choosing in residence at any given time, while each U.S. Senator, Congressman, and Territorial Delegate could name only one. Gaining admission by appointment from one of these officials was no easy matter.

Papa assumed charge of what would turn out to be a strenuous, extended, and suspenseful campaign to get his son into West Point. He fixed his eye firmly on Republican Senator Thomas R. Bard of California as the key figure. The cadet whom Bard had appointed to West Point was then in his third year and, of all the cadets from the state, the closest to graduation. If that cadet completed the course with his class, Bard would have the opportunity to send another cadet to the Academy in the summer of 1904. If George won Bard's nomination, he would have to wait a year between finishing the Clark school and entering the Military Academy. Papa considered the delay advantageous. George was young for his age, and another year would add to his maturity.

Several factors were favorable. Senator Bard had been associated with B. D. Wilson in several business ventures, notably the short-lived California oil boom, and would probably be sympathetic toward Wilson's grandson. Bard's son Tom had been George's schoolmate and might help boost his chances. Papa was well known in the area and belonged to the California Club of Los Angeles, an organization of substantial citizens. He could, he was certain, gain their support for George, mainly on two grounds: B. D. Wilson's standing in the community, and the Patton-Mercer martial blood.

The major obstacle was Papa's membership and activity in the Democratic party. He was involved in local politics and had run unsuccessfully for the state senate. Bard would be inclined to nominate the son of a Republican.

Papa asked a host of friends to endorse George, and they responded handsomely. Republicans and Democrats alike, all prominent men, bombarded the Senator by letter. They invited attention to George's family background and breeding, his health and military interests, and urged his selection for West Point.

While the Congress was in session, Bard's brother-in-law maintained the Senator's office at nearby Fort Hueneme, now the home of the Navy Seabees. He politely, and toward the end somewhat wearily, replied to every communication. He informed each petitioner of Bard's policy on appointments. Whenever the Senator could nominate another young man,

At top: **The cowboy image showing itself at an early age.**
Right: **Nineteen-year-old George with a 184-pound black sea bass he caught off Catalina.**

he intended first to hold an examination for applicants wishing to go, in order to determine who best merited selection. Although Patton's qualifications, especially his family inheritance, were impressive and compelled respect, he would have to compete with the others.

Knowing well George's educational deficiencies, particularly in spelling, and fearing his inability to win a fairly graded examination, Papa made additional plans. He inquired about entrance requirements at the University of Arizona, where a cousin was commandant of cadets, and at Princeton and Cornell, which also had Reserve Officer Training programs. He solicited the Morristown Preparatory School in New Jersey in case George needed an additional year of study before college.

But he had a trump card, the Virginia Military Institute, from which he and his father had graduated. Papa had many friends and relatives on the faculty and staff, and he was sure of gaining admission for his son. If George spent a year at VMI, he would be on his own and away from home and thus grow in maturity. If he survived Bard's test in the spring of 1904 and gained appointment to the Military Academy, his studies at VMI would have prepared him for the West Point curriculum. Best of all, as a regularly enrolled student attending a recognized college like VMI, George could enter West Point by certificate, without having to pass the Academy's entrance examination. If Bard chose someone else, however, George could continue at VMI and strive for one of the few Regular Army commissions offered to distinguished graduates.

This was finally Papa's decision. He enrolled George at his alma mater.

But he continued to put pressure on Bard, principally through his friend Judge Henry T. Lee, who had been a major in the Union forces and had seen Waller Tazewell Patton fall at Gettysburg. A prominent Republican well acquainted with Bard, Lee pressed for Patton's selection. When the Senator returned from Washington, D.C., to California, Lee arranged an interview with the Pattons, father and son. At that meeting, Papa had the distinct impression that Bard as good as promised to choose George. Whether the young man would have to return in the spring from the Virginia Military Institute to California in order to take Bard's competitive exam was left in the air.

In September 1903, Patton left California for the first time.

With his parents, Nita, and Aunt Nannie, he traveled to Virginia and visited relatives before reporting to VMI. Close to six feet tall, a handsome, slim young man who from time to time affected a stern visage, he worried about his military aptitude. To an uncle he confessed his fear "that I might be cowardly. He told me that no Patton could be a coward." George pondered the remark, then asked his father for elaboration. Papa explained. "While ages of gentility might make a man of my breeding reluctant to engage in a fist fight, the same breeding made him perfectly willing to face death from weapons with a smile." In other words, George, because of his blood, would never betray his heritage. Comforted, George wrote, "I think that this is true."

He hoped so, for throughout his lifetime he suffered qualms and doubts before important events and decisions. Shortness of breath, sweaty palms, sleeplessness, hay fever, hives, and intense nervousness assailed him. For he always questioned his ability to measure up to the standards he demanded of himself, the criteria set by his predecessors.

When he was fitted by the tailor for his uniform he was delighted to learn that he had exactly the same sizes as his father and grandfather before him, the height, shoulders, chest, and waist. The measurements were a good omen and gave him confidence.

A few days later, on a Sunday, wearing his military clothing in public for the first time, he accompanied Mama and a family friend to the Natural Bridge, a short distance from Lexington. They stopped at the hotel for ice cream. As he stepped from the carriage, self-conscious in his new clothes, he noticed several girls on the porch: "They became interested until I got out and with a look of disgust, one of them said, 'Oh, it's only a rat'"—a first-year student—"and then I first saw the necessity of chevrons."

When his parents and Nita departed, Aunt Nannie remained in Lexington, staying with friends, to help George combat homesickness. She was there most of the school year. Although her nephew needed little solace, she was a constant reminder of his family's interest in him.

At VMI, almost at once, his dyslexia caused trouble. He was unable to understand a posted handwritten notice on "the no hazing pledge," and as a consequence he made a minor mistake. Embarrassed, he wrote and told his father, who hoped "you managed some way to toss it off." Papa reminded him to

Virginia Military Institute, 1903. His VMI uniform had the same measurements as those of his father and grandfather before him.

★

practice reading all sorts of handwriting and to decipher each letter of every word until he comprehended the message. "When you start to read anything," Papa wrote, "keep at it until you work it out." Papa then repeated advice previously offered—to be polite to upperclassmen but to make friends among cadets of his class; to be a good soldier first, with weapon, brass, and clothing spotless, then to study hard.

George followed his father's instructions. So well did he function that at Christmastime he had received no demerits for appearance and behavior and stood well toward the top in his grades.

Actually, he was obeying his own inner convictions. He had started to learn his profession, and in that pursuit he was absolutely serious, thoroughly devoted, eager, even fanatical. Respecting, even liking, the discipline and the routine, he followed regulations to the letter. He performed his duties to perfection and with what might have seemed like exaggerated dedication. He was interested in every detail. Faultless in his grooming and clothing, erect in his posture and carriage, he was a model soldier.

He was well liked. In off-duty time, he engaged in horseplay with his classmates, but never broke the rules—or, if he did, as the commandant informed Papa, he had the good sense not to be caught. He was the first member of his class to be initiated into a secret fraternity, and as a result, he told Papa, "I am treated [by upperclassmen] almost as an equal. Theoretically, I do not approve of this"—for it was not according to the book, not in conformance with doctrine—"but practically I do."

Enchanted with VMI, Patton was never lonely there. In his eyes, most of the cadets were gentlemen. Many like himself were third-generation students. Some were the fourth of their families to attend the school. The military, it was clear, were members of an elite brotherhood, and young Patton belonged.

Beatrice invited Aunt Nannie and George to spend Thanksgiving with the Ayers in Boston, but they declined, perhaps because the Farmers and Merchants Bank had sold the winery and Papa was concerned with his finances and future. The correspondence between George and Beatrice continued on an occasional and intermittent basis. He had other things on his mind, specifically West Point.

His fervent wish to gain nomination to the Military Academy slightly marred his VMI experience. Almost constantly he reminded his father to prompt the Senator. "I *must* get that appointment."

Papa sought Judge Lee's help, Lee pressed the Senator, and Bard finally set the date for his competitive examination for February 1904, the test to be administered in Los Angeles by his brother-in-law. Because his son's absence for several weeks from his lessons might jeopardize his high standing if he failed Bard's exam and had to spend his four years at VMI, and possibly also because of the expense of a round trip to California, Papa asked whether George could take the examination in Senator Bard's office in Washington, D.C. Direct contact with the Senator was better than meeting with his brother-in-law. Or could George's class standing at VMI serve in lieu of the test?

Upon Bard's return to California early in 1904, Papa went to see him. Circumspectly, he suggested that Bard had implicitly promised to favor young George among the candidates. Bard rejected the notion. George would have to come to Los Angeles and sit with the other applicants. Yet he also assured Papa that the test was informal, the results were merely advisory. Bard took many other factors into consideration.

After receiving precise and detailed instructions in a letter from his father, George took the train to Los Angeles. During the long ride, he studied, particularly geography and spelling, memorizing the names of state and foreign capitals. Reunited with his family, he applied himself again to his books. In company with probably a dozen contemporaries, he submitted to the examination. Returning to VMI, he agonized over his performance.

Not long thereafter, three names, among them Patton's, appeared in the Los Angeles press. They had passed, and one of them would have Bard's nomination.

As Bard pondered, he received more letters from Papa's prominent friends urging George on him. Making up his mind, he telegraphed Papa of his decision to select George. Papa instantly wired his gratitude and told his son.

On the following morning, Papa leisurely wrote a long letter to George, telling of his emotions upon the success of what he called "a long and tiresome quest." Although George's parents regretted the separations from family imposed by military service, they both were happy for him. Papa added, "We are satisfied, because that which a man desires most strongly to do in this world . . . is what he is generally most fitted to do." After lunch at the California Club, where Papa opened champagne for the members in attendance, he added a rambling and somewhat blurred postscript. "You have in you good soldier blood. . . . Be honorable—brave—clean," he concluded, "and you will reap your merited reward."

The nomination elated George, not only the idea of going to West Point, but also the additional esteem generated among his classmates. But there was much to do, a note of thanks to Bard, letters and forms of all sorts to be filled out and signed for the Army. His relatives on the VMI staff helped him with the paperwork. And finally, when everything was properly executed and duly certified and in the mail, George wrote to his father of his pleasure. "Well I guess I have got it. And I am beastly glad and am sure you are. As for Mr. Bard I rank him and the pope on an equal plane of hollyness."

He and two other cadets took their West Point physical examinations at Fort McHenry in Baltimore to let "the government inspectors to examine this hundred and seventy pounds of meat" and to see whether "I am sufficiently sound to be killed." Somewhat belatedly he acknowledged his father's efforts in his behalf—he had the appointment "with the help of God and a vigerous use of your influence."

His year at VMI had been a great success. He had solidified his sense of Southern heritage and confirmed his Patton roots. He had matured. He had proved his competence to compete successfully with his peers, and this strengthened his self-confidence. Attention to duty and perseverance had paid off, for he had received no demerits for deportment and had excellent academic grades. Had he remained at VMI, he learned from an unofficial but no doubt impeccable source, he would have been promoted to be first cadet corporal, the first of his class to be selected in that grade during his second school year. In other words, he was judged to be the outstanding man in his class.

Coming east, his parents and sister took George to visit relatives and several Civil War battlefields before traveling to New York. Papa accompanied him to West Point in June 1904, and several cadets saluted Papa, who looked like an officer, thereby pleasing both Papa and his son.

George's initial impressions of West Point were in keeping with his sense of family worth. It was fitting for cadet gentlemen to have the tablecloths in the mess hall changed every day. Unfortunately, many of the cadets, unlike most at VMI, were hardly highborn, "just very respectable middle class fellows." Only Southerners were the true aristocrats.

He listened with his schoolmates to a Fourth of July oration on the meaning of the modern soldier and found himself in disagreement. "I belong to a different class," he wrote to Papa, "a class perhaps almost extinct or one which may have never existed, yet as far removed from these lazy, patriotic, or peace [-loving] soldiers as heaven is from hell. I know that my ambition is selfish and cold yet it . . . makes me exert myself to the utter most. . . . I may be a dreamer but I have a firm conviction I am not, and in any case I will do my best to attain what I consider—wrongly perhaps—my destiny." The majority of his peers were easygoing and had little desire to be out of the ordinary and superior, whereas he had his heart set on gaining the top, and toward that end he would strive with all his might.

Plebe camp was hardly the ordeal he had imagined—"they are almost too easy on us for our own good." He shared a tent with two gentlemen from families who were "strong on ancestors," like George's. At first, after his exhilarating experience at VMI, he relaxed and seemed to care very little how well he did. He berated himself and soon recovered his energy. He was again, he reported, "running with my usual eagerness." He had no time for fooling, and, in high spirits, applied himself to duty in a thoroughly serious manner. He enjoyed the respect for discipline and honor on the campus, but could not understand why most cadets had "a languid lacitude—or careless indifference or hazy uncertainty" about their profession and career. George, in contrast, was pressing hard to be an outstanding officer and man.

From the first he gave much thought to becoming a cadet corporal at the end of the school year. His studies gave him much concern. He worried constantly about his academic standing. Reciting and writing at the blackboard in class were very difficult. He felt worthless and stupid much of the time, for he had to work hard for everything, and he envied his classmates who made good grades with much less work. "I am either very lazy or very stupid or both for it is beastly hard for me to learn and as a natural result I hate to study." Yet he forced himself to his books with superhuman willpower and fought his tendency to "daudle" over his lessons, for he had to succeed.

1904: A West Point cadet at last, Patton receives a visit from his mother and sister.

☆

In moments of despair he felt that he had wasted his life and was getting nowhere, for he hated "so not to be first." He called himself a "characterless, lazy, stupid yet ambitious dreamer." He feared that he lacked "that small fraction of courage, will power, or what ever it is" to get ahead. Was he merely jealous of others? he asked. There was nothing worse to him than to be a failure.

Losing his confidence, he became uncertain whether he would be a cadet corporal and whether he would one day be a general. His letters home and to Beatrice were full of his "overpowering sense of my own worthlessness." He was "absolutely worthless."

"I have always thought that I was a military genius or at least that I . . . would be a great general." Increasingly he doubted. He had "ideals without strength of character enough to live up to them," that is, to study as long and as hard as he should. He was, he believed, smarter than many who outranked him. He was depressed because men who seemed not to care were above him even though he worked harder. He was, he confessed time and time again, stupid, and it was unfortunate to have such earnestness and tenacity and so much ambition and to be able to do so little except wish to do better. The feeling came, of course, from his dyslexia.

What sustained him and gave him courage, as always, was his parents, who understood his difficulties and knew that he was doing all he could. Papa wrote often to reassure him. Doing one's best, he said, whatever the results, was winning. George's exertions were praiseworthy. Aunt Nannie was at West Point much of the year, and Mama and Nita came to visit several times. All let him know that however West Point judged his performance, he would never lose their affection.

Increasingly Beatrice played an important role. Their correspondence became more frequent. He sent flowers for her coming-out party, and she chose to wear them instead of the other corsages she had received. He began to write her his innermost thoughts and fears, and she responded with perception and support.

In March 1905, when Theodore Roosevelt was inaugurated as President, the cadet corps marched in the parade in Washington. George thrilled to the applause and the approving shouts of the people lining the streets. He spent a wonderful evening with Beatrice, whose parents had come for the festivities. George and Beatrice danced and enjoyed each other's company. "If you had half as nice a time as I had . . . you must be dead with joy for actually I had the finest time in the world." To him, Bea, petite and brunette, was the prettiest girl he had ever seen. He admitted to Papa his long and severe crush on her.

Occasionally she came to West Point for a weekend visit, and he admired her courage in climbing a cliff with him, her ability to understand the West Point system, her willingness to learn about warfare and the military. He liked her presence and conversation as well as her hot temper. "You are one of the few people in the world," she wrote him, "who can be courteous without being idiotic."

It was foolish, he wrote, for "a general to wish for the first hours of a battle to return again [so] that [he] might profit by his experience and not make his initial errors a second time." Yet that was exactly what happened to him. At the end of the school year, his standing in French was so poor that he had to take an exam. If his score was high enough, he would be exempt from further tests in all subjects. Unfortunately, although he passed the French, his grade was too low, and he had to take a final in mathematics. This he failed. The authorities had remarked his cheerful willingness and his arduous efforts to succeed in his academic work. They could not help but admire his trim and precise military bearing and aptitude. They turned him back to repeat his first year.

Mama was then at West Point. George told her and then telegraphed the news to his father. Papa replied at once: "It is all right my boy and all for best God bless you." George and his mother took the train to California, where he spent the summer. His parents never reproached him. Their approval relieved him of guilt for his failure and stimulated him to further endeavor.

At Catalina, George studied much of the time and was coached by a tutor. He bought a notebook to record his thoughts, and his first entry was "Do your damdest always." Genius, he recorded, was the result of being careful with every detail. "Always do more," he admonished himself, "than is required of you."

He spent a few days with Beatrice and her family before returning to West Point. "To forestall the excuse that I did not invite you to any particular hop I hereby ask you to every dance and football game . . . from now until I graduate." She came as often as she could. "Don't argue with a man," she once told him. "If you can't convince him lick him. If you can't lick him keep still."

George went out for varsity football and played recklessly in practice—no doubt to test his courage. He soon hurt his arm and was unable to stay on the squad, so he took up the broadsword and tried out for the track team in the high hurdles. Mostly he had his eyes fixed on being appointed the first cadet corporal. Anything else would be less than perfect. He agonized, studied hard, maintained a respectable if not superior academic standing, and cultivated his military appearance by being exceedingly neat and sharp. Responding to his own adage, he accomplished not only what he had to but also all that he could. At the end of the school year, he passed his academic requirements and was appointed the second corporal for the following year. If he was somewhat disappointed to have second place, he was gratified to be so close to the top.

After a few weeks at home, he returned to West Point to break in the plebes at summer camp. He loved the authority he wielded. As second corporal he commanded a company, and when the first corporal was absent on guard duty, the whole battalion. Supremely happy in command, he felt powerful in his functions, gained confidence every minute, and was the embodiment of military efficiency and appearance. When he marched the men, the foolishness in ranks stopped, discipline reigned.

The plebes disliked him. Extremely severe, he reported more infractions of the regulations than anyone else. And at the end of camp, he was shocked and stunned when the tactical officers demoted him from second to sixth corporal. He had been, he told Beatrice, "too d— military." He had demanded too much.

Still devoting much effort to his studies, he passed his courses and was ranked in the middle of his class. There was, he wrote, "no one in my class who so hates to be last or who tries so hard to be first and utterly fails." He had plenty of ambition but seemed to lack the power to reach his goals. It was, he informed Papa, "exasperating to see a lot of fools who don't care beat you out when you work so hard." Part of his trouble, he admitted, was his lack of application and, perhaps referring guardedly to his dyslexia, "partly to other things."

He started to write poetry and sent sample verses to Beatrice, who corrected his spelling, a function formerly performed by Papa. He tried out for football, but injuries sustained in practice because he played too hard kept him off the team. He had more success in track and with the broadsword and impressed all with his horsemanship.

Ever concerned about courage, he tested his daring not only on the football field but elsewhere. At the small-arms firing range he committed a foolhardy act. While other members of his class fired their rifles, he was taking his turn in the pits— raising the targets for the shooting, crouching in a protective ditch during the rifle fire, then lowering the targets to read the scores. Wondering what it was like to be exposed to rifle fire and whether he was brave enough to face bullets without flinching, he suddenly stood erect and faced the firing line. The rounds sang about his head. Fortunately, miraculously, he was unhurt. He was gratified to know that he could be under fire without showing fear.

During a lecture on electricity, when the professor exhibited an induction coil with a twelve-inch spark, someone asked whether the shock would be lethal to human beings. The professor invited the questioner to submit to an experiment, but the student refused. After class, George asked whether he could be the guinea pig. Knowing that the professor would hardly administer a dangerous shock, he was curious about his reaction to the sensation. After some reluctance, the professor let the spark pass through George's arm. He steeled himself and felt little pain, although his arm was stiff for several days. He had again proved his courage to himself.

"I have always fancied my self [to be] a coward," he wrote Papa, but now he was not so sure.

Having been reduced from second to sixth corporal after plebe camp, he was happy in the spring of his sophomore year to be elevated to second corporal again. When the promotions for the following year were announced, he was named cadet sergeant major. That put him in line for one of the high positions in his senior year.

He was spending as much time as he could, during vacations, with Beatrice and her family. She came to West Point for football games and dances. Their friendship blossomed into love. She helped him overcome his habit of self-deprecation by accusing him, in a nice way, of fishing for compliments. She offered him the reassurance and reinforcement he needed. Although he would always have feelings of inadequacy, she diminished his sense of self-doubt.

When in the spring of 1908 he was named adjutant of the

Beatrice Ayer sent this photo of herself to Patton in 1918, when he was fighting in France.

corps of cadets, his joy was boundless. In that post, he would be the class leader. On the parade ground he would be at center stage when he read the orders of the day. He was known by the cadets as a "make," on the make for rank and honors, and the appointment crowned his ambitions and built his self-confidence, confirming what he had always hoped and believed: Success came from constant striving and from always doing his best. "Do you remember long ago," he wrote Beatrice, ". . . I said I would like to be adjutant but feared I never would be and you said I would."

He had always shown attention to discipline and recognition for rank, and one story, perhaps apocryphal, illustrated his firm beliefs. It was cadet custom to treat unpopular officers to "silence," that is, standing silently at attention until the officer left the room. Patton disapproved of the treatment, for rank, he believed, no matter who held it, required respect. Once when Patton was commanding the cadet battalion, he marched the men into the mess hall for lunch. They were standing at their tables and waiting for the command to take their seats when an officer whom they disliked entered. As the cadets started to stiffen to "silence," Patton abruptly marched them out.

In response to a question from Beatrice, he cited his reasons for deciding in favor of an Army career—the pull of heredity, the love of excitement, and the desire for reputation. "If you take away these three things, what is left in life?" What he wanted was not pleasure but rather success.

Feeling that his long friendship with Beatrice was building to a climax and required a statement of his intentions, George told Papa of his love for her and admitted his fear to propose marriage. She was far superior to him in every way, lived in a comfort quite unlike the rude rigors of Army life, and would probably be unhappy as an Army officer's wife. Furthermore, her father was old, well up in his eighties, and she was saying she wanted to stay at home as long as her parents were alive. (It was perhaps an excuse to explain why she was still unwed in her early twenties.)

Understanding that Beatrice was waiting until George was certain enough to propose, Papa encouraged him to go ahead.

He was still apprehensive. A certain Deborah at Catalina had made him forget Beatrice for a time. A Miss Dunn from the West Point area had fallen for him and engaged his attention. A beautiful girl at Vassar, Kate, attracted him immensely and, besides, possessed a fortune, which he figured he could use to buy his way to general officer rank. But in the end he preferred Bea over Kate, "ass that I am, when with the money"—Kate's—"I could be a general in no time." He did not know how rich the Ayers were, although he should have guessed from their homes and style of living.

During his Christmas vacation in 1908, while he was staying with the Ayers, he told Beatrice of his love for her and of his wish to marry her. But he prevented her from responding, perhaps because he was not altogether sure of his sentiments toward other young ladies, perhaps because he lacked courage, perhaps because the old feeling of inadequacy surfaced again. The implicit question was left unresolved.

In the spring of 1909, as graduation approached, he thought seriously of his profession, continued to write in his personal notebooks not only admonitions and reminders to himself and observations of particular meaning to him, but also military aphorisms, rules of warfare, perceptions of battles won and lost in the past. He came to an important conclusion: "In order for a man to become a great soldier . . . it is necessary for him to be so thoroughly conversant with all sorts of military possibilities that when ever an occasion arises he has at hand with out effort on his part a parallel. To attain this end . . . it is necessary . . . to read military history in its earliest and hence crudest form and to follow it down in natural sequence permitting his mind to grow with his subject until he can grasp with out effort the most abstruce question of the science of war because he is already permiated with all its elements."

Following this precept, he read widely in military history all his life, a practice that was fundamental for his later success. His knowledge of warfare in the past, his acquaintance with actual problems of battlefields distant in time, and his study of historical commanders enhanced his own leadership. Instantly aware of all the options involved in coming to a decision, he could choose the boldest course because he knew what the great ones had done.

Throughout his last year he agonized over choosing a branch of service. He rejected the artillery because the guns were too far from the scene of action. The infantry attracted him because of greater opportunities for rapid promotion. The cavalry drew him because of the horses and because the officers were said to be a better class of gentleman. Consulting with everyone, including the commandant of cadets, he weighed the advantages and disadvantages until he was almost physically ill as a result of his indecision. Finally he chose the cavalry. He would have a similar struggle with himself as he debated in World War I whether to go to the infantry or the tanks.

Graduating in June 1909 at twenty-four years of age, Patton had needed five years to complete the course. He had won his athletic letter by breaking the school record in the high hurdles. He was an accomplished swordsman and an expert sharpshooter with the rifle and pistol. By his fastidious attire and model bearing and behavior, as well as by his testing of himself at the firing range and elsewhere, he had established the beginnings of what would later be recognized as the Patton legend.

Apart from his family and Beatrice, he had no close friends. In order to reassure him about this isolation, which seemed to have some connection with his dyslexia, Papa had told him that a man who traveled alone went farther and faster than others who were encumbered by friendship.

He had enjoyed being the center of attention at West Point and particularly during his last year, when he had performed splendidly as adjutant. He loved to be the focus of large crowds watching him. He reveled in recognition and applause and always wanted more. Most important, he had largely mastered his reading disability, and in doing so had instilled in himself the need for sustained application and hard work, together with the driving will to overcome every obstacle hindering his march toward his goals. He understood that he had to work harder than others, but he was confident that devotion to duty paid off and led to victory.

It all made sense, he told Papa. "We are such superior people that we deserve to be successful." Triumph was their natural due.

He was eager to make his way to distinction and glory in the real world of the Army.

THE JUNIOR YEARS

During the first seven years of Patton's active service, he gave much thought to his objectives and how to attain them. The ultimate goal was, of course, fame. To reach that exalted aim, he had to learn his profession and gain proficiency in its practice. Both required concentrated study and conscientious application, which had become his habit. In the process he had to attract favorable attention to himself. Toward the latter end, he would use the influence of his family and social connections and cultivate the admiration of those who could help him advance in his career. These courses of action stamped him indelibly into the image of the soldier he wished to be.

After his West Point graduation, Patton spent a carefree summer in California—no academic worries, no more tutors. He had a very pleasant week with the Ayers on Boston's North Shore, dancing, going to parties, and sailing with Beatrice.

As the time approached for reporting to his duty station at

Fort Sheridan, Illinois, near Chicago, his normal nervousness appeared. He had hay fever and sneezed a great deal, but that was, he wrote to Aunt Nannie, "so old a story to me that it does not bother me much." He wanted badly to do well at Sheridan. "I suppose I shall," he said hopefully, "for I usually do."

His company—or, in the cavalry, troop—commander was Captain Francis C. Marshall, who had been a member of the West Point staff and was well aware of Patton's performance at the Academy. Very friendly, Marshall had Patton accompany him for several days to learn the routine. They inspected the mess hall and the kitchen, observed activities at the target range, did paperwork in the office, supervised the stable. Patton had "hay fever to beat hell," but a week later, he began to feel at ease. "My hay fever is much better."

What he looked at immediately was the quality of the officers on post. They were much like the cadets except for a fewer number of gentlemen among them. Some were awful, "not even decent," particularly former militia members who had entered the Regular Army after the war with Spain. The snobs, including Patton, referred to them as "the sin of 1898."

Of all his superiors, Patton judged Captain Marshall to be the best. He was certainly a gentleman, for, according to Patton, he and his wife were refined and, while living on their Army pay, had servants and gave regularly to charity. Marshall was an outstanding soldier, obviously on his way up. A brigadier general in World War I, he would be killed in an airplane accident shortly afterward. Lucky to have Marshall as his first commander, Patton tried hard to emulate him.

The enlisted men, although ignorant for the most part, worked well and quickly and when called "came at a run." He liked that kind of discipline. Whatever their lack of education and intelligence, if they knew their jobs and were clean and neat and obedient, they were good soldiers.

Much preferring outdoor activities to confinement in an office, more comfortable in field exercises where the troops played war and fought sham battles than in garrison life, Patton performed his duties energetically. They were neither onerous nor time-consuming. He had plenty of leisure. To keep himself occupied, he hunted to the hounds, laid out a polo field, coached a football team, and together with a colleague started a self-administered course of military reading and study. Always he strove for perfection in order to impress those over him. "Some day," he wrote with conviction or envy, he would have high rank and wage an important campaign and have "a big tent and a refrigerator and a stove and a trunk and a lot of men cussing me for having so much baggage." Marshall rated Patton as a young officer "of especial promise . . . the most enthusiastic soldier of my acquaintance and misses no chance to improve."

When he was in the stable one afternoon, he noticed a horse carelessly left untied in its stall. Locating the culprit at the other end of the building, Patton bawled him out, told him to run down, tie the horse, and run back, an excellent punishment designed to make the others laugh. The offender complied, but instead of running, he walked at a rapid gait. Patton lost his temper and shouted, "Run, damn you, run." He did so, and Patton reflected on the injury he had placed on the man by saying "damn you" instead of "damn it." When the soldier had run back after tying the horse, Patton called all the men together and in their presence begged pardon for his insult.

A public apology by an officer to an enlisted man was extraordinary, and the story made the rounds in the barracks. The Patton legend was taking root. Thirty-three years later in Sicily, he had to apologize in public again after slapping two soldiers who were hospitalized for combat exhaustion, a condition Patton considered to be cowardice; the act almost brought his career to an abject end in the middle of World War II.

Adding to the Patton legend was an incident that occurred while he was drilling his men. His horse bucked and the unexpected jolt sent his cap over his eyes; thus blinded, he was thrown immediately. He landed on his hand and knee and remounted at once. The horse bucked again and finally reared and fell, but Patton stayed on. As soon as he got his leg out from under the animal, he stood across it, so that when the horse rose to its feet, Patton was in the saddle. The horse threw its head back, struck Patton, and gashed his eyebrow. Probably dazed by the blow, Patton was unaware that he was bleeding until he saw the blood running down his sleeve. Not knowing what else to do, he kept his soldiers at drill for about twenty minutes more without so much as wiping his face. After dismissing the men, he went to troop headquarters and washed himself. As scheduled, he taught at the school for noncommissioned officers and attended the class for junior officers. Then he saw a doctor, who stitched and closed the cut.

Having been thrown from his horse embarrassed him, but his subsequent behavior, which showed composure, pleased him. The surgeon acknowledged with admiration Patton's nerve, but Patton ascribed his deportment to a lack of nerves. "And," he added, "a determination to be frigid." For "naturally I am not over bold and am inclined to show emotion—a most unmilitary trait." He had won out over his timidity, a basic fault, and had demonstrated strength of will.

To the enlisted men who had witnessed his exhibition, his continuation of duty while bleeding profusely from the face showed coolness and courage. The troops admired and had confidence in an officer who would lead despite being hurt. Soldiers' accounts of the event were no doubt embellished as they passed by word of mouth.

Patton was hardly satisfied. "Truly for so fierce a warrior, I have a damned mild expression." He started to practice before a mirror to change his countenance, to improve his fighting face. Although no transformation was immediately apparent, he eventually altered his youthful and buoyant appearance to glowering sullenness.

Leading an extensive social life, the normal due of a bachelor officer, he escorted a Miss Mishop, a Miss Fessenden, a Miss Page, and others to dances and parties and the theater, and was invited to dinners and formal balls at homes in the fashionable suburb of Highland Park. So many dates prompted remorse, guilt, and a sense of worthlessness. How could he have told Bea of his love for her? "I am nothing, have nothing, and have neither prospect nor possibility of either becoming some one [outstanding] or of obtaining some [great] thing." He was wicked to have caused "such a wonderful girl [as Bea] to love such a fool."

He spent Christmas with the Ayers and discussed marriage with Bea. They settled nothing, but they had to make a decision soon, "for I would look like an ass hanging around much longer."

Her father was reluctant to have Beatrice become an Army wife, and he tried to persuade Patton to resign from the military and to enter business. Patton informed Mr. Ayer of his affinity for the service. He had no logical reason for liking the Army, "I only feel it inside. It is as natural for me to be a soldier as it is to breathe and would be as hard to give up all thought of it as it would to stop breathing."

Understanding, Mr. Ayer asked Patton for a financial statement of his assets. Having no idea how much he was worth, he asked Papa for the information. Papa's response surprised Patton. "I had no notion I was so wealthy." Mr. Ayer was surprised too at "such a fine nest-egg in your property." He could not resist saying, "I would not sell the land."

Patton proposed by letter—"If you marry [me] in June— please do," and Beatrice telegraphed, "Pa and Ma willing for June if you are rejoice." He told Mama, "Being thus importuned? I accepted her." He noted her "pretty good taste in most things," but with his usual self-depreciation added, "Except husbands." Mr. Ayer gave his blessing and informed Patton of his practice of sending his married children a monthly income and of his intention to do the same with Bea. Their engagement was announced, and when Patton reluctantly told his girlfriends at Fort Sheridan and Highland Park, his popularity plummeted. Bea set the date, Patton obtained leave, and they decided to honeymoon in Europe. Only one problem was bothersome. No quarters on post were immediately available for married officers. Where would they live? A house or apartment off post was the last thing he wanted.

While Papa stayed home to seek, vainly it turned out, the Democratic nomination for the U.S. Senate, Mama and Nita met Bea and her parents in Chicago and visited Fort Sheridan. After Bea's mother and father departed, Patton's squadron commander gave a reception honoring Mama, Nita, and Beatrice. Although inexperienced in military matters, Bea charmed all the guests. She paid particular attention to the post quartermaster, who assigned housing and determined where officers resided. "She made such a hit," he told Papa, ". . . that I think our chance of getting a house went up a number of points."

Patton soon secured half of a two-family house and was excited. He was uncomfortable, too—over the contrast between the accommodations he was providing and Bea's life of luxury with her parents. She would have to make a great adjustment. And he would have to rise quickly. "Beaty," he wrote, "we must amount to some thing."

His last letter before marriage made a confession. She was "the inspiration for a week and cowardly nature"—his own. "I have always so wanted to win that I have ever feared lest I might lose. . . . May our ambition [be] as fortunate and great as our love."

Their wedding was a social event. A special train took the

George and Beatrice were married at Beverly Farms,
Massachusetts, in May 1910. This photograph was taken
afterward at her family home, Pride's Crossing.

★

guests from Boston's North Station to Beverly Farms, where carriages waited to drive them to St. John's Episcopal Church. After the ceremony there was a grand reception at the Ayer home in Pride's Crossing. Unfortunately, Mama Patton was ill and remained in her room at the Hotel Touraine. Papa and a radiant Aunt Nannie, who had her brother-in-law all to herself, stood with the Ayers. A full orchestra played for dancing on the terrace overlooking the sea.

George and Bea traveled to New York. Their bridal suite on the steamship was full of flowers and gifts. He carried a black leather notebook to record their trip but made few notations. They drove through the English countryside and spent some time in London, where Patton bought military books, among them a copy of Karl von Clausewitz's *On War*.

Many years later Patton apologized for being so rough and for hurting Beatrice on their wedding night. Was his brutality the result of inexperience? Or was he trying to prove his manhood and to show a macho image?

A year afterward, when Bea was in Massachusetts for the summer and Patton at Fort Sheridan was embarked on a frenzy of activity to overcome his loneliness and physical desires, a letter from Bea incensed him. She pictured him in her imagination as engaged in his favorite occupation, reading. Chagrined to have his manliness apparently challenged, he replied, "Darling One: You are one fierce woman. What in H do you mean by 'Doing what I like best to do—reading.' I would rather a damned sight look at some thing else than book and you know what it is too. It looks like a skunk." Her observation seemed to question his masculinity, which he equated with military prowess. Sex drive and hot blood went with soldiering, and he was doing his utmost to establish himself as a fearsome and virile warrior.

Accompanying his troop into the field for extended exercises, Patton was busy. But he found time to study some of the military books he had purchased in London. Clausewitz was hard to read and was "as full of notes . . . as a dog is of fleas." He had a surge of confidence and reported: "There is probably not a shadow of doubt that even with out a war I will be a general."

Bea had qualms about fitting into a military life, but she was gracious, and everyone adored her. She smoothed her husband's rough edges, taught him the art of flattery, and helped him overcome his feelings of inferiority. She dedicated her life to his advancement. Controlling his temper, soothing his hurt feelings, she provided him with diplomacy and finesse.

They always dressed for dinner, but the practice seemed out of place, even faintly ridiculous, in their modest quarters. She questioned whether they ought to continue. "The poorer the surroundings," he replied, "the more important it is to keep up your standards."

Expecting a child in the fall of 1910, Bea began to translate an article in a French military journal. As the cold and dreary weather closed in and limited Patton's outdoor activities, he rephrased her language into proper American terminology. Publication of the piece in a service magazine would make Patton better known in the Army. A horse show in Chicago caught his fancy, and he decided to enter the competition in the following year, for participation was "a fine advertisement" for an officer.

Their daughter, whom they named Beatrice, Jr., was born in March 1911. Patton was immediately jealous of the baby because she took so much of Bea's time. To compensate, he bought a typewriter, which freed him from his all but illegible script, and he started to write articles on military subjects. He found it stimulating to set his thoughts on paper, and he soon formulated recurring themes that would always be associated with him, for example, "Attack . . . push forward, attack again until the end." He became identified with offensive warfare— "Blow follows blow" in the ideal battle. Reflecting his interest in training, he set down, "No machine is better than its operator."

Patton often turned his thoughts to the future. How could he make a name for himself? How could he do so if the United States remained at peace? If something interesting, a war, occurred in Europe, he would resign his commission and fight as a mercenary. But before that happened, he would probably have to serve a tour of duty in the Philippines, an obligation for every officer. With the insurrection there at an end and the islands quiet, he considered possible assignments better suited to his aims.

If he could attend the cavalry's Mounted Service School at Fort Riley, Kansas, as a student, he would enhance his military knowledge; but he was too junior in rank to expect the assignment soon. The choicest place was the French Cavalry School at Saumur, but, for the moment at least, this was out of his reach. Washington, D.C., where all the important people lived, was tempting.

Having learned all he could at Fort Sheridan, eager to advance his career, wanting to avoid service in the Philippines, he inquired of Marshall, his troop commander. How did one, he asked candidly, pull wires in the Army? He and his family knew General Fred C. Ainsworth, the Army's Adjutant General. The Ayers were acquainted with prominent persons in Massachusetts and in the Republican administration of President Howard Taft. Papa had friends in California and Texas. "There are the weapons," he concluded, "now please show me how to use them."

Exactly how the influences worked to free Patton from Fort Sheridan remained obscure. Marshall was a friend of the personal aide of General Leonard Wood, the Army Chief of Staff. A major who was courting Bea's sister Katharine and who was stationed in the capital looked for openings. The Ayers and the Pattons exerted subtle pressures in high places. And in December 1911, orders transferred Patton to Washington, D.C., to Fort Myer, Virginia, a showplace where the Army Chief of Staff resided, where officers who were the best kind of gentlemen exhibited polished horsemanship, played a high quality of polo, and managed impressive military funerals. Moving from a post of routine duties to the hub of the U.S. Army, close to those who mattered, not only high-ranking officers but also official Washington, was truly, as Patton said, "nearer God than else where and the place where all people with aspirations should attempt to dwell." Lunching at the exclusive Metropolitan Club as a member's guest soon after his arrival, he reported with great satisfaction, "All the big men were there."

Serious about his troop duties and exhibiting his usual zeal, Patton lived in grand style, bought thoroughbred horses for racing and show, and dined and danced in the best establishments. He quickly became known among the Washington elite and was soon being mentioned as a participant in the Fifth Olympic Games to be held in Stockholm in the summer of 1912.

The Modern Pentathlon, consisting of five events, was tailored to the military man and seemed especially fitted to Patton's strengths. The scenario explaining the competition had an officer carrying a message on (1) horseback, encountering an enemy force and (2) firing his pistol, then (3) fencing with his sword, escaping and (4) swimming a river, then (5) running cross-country to his destination. Patton was an excellent horseman, swordsman, and pistol shot, had been on the track team at West Point, and had swum off Catalina. He was in good physical condition, handsome, precisely military, likable, dedicated to the service. Chosen to represent the Army and the United States at the games, he started training at once, went on a diet, and abstained from alcohol and tobacco.

He and Bea, Papa, Mama, and Nita sailed for Europe. Patton practiced and exercised on the ship regularly and rigorously. He competed fiercely and won fifth place. He might have stood higher, for, inexplicably, he missed the target twice when firing his pistol, unless two bullets passed through the holes made by previous rounds and could not be counted. He collapsed after crossing the finish line in the cross-country run and was the only fencer to beat the French champion. He impressed everyone with his enthusiasm and sportsmanship.

All the contestants whom he asked considered the best swordsman in Europe to be Adjutant Cléry, the professional champion of Europe, instructor of fencing at the Saumur Cavalry School. The opportunity was too good to miss. While Papa, Mama, and Nita toured the continent, Patton and Bea traveled to Saumur. They stayed two weeks while he took private lessons from Cléry and improved himself in the dueling sword and saber. He also learned Cléry's method of instruction.

Returned to Fort Myer, Patton was asked to dinner, along with Secretary of War Henry L. Stimson, by Leonard Wood, the Army Chief of Staff. Both listened to Patton's account of his experiences in Stockholm and Saumur. Wood invited Patton to ride with him for exercise on the following morning. Patton was enchanted. Still a second lieutenant, three years out of West Point, he was making the right connections. When he dined at the Chevy Chase Club with two major generals, a major, and a captain, he enthused, "I am going some," then added his usual caveat, "though they have probably forgotten me by now." He joined the Metropolitan Club, where the socially prominent gathered.

Carrying out his program of gaining notice from the well-placed, Patton rode in many flat and steeplechase races around Washington and elsewhere during the fall of 1912. He explained to his father-in-law: "I am working myself pretty

**Patton competing in the modern pentathlon at the Olympic
Games in Stockholm, 1912. He came in fifth.**

☆

hard but it is not done in a thoughtless way nor without good reason. If you had not done more work than other people when you were my age, you would not be now what you are. . . . What I am doing looks like play to you but in my business it is the best sort of advertising. It makes people talk and that is a sign they are noticing. . . . The notice of others has been the start of many successful men."

The most fruitful part of his campaign to become known was his identification with the saber. With Bea's help, he wrote a report of his work with Adjutant Cléry. "The French," he said, "use the point far more than we do. . . . The whole French system of mounted saber fencing is concentrated in the word: 'Attack!'" Thrusting with the tip like the French was far more effective than wielding the edge as an ax, as was American practice. The thrust brought a cavalryman into contact with an enemy more quickly and had other advantages. The curved sword in vogue with the American cavalry stressed the cutting edge, and Patton advocated changing to a straight blade. He made no mention of the parry, a defensive action. His thought was fixed firmly on the offensive.

His paper, addressed to the Army Adjutant General, went through channels and thus passed across his regimental commander's desk. Sending it forward with a favorable endorsement, he suggested that Patton enlarge his message into an article for publication in a military journal. The idea of obtaining notice among readers was attractive, and Patton agreed. He decided to try to have the sword changed. "I may get some prominence yet," he told Bea. "I hope so."

Ordered to temporary duty in the Office of the Chief of Staff in December 1912, he stayed several months. He wrote papers on a variety of assigned subjects—on the war in the Balkans, why racing and polo were good for Army officers— and his writing featured his wide knowledge of military history as well as lucid and authoritative prose. He talked constantly to his colleagues about the saber. Occasionally he acted as aide to Wood and to Stimson, and he became friendly with both.

His article appeared in the influential *Army and Navy Journal* and persuasively advocated the straight sword for the cavalry. A few months later, early in 1913, the Secretary of War instructed the Army Chief of Staff to direct the Chief of Ordnance to manufacture 20,000 cavalry sabers in accordance with the specifications of an enclosed model. The weapon was of Patton's design, and it was known as the Patton sword. When the first new ones appeared, Wood sent Patton to the Springfield Arsenal for a few days to be sure of their conformance with Patton's requirements. Shortly thereafter the *Cavalry Journal* published another piece by Patton, this one a full-scale treatment describing the history of the sword in combat, mentioning, among others, German mercenaries in the Italian wars, Cossacks, Poles, Turks, and Arabs with good effect, and drawing lessons from the past. Patton's reputation grew.

The campaign waged by Patton on the printed page and in enthusiastic conversations with senior officers in the War Department came to complete fruition in the summer of 1913. He received permission to travel to France at his own expense in order to perfect himself in swordsmanship. He was then to report to Fort Riley, Kansas, no later than October 1. He was to be a student at the Mounted Service School and also the instructor in fencing. In the latter position he was to have a magnificent title, Master of the Sword. The first to hold this appointment, he was thus acknowledged as the foremost expert in the Army. He had made his wishes for Washington, Fort Riley, and Saumur come true.

For six weeks Patton worked with Cléry, not only to improve his fencing techniques but also to learn how to instruct. Bea translated Cléry's lectures. The Pattons made many friends among the French cavalry officers. He had long discussions with them, particularly on the reasons for Napoleon's ability to dominate warfare for so long. He learned to speak fluent French. He bought a saddle as a gift for Leonard Wood.

After packing their household goods at Fort Myer, Bea went to Massachusetts, Patton to Fort Riley. He had his usual nervousness but quickly settled in. "I have had little bother from hay fever." The house assigned to him was mediocre. "You certainly have to give up a lot on my account," he wrote Bea.

Patton found teaching difficult. Most of his students were senior to him in rank and age, and it was hard to hold their attention. In addition, he was taking the cavalry course and had to keep abreast of his lessons. At the end of the day he was always tired. Yet when the Cavalry Board asked him to write regulations for the new sword, he agreed. He also had enough energy to edit a book on Army racing records.

When American troops occupied Vera Cruz in April 1914, Patton hoped for an immediate war with Mexico. Prophetically he remarked that if the conflict was of short duration, he would have no chance as a second lieutenant "to make any reputation as a leader of men." But perhaps he could "make a personal record on which to base something in the future."

He was among the dozen officers selected to take the second-year course at the school, a tribute to his promise as an officer. He was also to continue to be Master of the Sword.

Upon the outbreak of World War I, Patton thought immediately of requesting a year's leave of absence to fight in the French army, an arrangement he had discussed with friends at Saumur. He wrote to Leonard Wood, now commanding general of the Eastern Department, and asked what he thought of the idea. Wood discouraged and flattered him. "We don't want to waste youngsters of your sort in the service of foreign nations," he replied.

In November 1914, on his twenty-ninth birthday, Patton told Papa, "I certainly am aging. . . . I fixed twenty-seven as the age when I should be a brigadier and now I am twenty-nine and not a first Lieutenant." He was losing his hair, and he wrote Beatrice, "When I get less hair than I now have I will look like a German duelist."

Bea traveled to California to be with the Pattons for the birth of their second child. Patton wanted their daughter named Bea II, like a racehorse—perhaps he was joking—but Beatrice called her Ruth Ellen after her mother-in-law and mother.

Patton was riding across the prairie one day when his horse stepped into a hole, fell, threw Patton, and rolled on him. While getting up, the animal kicked Patton in the head. He bled, but rode about two miles to the post hospital and had five stitches to close a bad cut. Exactly two years earlier, he had fallen when riding in a steeplechase and had incurred injuries to his skull. Being kicked and butted by horses was becoming routine for him, and, besides, he was accident-prone. The shocks continued and may have eventually produced a permanent condition, perhaps a subdural hematoma, a pool of blood around his brain. This condition could sometimes have made it difficult for Patton to stifle his aggressions and his emotions, his temper as well as his tears. The ferocious face that he cultivated enhanced his projection of toughness, but toward the latter part of his life, he could no longer altogether control his tendency to flare up in anger, then subside into abject contrition.

Following closely the developments of the war in Europe, Patton was indignant over what he considered to be President Woodrow Wilson's timidity. Wilson's too-proud-to-fight was nothing more, Patton believed, than cowardice. The sinking of the *Lusitania*, which outraged him, should have prompted immediate American entry into the war.

When he graduated from the Mounted Service School in June 1915, he was declared eligible to take an examination for promotion. He was also to return to his regiment, which was about to leave for the Philippines. Unreconciled to that destination, he obtained a special leave of eleven days and went to Washington, D.C., to seek another job. Only the doorkeeper at the Metropolitan Club, where he stayed, recognized him. "No one else did. Some day I will make them all know me." His friends secured him another assignment, and he was transferred to a cavalry regiment stationed at Fort Bliss, Texas, at El Paso, on the border with Mexico, where troubles threatened to break into open conflict.

As various Mexican groups competed for power, American troops took positions along the border to prevent incursions by Mexican armed bands into the United States. Among these American forces was Brigadier General John J. Pershing's brigade, which had moved from the Presidio of San Francisco to Fort Bliss and was ready to invade Mexico. Pershing was about to bring his family to Fort Bliss when a tragic fire at the Presidio destroyed his home and killed his wife and three daughters; only his young son survived. When President Wilson favored Venustiano Carranza and gave his government de facto recognition, together with permission to use American railroads to transport his troops, Francisco Pancho Villa turned anti-American.

Patton arrived at Fort Bliss and could find no one to tell him what he was supposed to do. He finally learned that he had no duties until his regiment arrived on post. Until then, he was to prepare to take his promotion test. Unsure of his ability to pass, he requested and obtained a postponement. "My hay fever is *gone*."

While he studied for his exam, he kept busy. "I have a method in this." He was attentive to members of his examining committee. He helped the president of the promotion board train polo ponies. His former troop commander at Sheridan, now Major Marshall, was luckily on an official visit and staying with the second member of Patton's promotion board, so Patton called on them and quoted history "to show what a hell of a soldier I was. I hope it had the results desired. Anyhow Maj. M will blow my horn." Eventually he passed and was certified as qualified for promotion.

He met his new regimental commander, who was pleasant and fat, took temporary command of a troop because the captain and first lieutenant were still absent, and taught his men to groom and feed the horses in the proper manner—that is to say, according to his practice. A regimental review with sabers drawn, all of them the swords he had designed, brought tears to his eyes. What moved him was "the call of ones ancestors and the glory of combat."

Two cavalry troops, including Patton's, departed for several weeks of field duty. They marched ninety miles to Sierra Blanca, a frontier town high in the mountains. They set up camp and patrolled, their task to protect isolated ranches threatened by bandits and to guard the main line of the Southern Pacific railroad, which passed nearby. They made periodic visits to outposts about thirty miles away.

A settlement of about twenty houses and a saloon, Sierra Blanca was a curious place, tough and exciting. The men wore boots and spurs and carried weapons. The marshal, who had white hair and a sweet face, was a noted gunman. Seven brothers named Love, who dressed like laborers and were very rich and amiable, owned practically the whole country and had a hired gun fighter. Patton came to know many of the inhabitants, who intrigued him.

The land was wild, desolate, and dangerous. Game abounded, including quail, duck, and rabbit. By sheer luck Patton shot a running jackrabbit at about fifteen yards while riding at a trot. "My reputation as a gun man is made," he wrote. Traveling to one outpost or the other, he spent long hours in the saddle with his men, went with little sleep, hunted for food, guarded against ambush. "I like this sort of work a lot." In this he resembled his Grandfather Wilson.

On Thanksgiving Eve he was in command of Troop A—the senior officers were on the trail—when, at sundown, a wire from El Paso alerted him to a possible raid on the town by 200 Mexicans. Patton made his plans to repel the attack, instructed his soldiers to sleep with their weapons beside their beds, and directed them where to go in case of alarm. He hoped for action. With about one hundred men under him, he was ready to give the enemy a warm welcome. "If this is the eve of battle, it is not at all interesting nor so exciting as a polo game." To his disappointment, the night passed quietly.

Late on the following day, orders from El Paso directed him to march on about eighty Mexicans who were camped on the American side of the Rio Grande. He was to drive them across the river or capture them. He issued instructions to his men. They would start at 3:30 A.M. so as to reach the Mexicans around daybreak. He would lead them in a saber charge. In bed, "I thought I had a medal of honor sewed up and laid awake planning my report." His bubble burst when a captain and a first lieutenant showed up. They ordered the sabers left home. The party rode out early, found no one, and returned after being in the saddle for eleven hours and traveling between sixty and seventy miles.

When he got back to Fort Bliss, Bea came and spent two months with him. During a terrible windstorm, she broke down and cried and begged him to resign from the Army. The crisis passed, the weather improved, and Bea decided that El Paso was suitable for her and the babies. Patton asked for quarters on post, Bea brought the children, and they moved into a house. "I am still and ever will be jealous even of B Jr. and R.E.," for in his eyes they monopolized Bea's attention.

Nita visited them and in the normal course of the social activities met Pershing. They liked each other and became friends. Straight as a ramrod, he was a widower of fifty-five. Big-boned, the outdoor type, she was twenty-nine and unmarried. She stayed with the Pattons longer than planned.

On March 9, 1916, when Pancho Villa raided Columbus, New Mexico, and killed seventeen Americans, Pershing received orders to take a "punitive expedition" into Mexico and hunt down and capture Villa. As Pershing organized a force and selected units for the invasion of Mexico, Patton worried. Would Pershing leave Patton's regiment at Fort Bliss because the commander was too fat for active campaigning? If so, how could Patton manage to go along on what was bound to be a marvelous adventure and a great opportunity to gain combat experience and glory?

Three days later, when Patton happened to be the officer of the day, his worst fears were confirmed. His regiment would not go to Mexico. At once Patton asked his squadron adjutant to recommend him as Pershing's aide. He asked the same thing of Major John L. Hines, who was to be the adjutant gen-

1915: The Pattons with their daughters Beatrice (left) and Ruth Ellen.

☆

eral of the expeditionary force. He repeated his request to Lieutenant Martin C. Shallenberger, one of Pershing's two regular aides. Because the other, James L. Collins, was temporarily absent, Pershing asked Patton if he really wanted to go. Patton answered, "More than anyone else." Pershing agreed to take him if he could. After dinner, Patton called on Pershing and mentioned his ability to work with newspaper correspondents. He had never done so. On the following morning, Pershing chose Patton as a provisional aide until Collins returned. Patton promised himself to show his capabilities and prove his merit. Knowing how excited her husband was over the prospect of engaging in war, and since she had Nita with her, Bea showed no emotion "and did not cry or anything."

In later years, Patton elaborated dramatically on how Pershing came to select him. He failed to mention Nita's presence at Fort Bliss. To some extent at least, Pershing took Patton out of friendship for his sister. As for the regimental commander who was presumably too fat for field duty, Patton never forgave him. In World War II, when Walton Walker, who was fat, was one of Patton's corps commanders, Patton was at first suspicious of Walker's capacities. He later regarded Walker as one of his best. "Inspite of being fat, Walker is good."

Patton helped Hines decode telegrams most of the day. Toward evening, while Shallenberger went ahead in the general's car to decoy the newspapermen, Pershing, Nita, Bea, Hines, and Patton, in his automobile, drove to the train. Bea and Nita returned to the post while the men boarded for the trip to Columbus.

As a proper aide, Patton got the general something to eat. When the train stopped about a mile outside Columbus, Patton descended, located Pershing's staff, and brought them to the general. Patton took off Pershing's baggage and unloaded the headquarters horses.

During the subsequent foray into Mexico, Patton proved himself indispensable. He assisted Pershing on inspections, rode with him for exercise, carried messages, looked after the mess, the horses, the motor vehicles, the guards, the escort troops, and the clerks. As he had promised, he was good with the war correspondents. When Collins, the regular aide, joined, Patton continued as an unofficial aide and stayed on as an extra member.

The excitement prevailing during the early push into Mexico soon evaporated. The weather was too hot or too cold, and frequent rain, sleet, and snow added to the general discomfort. The columns pursuing Villa had no success in finding and trapping him, although Pershing eventually had 15,000 men and traveled 400 miles into the country.

The highlight of Patton's service and one of the few notable incidents in the campaign occurred in May, six weeks after his arrival. Just above the town of Rubio, two ranches, one near the hamlet of Saltillo, the other near San Miguelito, attracted Patton's attention. A well-known Villista officer named Julio Cárdenas lived in one, his uncle in the other. Patton stopped at Saltillo and searched the house. Nothing aroused his suspicion. Continuing to San Miguelito, he found the uncle together with Cárdenas's wife and baby. Perhaps Patton and his men tortured the uncle as they questioned him, and perhaps the uncle revealed some information. "The uncle," Patton wrote Bea, "was a very brave man and nearly died before he would tell me any thing." In his diary, Patton recorded, "Tried to get information out of uncle. Failed."

Two weeks later, Pershing dispatched Patton to purchase corn from neighboring farmers for delivery to the headquarters. Accompanied by ten soldiers and four civilians—two scouts and two drivers—in all a party of fifteen traveling in three automobiles, Patton obtained corn at the villages of Coyote and Salsito. He drove to Rubio and found a number of rough-looking men in the town. Whether their presence made him suspicious or whether he acted on impulse or a hunch, he decided to go to Saltillo, about six miles to the north.

Once out of sight of the town, he stopped his party and explained what he wanted to do. He knew the house because he had been there before. It stood about 200 yards east and to the right of the road running north from Rubio. It was built in a rough square about an interior courtyard. The main entrance to the house was away from the road and looked toward a stream running parallel with the road.

As soon as the driver of the first car, Patton's, saw the house, he was to go at full speed, pass the structure, and stop just beyond. Patton and two others were to sprint across the northern end of the building. The second and third cars were to halt just short of the house, and three men from each vehicle were to race across the southern end of the house. These nine men were to converge on the main gate and search the

Lieutenant Patton in Mexico, 1916. He was aide to Major General John Pershing.

interior. The six men remaining with the cars were to cover the road.

It was a simple plan, very clear to the men, and they carried it out at Saltillo. The uncle was there, and he sold some corn and promised delivery. Something in the uncle's face or behavior led Patton to wonder whether Cárdenas was home at San Miguelito.

The house there resembled the one at Saltillo, and Patton and his men repeated their performance. The only thing different was the sight of three old men and a boy skinning a cow. As the cars appeared, one of them ran inside for a moment, then returned. The four Mexicans paid no attention to the Americans and continued their work.

Carrying a pistol and a rifle, Patton reached the eastern side first and started to walk toward the gate, a large arched door leading to the patio. Three armed men on horseback dashed out. When they saw Patton, they wheeled to the southern corner. With several of Patton's men running toward them, they turned back to Patton, who was standing with his pistol drawn. They fired at him, and he discharged five rounds. Two of his bullets found their mark, one entering the belly of a horse, the other breaking the arm of the rider.

Because his soldiers were shooting and he was in their line of fire, Patton retired around the corner and reloaded his pistol. He could not see the rider whom he had hit turn into the courtyard.

When Patton came around the corner again, he was almost run down by a horseman. Patton fired at the animal, broke its hip, and brought it down. When the rider disentangled himself and rose with a pistol in his hand, Patton and several other Americans who were now with him cut the man down at a range of about ten yards. The second was a hundred yards away and escaping until the fire of several soldiers and Patton, who discharged three rifle rounds, brought him down.

The third man, who had reentered the inner patio, dismounted from his wounded and bleeding horse, dropped out of a window, and was running along a wall when shots from soldiers felled him. One of the scouts went to him, and the downed man made what seemed like a motion to surrender. Instead, he raised his pistol and fired, but missed. The scout killed him.

Feeling it necessary to search the house in case other Villistas were hiding, Patton called over the four men skinning the cow. He and three others used them as shields and entered the building. They found several old men and women, who revealed the identities of the three dead men. One was indeed Cárdenas. While Patton's men tied the bodies to the hoods of the cars, Patton put Cárdenas's silver-studded saddle and sword into his vehicle.

They noticed about forty horsemen in the distance and coming at a gallop. They fired a few shots at them, then cleared out. Beyond Saltillo, remembering the tough hombres in Rubio, Patton had one of his men cut the wires along the road to prevent word of his skirmish from reaching the town before they arrived. The appearance of the three cars and bodies in Rubio caused great commotion, but Patton and his party sped through and reached headquarters without further incident.

Patton was elated, and so was everyone else. Pershing permitted him to keep his trophies, and Patton planned to send the saddle to Papa for his office. The war correspondents crowded around for a firsthand account of his adventure, and the stories they filed made Patton a national hero for several weeks. His photograph appeared in newspapers around the country. The New York *Times* headlined, "Cárdenas' Family Saw Him Die at Bay—Shot Four Times, Villa Captain—Dramatic Fight at Ranch—Lieut. Patton and Ten Men Killed Three Bandits—Peons Kept On Skinning a Beef." What was more important for his career, Pershing mentioned him in dispatches and in his official report. The Patton legend received nourishment.

He informed Bea, Papa, and Mr. Ayer, "I have at last succeeded in getting into a fight." He had always expected to be scared, but had no fear and was not even excited. His dominant emotion: "I was afraid they would get away."

Was Bea wondering whether his conscience hurt for killing a man? No, he felt the same way he did when he hooked and landed his first swordfish, surprised by his luck. The exchange was a fair fight and a military act. As for the presence of Cárdenas's wife, mother, and baby, he preferred to avoid thinking of them.

The incident was rather prophetic. It was the first time in U.S. Army history that a unit had motored to battle. Eventually it was called motorized warfare, and this earliest example foreshadowed Patton's later expertise in this kind of combat.

In compliance with President Wilson's orders, Pershing

withdrew his force to within 150 miles of the border. A terrible boredom set in. Pershing instituted a series of competitions and games to keep the troops occupied, riding and shooting contests, boxing matches, field days. He carried out wholesale inspections of all the men, horses, and equipment, appointing Patton to one of his teams. He conducted tactical exercises and mock battles.

Pershing took a few days of vacation in Columbus, and Patton and Collins accompanied him. Bea, Mrs. Collins, and Nita were there, and they spent much time together. After the men returned to Mexico, Pershing kept talking to Patton of his sister, whom he called Miss Anne. "Nita," Patton wrote Bea, "may rank us yet."

When Papa retired from the Huntington Company in 1916 and secured the Democratic nomination to run for the U.S. Senate, his son offered ruthless advice. "Dear Senator," Patton wrote, Papa was bound to win, but even if he lost, he could probably obtain some high appointment in Washington if "as seems probable that creature Wilson wins" the presidency again. Papa was not to go at the election in any halfhearted way, "but whoop it up" and tell the people "all sorts of lies" for their votes. He urged Papa to use "rough stuff" against his opponent, Republican Governor of California Hiram Johnson. If Johnson threw mud at Papa, "you sling rocks. In fact I would start it as you have more on him than he can have on you. Go after each and every vote as if it were the only one you had. . . . You are not polite enough to people in general. Treat each one as if he was an army officer you were friendly to on my account. Get a lot of cigars and give them to people and ask about the children and the crops. It is perfectly possible to be for every policy under heaven to the man who is interested in that policy. . . . I hope you will win and I know you will."

A few weeks before the election, Patton was working in his tent, writing a paper, when his gasoline lamp exploded and badly burned his face and head. Hospitalized, he waited several days to reassure Bea. The worst thing he had feared, he said, was to be blinded and unable to see her again.

As the electoral campaign was coming to a climax, Patton was granted sick leave. His face heavily bandaged, he rode in a truck convoy to Columbus. Bea met him, and they took the train to California. Patton accompanied his father on several trips where Papa made speeches. Attracting notice as the hero of the Rubio ranch and sympathy because of his bandages, Patton made no comment on Papa's discourses, perhaps because he was uninterested in the substance of Papa's remarks or disappointed by Papa's failure to stir his listeners.

Teddy Roosevelt's Progressive party split the Republican vote, but Papa was unable to capitalize on the division, and Johnson won. Patton was with Papa at the California Club when the returns came in. "He never flinched," Patton recorded, "and took it with a smile." Because Wilson carried California and thereby obtained a majority in the electoral college, Patton urged Papa to push himself for a cabinet appointment, most of all for Secretary of War. It was not to be. Papa was "too high souled to be a good advocate for him self."

As the Punitive Expeditionary Force prepared to leave Mexico, Patton reflected on the advantages he had gained. Service in Mexico made unnecessary a tour in the Philippines. He had been promoted to first lieutenant. He had attracted notoriety in the Rubio ranch affair. He had met and become friendly with excellent officers whom he would encounter throughout his career. He had become acquainted with the primitive motor vehicles used by the U.S. Army and employed them for the first time in extended operations. He had observed the reconnaissance efforts of the Aero Squadron, also an innovation, and noted the difficulties of landing on rudimentary fields and of maintaining an adequate reserve of spare parts. He had become aware of the importance of logistics as he studied the supply system. He had worked with signal communications. As a liaison officer carrying some of Pershing's messages over long distances to widely dispersed units, he had learned the importance of coordination. Watching exercises and maneuvers designed and conducted by Pershing had given him a high appreciation of the value of mobility, particularly the use of cavalry to outflank and defeat infantry.

Best of all, he had come to know Pershing quite well, not only as a friend but also as a professional officer. Observing Pershing closely, Patton modeled himself after him, the manner in which Pershing carried himself and issued orders, his insistence on discipline and loyalty, his attention to detail. Nothing was "too minute to escape him," and it was "personal care which gets the results and only this *personal* care will." Pershing's interest in all phases of training impressed Patton. The results, he noted, were clear. "Every horse and man was fit; weaklings had gone; baggage was still at the minimum, and

Back in California with bandages, after being burned in Mexico by an exploding gasoline lantern.

★

discipline was perfect. . . . By constant study General Pershing knew to the minutest detail each of the subjects in which he demanded practice, and by physical presence and personal example and explanation, insured himself that they were correctly carried out." That would be Patton's method too.

In short, he told Beatrice, "I have learned more useful soldiering while in Mexico than all the rest of my service put together."

As for his own ambitions, he confessed to Bea that if he were sure of being no more than an average soldier, he would leave the Army. He disliked the dirt and the inconveniences "except as a means to fame. If I knew that I would never be famous I would settle down and raise horses and have a good time. It is a great gamble to spoil yours and my own happiness for the hope of greatness." Worst of all, he was occasionally beset by doubt. Sometimes when he thought he was doing his "damnedest," he really was not performing as well as he could.

He was glad to march out of Mexico early in February 1917 and to enter El Paso to the acclaim of cheering crowds. Some of the applause, he was sure, was directed to him.

THE GREAT WAR

Two months after Patton returned from Mexico with Pershing, the United States declared war on Germany. Less than two months later, both men were on their way to France.

Patton continued to serve Pershing as an acting aide. Pershing, who had made his reputation in Mexico and received his second star there, then succeeded Frederick Funston as the head of the Southern Department in San Antonio. Remaining in El Paso with his cavalry regiment, Patton took command of a troop, passed his promotion examination, and became eligible for captain.

The friendship between Pershing and Nita blossomed into romance and talk of marriage. Pershing visited the Patton family in California and on his way back stopped at El Paso and had George and Beatrice to dinner. Upon the outbreak of war, Papa Patton decided to go to Washington to look for a suitable job or government appointment. Mama and Nita accompanied him. They made a stopover in San Antonio and saw Pershing just as the War Department summoned him to the capital. All four traveled together.

Pershing received orders to organize a division with himself in command and to take the formation to France as the first American unit to fight alongside the Allies. He submitted a list of officers whom he wanted on his staff and included Patton's name. Several days later, Pershing was appointed the commander in chief of the American Expeditionary Force, all the troops to be sent to France. He wired Patton to join him in Washington.

With a small headquarters party, Pershing was to go overseas at once as a symbol of reassurance and promise to the war-weary Allies, who had fought immense battles of attrition for three years. Although the American entrance into the war was a great psychological boost for them, the United States was unprepared to join in the massive clash of arms on the Western Front. Positioning units along the Mexican border and pursuing Villa had been a small start toward mobilization, but now the U.S. Army had to raise, equip, and train a much larger force. The War Department planned to ship Pershing 2,000,000 partially trained troops. He would bring them to combat readiness over there.

As for the question of the marriage between Pershing and Nita, they decided to wait. In view of Pershing's awesome responsibilities and the fact that he was leaving the country, they agreed to postpone their wedding until the end of the war.

In Washington, Patton took charge of orderlies and other miscellaneous personnel in Pershing's contingent. Late in May, he and Bea, the Pattons, and Pershing went to New York, where they made their farewells. Sixty officers and 128 civilian clerks and soldiers of Pershing's initial group boarded ship and sailed for Europe. Papa was unable to find a place in Washington, and the family returned home. Nita threw herself into war work and wrote long letters to Pershing. Bea settled down in Massachusetts.

Patton in Paris performed much the same duties as he had in Mexico. He looked after the orderlies, posted guards, handled the motor-pool drivers, occasionally acted as aide to Pershing. Once in a while, when invited by Pershing to come and chat, he listened to Pershing talk of the war and also of Nita. "It certainly is the most intense case I have ever seen," Patton remarked.

Pershing was in almost constant consultation with the French, and late in July he visited the British commander in chief, Field Marshal Sir Douglas Haig. He took two colonels with him and, as his aide-de-camp, Patton. Driving to the British General Headquarters, they toured installations and listened to briefings on how the center worked. The Americans had dinner with Haig at his chateau, and Pershing impressed Haig with his "quiet and gentlemanly bearing," the awareness of his gigantic task, and his desire to learn. "The ADC," Haig added in his diary, referring to Patton, "is a fire-eater and longs for the fray." Patton liked Haig, a cavalryman who enjoyed hunting and polo and who talked with him about the saber. Haig was, said Patton, "more of a charger than I am."

He acted again as Pershing's aide during an inspection trip to St. Dizier, where American troops were training. The soldiers were sloppy, the officers lazy, the exercises listless. Patton resolved that if ever he had men at drill, he'd remedy these deficiencies. Pershing realized how far he had to bring his men before he could commit them to battle.

Paris was, Patton wrote Bea, "a stupid place with out [you], just as heaven would be under the same condition." He was happy to be with "real people," that is, the good ones, and he was lucky to have always served with the best officers. "I can't see for the life of me where I am going to do much in this war personally but my luck will hold I suppose and I will run into something. I wish it would be you." He had learned of his promotion to captain, and he expected, like everyone, to go at least one step higher during the war. "I certainly don't see any stars in prospect for me but one can always try. Sometimes I think I don't try as hard as I ought but probably I do. . . . I would give a lot to have you consol me and tell me that I amounted to a lot even when I know I don't."

Despite regulations forbidding officers' wives to travel to France, Patton urged Bea to pull strings and come as a tourist, a secretary with a government agency, an accredited correspondent to a Boston newspaper, or a buyer for a department store. Bea finally decided to go neither to Paris nor to London, where her sister Katharine lived with her State Department husband. Her presence in the war zone might jeopardize Patton's career. He might even be sent home. Both were disappointed, and Patton tried to comfort her—"Things with us have always turned out for the best. . . . We have both always done our duty as we saw it to the best of our ability and God or Fate never forgets that."

The Allies had decided by September to place the Americans eventually on the front in Lorraine, so Pershing moved his headquarters out of Paris and its distractions about 150 miles to Chaumont, a small city in eastern France. From there he directed an expanding number of training camps and specialists' schools for the stream of American units and soldiers arriving in the country.

The post adjutant at Chaumont, Patton commanded the headquarters company of about 250 men and a motorcar detachment of ninety automobiles. He was in charge of anti-aircraft defenses and performed odd tasks. He also took it upon himself to dress down savagely officers and men who were dirty, who failed to salute, who were derelict in military discipline and courtesy. Although Pershing's headquarters was bound to grow and thus to make Patton eligible for promotion, he was restless, disgustingly safe, and "darned sick of my job."

He became vaguely interested in tanks, a new and as yet unproved weapon. Having invented them about the same time, the British experimented with heavy tanks, the French with light ones, but neither army had meaningfully employed them in combat. Theoretically, tanks could destroy defenses and restore offensive mobility to the battlefield, for the machines would protect tankers from small-arms fire in no-man's-land while they crushed barbed-wire entanglements and machine-gun nests, thereby permitting the infantry to advance. The Americans had no tanks, but staff officers were talking of obtaining them.

Although still not altogether sure of his course, Patton placed his name into consideration for assignment if a tank service was organized. A letter set forth his qualifications. The use of light tanks, he said, resembled cavalry operations, and he was a cavalryman. He had commanded a machine-gun troop, was well acquainted with weapons, and had successfully instructed on the firing range. He had repaired automobile engines and knew how the motors worked. He spoke and read French fluently, got on well with Frenchmen, and could thus consult French tank manuals. Willing to take chances in war, he believed in getting close to the enemy. While teaching for two years at the Mounted Service School, he had roused "the aggressive spirit in the students." Referring to the Rubio ranch, he pointed out he was the only American officer "who has ever made an attack in a motor vehicle."

Pershing asked Patton where he preferred to serve if he was promoted to major—on the staff or in command of an infantry battalion? A staff position held little interest for him. He wanted to be with troops. Whether he commanded 1,000 infantrymen or a unit of tanks, "with luck I might go a long way."

In mid-October, Patton came down with jaundice and went to the hospital. Put in the same room with Colonel Fox Conner, he talked about infantry and tanks and asked Conner's advice. Noting the untried capacities of tanks, Conner inclined toward the infantry as leading more surely to action and advancement. Patton agreed and so decided. But when a friend visited him and brought news of the decision to start a tank school in the nearby town of Langres with Patton as director, Patton forgot his earlier resolution and accepted the challenge.

Patton was still up in the air when he was promoted to major. No matter where he landed, he decided, apparently leaving the choice to fate, what was important was to sever his close association with Pershing. He had to be successful on his own, to "stand on my own feet. Then if I can't make a go of it why it is my fault." If Patton stayed with Pershing and if Pershing married Nita, everyone would accuse Patton of getting ahead by pull.

When orders assigned him to direct the new tank school, "I did not sleep a bit that night" for fear of having made the wrong decision. He then reconciled himself to his destiny. The tanks were to be his "way to high command if I make a go of it." As against a hundred majors of infantry, he would be the only one of light tanks. Besides, infantrymen were in the trenches most of the time while tankers fought only in attacks and were comfortable the rest of the time. Tanks, of course, might prove to be useless, but if they worked on the battlefield, they "will work like hell."

"Here is the golden dream," he confided to Bea. Patton would open and run the school, then organize and command a tank battalion. If he did well, he would eventually command a tank regiment or brigade and be eligible for high rank. In the infantry, he might happen to be in reserve during an attack, and someone else would have the opportunity to gain credit for heroism in battle. Furthermore, newspapers and illustrated magazines featured tanks because they were a novelty, and he would get more publicity. Finally, tankers had less chance of being wounded, for they were either untouched or blown to bits by a direct shell hit.

To become thoroughly familiar and proficient with tanks before opening his school, Patton spent two weeks at the French tank training center near Compiègne. Lieutenant Elgin Braine, an engineer in civilian life and a reserve artillery officer assigned to the tank corps, accompanied him. Patton became increasingly enthusiastic as he drove the small two-man Renault tank, where the driver sat on the floor and the gunner stood in the turret, directing the tank by touching the driver on the head and shoulders with his foot. Tanks were armed with a machine gun or cannon, and Patton fired both. He examined the tank's structure and machinery, observed training maneuvers, inspected repair shops, and had long discussions with faculty and students on tank employment.

While he was there, the first real tank battle took place at Cambrai. Although some tanks had earlier been in combat, Cambrai marked the birth of armored warfare in the twentieth century. Three brigades of British tanks, almost 500, supported by a thousand guns and six divisions of infantry, attacked without preliminary artillery and gained complete surprise. In little more than four hours, the leading troops advanced more than seven miles. Despite this enormous initial success, the tanks were unable to maintain their momentum and to exploit their breakthrough. A week later the Germans drove the British back to their original starting line.

Despite this result, the tanks had proved their value if employed in large numbers. They could destroy and overrun defenses on the Western Front. They had punch and go. The shortcomings that had prevented them from sustaining their triumph were inexperience and a lack of doctrine. It was clear to most that with improved battlefield techniques, the tank could turn into the premier weapon of the war.

The realization brought a resurgence of interest in tanks, together with a flood of applications to join the new combat arm. Patton felt lucky to be the first American tanker. He visited the British near Cambrai, spoke with the brigade commander and his chief of staff, J.F.C. Fuller, and gained insight into tank procedures. During the months that followed, whenever tanks were in action he always went to the scene afterward to talk with the tankers.

Driving to Paris, "I had my usual yearly accident." The car ran into a closed railway gate and the jolt sent Patton's head through the windshield. He cut an artery on the temple, hurt his chin, and bled a great deal before the American hospital in Neuilly patched him up.

At the tank factory in Bilancourt outside Paris for a week, Patton, together with Braine, meticulously examined the mechanism and the parts. Returning to Chaumont, they set their observations on paper. With Braine's assistance on the mechanical aspects, Patton composed a long and thorough report. He explained the nature of the tank, the organization of tank units, the tactics of tank forces, and the instructions and drills for tankers. His study laid the groundwork and became the basis of U.S. tank operations. If he was successful, he wrote to Beatrice, "I may have the chance I have always been looking for."

About to open his tank school in Langres, he confessed to her: "Actually I am in quite a 'Funk.'" Although all his friends were confident of his ability to do the job, "I wish I were as sanguine. I am sure I will do it but just at this moment I don't see how. I will have to grow and grow a lot. But I *will*." He added, "I miss you in all I do or think. We are so united that I don't function well alone."

He had an awesome task. Virtually singlehandedly, as the only American who knew much about tanks and as the recognized expert in this new form of warfare, he was about to bring a new branch into being, a service with men and machines, then teach the men and show them how to fight, and lead them in combat.

In mid-December, just before he left Chaumont for Langres, he wrote, "This is my last day as staff officer. Now I rise or fall on my own." He was nervous but had no reservations. He could have obtained appointment to a staff. But "I have always talked blood and murder and am looked on as an advocate of close up fighting. I could never look myself in the face if I was a staff officer and comparatively safe."

The site of a Roman military camp and of a medieval strongpoint, with ramparts and walls, Langres, about twenty miles from Chaumont, was a small town on a high plateau dominating the countryside. A later and apocryphal story told of Patton's arrival at night during a rainstorm; it alleged that in keeping with his belief in reincarnation and his conviction that he had served in Caesar's legion, he experienced a sensa-

Patton, a lieutenant colonel, as commander of the Tank
Corps school in Langres, France.

tion of déjà vu: He knew the layout of the streets and the locations of the amphitheater, the forum, the temples, and where Caesar had pitched his tent. In truth, he came in daylight and took a room at the hotel until he found a house to rent.

Creating a context for the tank effort, the American Expeditionary Force named Colonel Samuel D. Rockenbach to be chief of the Tank Service at Pershing's headquarters. Rockenbach had a dual position. As a commander, he was the boss of the American tankers training in England in the heavy British-type tanks, and of Patton in Langres, who was to instruct Americans in the light French tanks. As a staff officer, Rockenbach was the adviser to Pershing on tank matters and the focal point for administration, procurement, supply, and the like.

A mature if somewhat pompous officer, a graduate of the Virginia Military Institute, Rockenbach was good at operating in a large headquarters. Although he and Patton were at first cool and suspicious toward each other, they had to work together and to depend on each other for the sake of the war, the tanks, and their own personal fortunes. Rockenbach came to respect Patton's tactical sense, and Patton admitted Rockenbach's staff competence. Gradually they established a close relationship. If they never developed a warm friendship, they gave mutual support, and each came to have a grudging admiration for the other.

Looking for a place to lodge and train the tankers to be assigned to him, Patton found exactly what he wanted about five miles south of Langres. On the road to Dijon and beside the railroad from Langres, around the hamlet of Bourg, an expanse of land gave him room for a school, a tank park, and a maneuver ground. After visiting the location several times and becoming increasingly enchanted, he showed the place to Rockenbach, who approved. When Patton sought to requisition the land, the French authorities at first refused to make the ground available, mainly because they feared stray rounds and shells from tanks in training. By a superb demonstration of firmness, pressure, anger, and diplomacy, Patton secured the land.

Then he took Rockenbach on a whirlwind visit to the French and British training schools. He was very patient, explained all technical affairs meticulously, and smoothly talked Rockenbach around to his ideas and outlook.

Near the end of the year, Patton received his first tankers. Two dozen Coast Artillery Corps officers who were former sergeants were the nucleus of his new unit. Having been appalled by the lack of saluting and the unsoldierly conduct in Langres, Patton resolved to have model troops under him. The Tank Corps,* he said, "will have discipline if nothing else." His first memo as director laid down a strict policy on personal appearance, dress, cleanliness, shaving, haircuts, and proper saluting.

Asked to speak on tanks to fifteen senior officers, Patton stressed the need for cooperation with the infantry. Very much aware of widespread doubts on the value of tanks in combat, Patton was careful to stress the supremacy of the infantry in battle. The tanks operated simply to help foot soldiers gain and hold ground and win victory. The talk was good and well received, but, as always, he wondered about his performance. "I don't feel that I am doing my best some way. I never do. If I ever do feel that I am earning my pay I may really begin to get somewhere."

The French had promised to furnish several tanks for Patton's training program, but none came to Bourg. Patton persuaded Rockenbach to send Braine, whom he admired for his competence and loyalty, to the United States to speed the American production of tanks. While he waited for machines and soldiers, Patton drew up tables of organization and equipment, drill regulations, and courses of instruction.

A replacement center sent him 200 men, and Patton met them at the Langres railroad station. He marched them to his area, where he had prepared for their reception: A hot meal was ready, a latrine had been dug, and billets had been found in barns and farmhouses. He provided the best accommodations he could and looked after his soldiers as well as he could—this too was already a Patton trademark and part of the legend. He was tickled to have them under him. All drafted, some college graduates, they were, he judged, "really a very fine bunch of men much above the ordinary."

Around the end of February 1918, he moved his soldiers to more permanent and more comfortable barracks in Bourg, his own village, where he was "the absolute boss." He maintained a strict discipline, which he believed saved lives in battle and which he defined as "instant, cheerful, unhesitating obedi-

*The names Tank Corps and Tank Service were used interchangeably. Patton tended to use Tank Corps.

ence" rendered automatically. With order, he believed, troops were irresistible. Together with simple movements and elastic formations, iron discipline was the essential to success in battle. Saluting, a mark of military brotherhood, was important as an indication of morale and alertness. A commander who was unable to have his men salute properly had little chance of getting them to perform their jobs in the midst of battlefield danger. Hard training made combat easy.

He lectured his officers often on the need to accomplish their tasks perfectly. They were to teach uniform doctrine and create an elite body of men who were determined to win. Leaders were to explain and demonstrate lessons in an interesting manner and to cultivate an aggressive, offensive spirit in all ranks.

Patton appeared everywhere, encouraging and bawling out his men. He wished to turn them into images of himself— ruthless daring and dash. His words were moving and dramatic, and his troops embellished and spread them.

Mr. and Mrs. Ayer died a few weeks apart in the spring of 1918, and Patton wrote tenderly to Bea.

Late in March, when Patton had about 250 officers and men under him, a train brought ten French tanks to a place near Bourg where Patton had had a platform and a ramp constructed. During the night, Patton drove the tanks off, showed nine of his most experienced drivers how to operate them, and moved them about a mile from the railroad into a woods, where they were camouflaged. French railway officials had expected the unloading and removal to consume fifteen hours; Patton's men efficiently did it in three.

Promoted to lieutenant colonel, "I feel more or less a fool being a colonel," he wrote Bea, "but it will wear off. . . . How do you feel being a Mrs. Colonel. We never thought to reach it so soon did we."

Patton planned and conducted his first maneuver for tanks and infantry working together. A series of exercises and practice movements in simulated combat followed. Patton learned by trial and error how to group and regroup, how to deploy and redeploy. He prepared the field orders, the instructions, the directives, and then like Pershing in Mexico, personally directed the operations. Often he staged demonstrations for officers attending the schools in Langres in order to promote understanding of tank capabilities.

Patton received frequent compliments on the "very soldierly" appearance of his troops and the neatness of his area. Senior officers considered the tankers to be the best in smartness, enthusiasm, and saluting. Patton was pleased, "for the good opinion of those above you is a source of great advantage." Furthermore, "if a person does his best and keeps doing it, it usually pays, though not always." Yet at the end, "luck always changes [for the better] if you do your best with what you have." On the other hand, he worked very hard and seemed to accomplish very little.

At the end of April he organized the 1st Light Tank Battalion. He himself was in command, and Joseph Viner, Sereno Brett, and Herman Compton were the company commanders. Two months later he established the 1st Light Tank Brigade, again under his command, with Viner and Brett as the battalion commanders, each with three companies, and a repair and salvage company to service the tanks. Officers and men gained assurance in their duties and showed it. "I have traveled far and fast" since Mexico, he told Beatrice. He reported a song composed about him. One line said, "We will follow the colonel through hell and out the other side." Flattered, he was at a loss to understand why the tankers liked him, for he cussed them freely, he said, all the time. "I am with out question a very superior soldier" despite "my many shortcomings." What he had in abundance was the ability to establish strong rapport with his troops.

He agonized through the early months of 1918 whether he would have enough tanks and trained men to enter the fight before the war ended. Was he right to have chosen the tanks? Had he selected the infantry he would probably have already seen action, for a few American units, responding to the danger of the Ludendorff spring offensive, had joined the Allies in combat, at Cantigny, Belleau Wood, and Chateau Thierry. Patton dreaded that the war might be over before he engaged in battle. "That would destroy my military career or at least give it a great set back." He woke up at night in a cold sweat fearing the coming of peace. The advantage he clung to was being the only American light tank commander instead of one of many infantry battalion commanders. He continued to work despite difficulties and discouragements, which, he acknowledged, were doing his character a great deal of good. But unless he participated in battle, all his effort was wasted.

With five of his lieutenants, he visited a sector of the French front and for several days observed how troops entered the lines and behaved under fire, how artillery was placed in support, how business was conducted. Vastly interested, he found the experience curious, even funny, hardly dangerous.

Although Patton had no wish to be a staff officer, he decided to attend the Army General Staff College in Langres. Keeping up in his course work at the same time he remained in close touch with his tank center would be double duty, but he preferred to be busy. The schooling would contribute to his professional knowledge by teaching him how modern mass armies were organized and operated. His days were full of activity and study. Occasionally he lectured to the staff college students on the employment of tanks. There he came to know many of the best soldiers of his time, among them George C. Marshall and Adna R. Chaffee.

With tank production in the United States in chaos, the factories unable to provide the machines required, Pershing secured a promise from the French to equip Patton's battalions. The first installment of fifteen arrived at Bourg. The men drove them off the train, down the ramp, and to the tank park in record time. With a total of twenty-five tanks now on hand, the tankers practiced unit exercises and company drills. Morale was high. Everyone had absorbed Patton's enthusiasm and, like him, believed proficiency and boldness to be the keys to victory.

By August 1918 he was commanding fifty officers, 900 men, and twenty-five tanks. "I will have to develop even a meaner look than I now have but that will only be my official face," he told Beatrice. He probably would leave the tanks and go back to the cavalry after the war because tanks were a specialty, and specialists "don't get supreme command." Also, he expected the next war to be in Mexico, where tanks would be useless because of the lack of roads.

He had been brought up in the cavalry, which stressed mobility, and his thinking on tanks was much the same. He preferred relatively light machines. Less armor and more speed made them maneuverable and gave them greater range. Because tanks were to assist the infantry, coordination between the two had to be detailed and careful. Tanks were not to be used as pillboxes placed along the front but rather employed to deliver shock by rapid movement. Tankers had to be extremely bold, even rash. He would soon have the opportunity to prove his beliefs.

On August 20, while Patton was listening to a lecture at the staff college, someone handed him a note. He was to report to the chief of the Tank Service at once. At Chaumont, Rockenbach told him of the first large-scale and independent American attack scheduled for early in September. The tanks were to take part.

In great excitement, Patton and Rockenbach drove to the First Army headquarters, where they were briefed on the operation. Rockenbach remained to coordinate various matters while Patton went forward to consult with corps and division staffs and to inspect the region. To see whether the ground was hard enough to support tanks, Patton accompanied a night patrol of French soldiers into no-man's-land. He hoped for a fight, but the French and Germans merely exchanged whistles. He checked detraining points for his tanks, plotted routes to a nearby woods to conceal them, found paths to the jumpoff line, wrote a terrain appreciation and a preliminary plan, asked the artillery to use smoke shells to mask the tanks from enemy observation, requested road space to be reserved for gasoline trucks, and wanted a specially designated airplane to locate enemy strong points and to direct artillery shells on these targets.

Three American battalions of about 150 heavy tanks coming from England were supposed to participate in the attack, but they arrived too late. To compensate for their absence, the French contributed two battalions of about 225 light tanks to the offensive. Patton's brigade was to have 144 tanks, and they were then in the process of being unloaded at Bourg. Because Patton would be with the attacking forces, he appointed Viner to take charge of the school and center. He moved Brett to command the 1st Battalion and installed Compton at the head of the 2d. Setting up his command post, Patton established observation posts, selected assembly points, laid telephone wires. He conferred with the two division commanders he was to support, found both eager to cooperate, and had them send ninety infantry officers to a tank-infantry demonstration at Bourg.

Everything was set when everything was changed. The tanks were now to work with another corps in a different area. Patton again personally reconnoitered the ground, wrote a new plan of attack, and repeated his activities in the new zone. He established a dump of 10,000 gallons of gasoline. The trains bringing his units to the front made mistakes, and there was much confusion. With everything straightened out on the eve of the battle, Patton issued an order of the day. He exhorted his troops to do well, to keep moving forward, to help the infantry. "This is our big chance: what we have worked for. . . . make it worth while." Now, at last, after a lifetime of yearning, Patton would go into battle.

Pershing's First Army was to eliminate the St. Mihiel salient, a bulge carved into the Allied line generally east of Verdun as early as September 1914. No serious fighting had taken place there for two years. In that quiet zone, the Germans constructed heavy defensive works and manned them with inferior troops; they planned to withdraw in the event of an Allied attack. Without knowledge of the German intention, American units came together and concentrated near St. Mihiel from dispersed locations, all moving at night in great secrecy. Pershing organized a converging maneuver by 550,000 Americans and 110,000 French soldiers. While the French exerted pressure, two U.S. corps side by side were to drive the southern face of the salient and go north to meet another U.S. corps coming eastward from the western side. The tanks were to support the advance from the south. One battalion of the French tanks was to be with the corps on the right, and Patton had no responsibility for that unit. The other French tank battalion, plus Patton's tanks, all under him, were to be with the corps on the left.

According to Patton's plan, Brett on the left was to lead the infantry of the 1st Division to their objectives around the village of Nonsard. The French tankers in the center were to follow the infantry. Compton on the right was to start behind the infantry of the 42d Division, pick up speed, pass through the foot soldiers, then lead them into Essey and Pannes in turn. Patton had confidence in Brett, who was a tough infantryman turned tanker, and the 1st Division had had experience working with tanks at Cantigny. On the other hand, the 42d Division had never operated with tanks, and Compton was less strong and sure of himself. Patton positioned himself closer to Compton's men.

Tired from his exertions and lack of sleep, worried because rain threatened to turn the ground into mud that would render tanks helpless, Patton was at a high pitch of tension on September 12, the day of attack. At 5:00 A.M., after a four-hour barrage, the troops started to advance. At 6:10, on a hill where he could watch Brett on the left, the French in the middle, and Compton on the right, Patton telephoned the corps headquarters and reported Brett's tanks passing Xivray; the French were invisible because of heavy fog. At 6:30, all the tanks were advancing except several bogged down and stuck in trenches. Irritated, he walked two miles to the scene, got them dug out, and started them moving. He and his staff continued forward on foot.

Patton was now experiencing what has been called the dilemma of command: Where should the commander be in battle? If he remains at his command post, he ensures good communications with his reserves and the artillery, maintains his contact with superiors, permits them to visit him with the least inconvenience and personal risk, and is on hand to offer advice and counsel and to receive new orders and missions. If he accompanies the combat elements and leads in person, he becomes vulnerable to disablement or death and loses touch with his superiors, but his presence will enhance the performance of his men. Patton preferred the latter course—to be available to make instant corrections and adjustments and to spark morale and drive where the fight was won or lost. He embraced the notion that a leader belonged in the midst of the action as a visible symbol of skills learned and attitudes inculcated. Perhaps for Patton the excitement was too attractive. Perhaps he felt a need to prove his courage, to test his nerve.

When Patton's telephone wire ran out, he left his adjutant there and walked forward with a lieutenant and four runners. At 7:30, he reported that at least sixteen tanks were heavily engaged, and that the artillery smoke screen was excellent. An hour later, from a hill near Seicheprey in Compton's zone, he saw tanks preceding infantry in both the 1st and 42d Division areas. Five tanks were out of action, but he did not know the cause.

At 9:15, a runner from Compton told Patton of tanks being held up by difficult ground. He, an officer, and three runners went forward, passing huge trenches, many of them eight feet deep and ten to fourteen feet wide. He walked through shell-fire so close that the explosions threw dust on him. Although he wanted to duck, he wrote to Bea, he soon recognized "the futility of dodging fate." He was "the only officer around who had left on his shoulder straps"—the others, he noted, had discarded them for fear of attracting the fire of German sharpshooters—"and I had to live up to them. It was much easier than you would think and the feeling, foolish probably, of being admired by the men lying down is a great stimulus."

Reaching St. Baussant under shelling, an experience "not pleasant," he found several French tanks stuck. The French major was working to get them going, so Patton proceeded toward Essey, where infantrymen were lying in shellholes and firing. Shells were passing overhead, but Patton kept walking, furiously smoking his pipe. He followed the firing line until he saw Brigadier General Douglas MacArthur, "who was standing on a little hill. . . . I joined him and the creeping barrage came along toward us. . . . I think each one wanted to leave, but each hated to say so, so we let it come over us. We stood and talked but neither was much interested in what the other said."

From another hill, Patton saw Germans running beyond Essey. The town seemed ready for the taking, and Patton went toward it. When five of Compton's tanks came up, Patton told them to go through Essey. A Frenchman at the bridge just before the town turned them back because, he said, the bombardment was too intense. An angry Patton sent them forward. On foot, he himself led them across the bridge into the village. Patton later said he did not know whether the bridge was mined or wired for demolition and would explode as he crossed.

Walking behind the tanks, Patton had some Germans surrender to him. He sent them to the rear. MacArthur was in Essey, and Patton asked whether he could attack the next town, Pannes, about two miles ahead. MacArthur said sure, so Patton and the tanks continued. Just before Pannes, riflemen were firing but unwilling to enter the town. All the tanks but one ran out of gas, and Patton directed the sergeant to go in. Because he seemed a little nervous, Patton climbed up and sat on the top of the tank to encourage him. A lieutenant and sergeant kept Patton company on the tail of the tank. These two, once in town, departed to take about thirty Germans prisoner.

Still atop the tank as it left Pannes, Patton saw paint fly from the side as bullets struck. He jumped off and lay in a shellhole. While Germans shot at him, the tank continued advancing. The infantry, about 300 yards behind Patton, made no move to come up. Patton ran back to the infantrymen, falling flat every time he heard bullets around him. He located the infantry commander and asked him to get his men to go after the tank, still moving ahead slowly. He refused.

Taking off at a hard run, while bullets sang about him, Patton caught up with the tank and tapped on the back door with his walking stick. The sergeant inside looked out, saluted, and said, "What do you want now, Colonel?" He told the tanker to turn around and go back. The man seemed disappointed. Patton, walking in front of the tank for protection against the small-arms fire, led the tank back to Pannes.

When four tanks came by, Patton put them in line and sent them through Pannes to attack the next town, Beney, while he followed on foot. The Germans were leaving, and the tankers took the town and captured four artillery pieces and sixteen machine guns.

Satisfied that Compton's battalion had done well, Patton decided to see how Brett was doing. Trudging across what had been no-man's-land, he found Brett and twenty-five tanks at Nonsard. They were out of fuel.

Patton walked to the rear to have gasoline sent up, then reported to the corps headquarters. The tankers had attained their objectives and more. During the hours of darkness, because the infantry failed to come up, Brett's and Compton's tanks withdrew several hundred yards from Nonsard and Beney. Gasoline came up during the night.

Tank casualties during the first day were two lost to artillery fire, three to engine failure, two to broken tracks, forty stuck in trenches and being towed out, thirty stalled by lack of fuel. Ready for action on the following morning were eighty American tanks and twenty-five French. Brett advanced to Vigneulles, Compton to St. Benoit. The Germans were in retreat, the salient had been erased, the Americans had captured 15,000 prisoners and 450 guns, and Pershing ended the battle.

Of the 174 tanks engaged, three were destroyed, twenty-two were ditched, and fourteen had broken down. Five men had been killed, four officers and fifteen men wounded. The attack had gone well against little German resistance. Although the action hardly tested the tankers, Patton's "Treat-'em-Rough Boys," as they were called, performed valiantly in their initial operation under fire. They acted like veterans, demonstrated coolness and efficiency. They proved their ability to fight and win under Patton. The tankers had showed the Patton mark, the spirit to confront and defeat the enemy, the ardor to fight, the desire to advance aggressively. Newspaper stories were numerous, and many featured Patton riding on a tank.

Although Rockenbach reprimanded Patton for going into battle instead of remaining at his command post, Pershing sent a letter of congratulations to Rockenbach on the tank performance. Rockenbach then complimented Patton and his men.

There was no time to rest, for the First Army was to move at once about sixty miles to a new attack zone west of Verdun and initiate the Meuse-Argonne offensive with three corps in the line, the tanks to support the I Corps. Before American troops relieved French units, Patton borrowed a French uniform and thoroughly inspected the ground. He planned to use his tanks in depth for a concentrated thrust to penetrate the German defenses. This was to be followed by a pursuit, much in the manner of the later blitzkrieg. Putting his battalions in column, he instructed Brett, leading off, to take the initial objectives, Compton, following, to pass through to the second objectives, and finally, the French to go through and move as far forward as they could. He did his best to collect and store, just behind the front, adequate supplies of gasoline for the 140 tanks to be employed.

Physically and mentally weary, Patton complained to Bea about his officers who came running to him to solve their problems. "Some times I think I am not such a great commander after all. Just a fighting animal. Still I will improve in time. At least if one learns by mistakes I ought to be wise. I have made all [the mistakes] there are." He was "always nearvous about this time [before battle] just as at Polo or at Foot Ball before the game starts but so far I have been all right after that. I hope I keep on that way."

The terrain was extremely difficult, and the German defenses were elaborate and ingenious. The Americans faced a labyrinth twelve miles deep, with mutually supporting machine-gun nests, set in concrete and protected by barbed wire, on the heights of Montfaucon, Cunel, Romagne, and Barricourt.

The artillery preparation commenced at 2:30 A.M. on September 26, and three hours later the troops started forward in a heavy mist, which concealed the tanks from the enemy and from Patton at his observation post as well. With two officers and about a dozen runners, he walked toward the sound of the guns to see what was going on. By 9:00 A.M., the tanks had advanced five miles and captured the village of Varennes and proceeded toward the hamlet of Cheppy. As Patton approached Cheppy, shells and machine-gun fire came in on his party. They took cover in a railroad cut. Panicked soldiers were running toward the rear, and Patton stopped them and collected about 100 men.

When the enemy fire subsided, Patton led them out and placed them in spread formation across the reverse slope of a hill. At the bottom of the rise, behind him, several tanks were unable to cross two large trenches. Patton sent several men down to hurry them, but nothing happened. He finally descended the hill himself. Men were digging to break down the walls of the trenches and allow the tanks to proceed, but whenever enemy fire fell nearby, they all jumped into a trench and took cover.

Patton put an end to that. Organizing a concerted effort, personally unstrapping shovels and picks from the sides of tanks while bullets splattered the hulls, exposing himself to enemy fire, hitting one man over the head with a shovel to get him to work, Patton soon had the sides of the trenches torn down. Five tanks crossed the barrier, and Patton sent them up the hill. He followed.

When the tanks disappeared over the crest of the hill, Patton waved his large walking stick around his head, shouted, "Let's go get them. Who is with me?" and strode forward. The men who were spread across the reverse slope got to their feet and followed in his wake. As they crossed the top, incoming machine-gun fire washed over them. Everyone fell to the ground.

Patton "felt a great desire to run, I was trembling with fear when suddenly I thought of my progenitors and seemed to see them in a cloud over the German lines looking at me. I became calm at once and saying aloud, 'It is time for another Patton to die' called for volunteers and went forward to what I honestly believed to be certain death." When the fire abated, Patton rose to his feet, waved his stick, shouted, "Let's go," and went ahead.

Six men were with him, including his orderly, Joc Angelo, but one by one the soldiers fell, until Angelo said, "We are alone." Patton replied, "Come on anyway." He took a few

113

steps, and a bullet entered his left thigh, came out near his rectum, and dropped him.

Angelo helped him into a shellhole, cut his trousers, and bandaged his wound, which was bleeding a great deal. Several tanks appeared, and Patton sent Angelo, who crossed the ground by rushes, to point out the locations of German machine guns about forty yards away. A sergeant came by, and Patton told him to carry back word of his wound. Brett was to take command. No one was to come for Patton because the firing was too dangerous. Several more tanks passed, and Patton again sent Angelo to give directions and to point out targets. A medic happened by, changed Patton's bandage, and continued looking for other wounded men. An hour or so later, when there was no longer fire in the area, three men came with a stretcher. Together with Angelo, they placed Patton on the litter and carried him about two miles to an ambulance company. Patton insisted on being taken to the division headquarters, where an officer came out and listened to Patton's report of the action. Then he was driven to an evacuation hospital.

He awakened on the following morning to find two of his tank officers in beds adjacent to his. Newspaper stories called Patton the "Hero of the Tanks," for he had directed his men though lying wounded in a shellhole.

After three days he was transferred by train to a base hospital south of Dijon. Although he was absent from the continuing combat, he contributed to the continuing tank exploits not only by his teaching and training but also by his indomitable spirit. He had passed the final test of leadership, leaving behind him in other men the conviction and will to carry on. With dwindling numbers of machines on hand, the tankers fought through the middle of October. They worked with infantrymen to clean out difficult pockets of resistance, helped the foot soldiers establish a consolidated front, and frequently operated ahead of the riflemen. The Germans resisted fiercely. The campaign lasted for forty-seven days and the Americans lost more than 26,000 dead and 95,000 wounded.

Rockenbach recommended Patton for promotion to colonel. Pershing, well aware of what he called Patton's gallantry, wrote Bea of her right to "be prouder of him than ever."

"Peace looks possible," Patton informed Bea, "but I rather hope not for I would like to have a few more fights. They are awfully thrilling like steeple chasing only more so." His wound was miraculous, and he ascribed his good luck to fate. The bullet had missed his hip joint, sciatic nerve, the big artery, and all the vital parts. He walked normally. "I am a lot older in some things," he told Bea. He had often wondered whether he could command a battalion. "Now I know I could command a Division."

Three weeks before his thirty-third birthday, quite a young man, he was promoted to colonel. "What do you think of me," he asked Beatrice. "I feel quite elated though as a matter of fact I don't believe I deserve it very much." Healing nicely, he was transferred to the hospital at Langres, and he visited his men at Bourg. There he was pleased to find many complimentary letters on the performance of his tankers in combat.

To Bea he admitted he'd been afraid to march forward just before being hit—until he thought of "my ancestors." After that, remaining on the ground and trembling would have stamped him as false to his caste. To Papa he wrote: "I have always feared I was a coward at heart but I am beginning to doubt it."

Discharged from the hospital and back to duty at Bourg, Patton issued an immediate order on "dress, comportment, and discipline." He recommended officers and men for decorations. He was working on tank tactics, how to increase the range of tank operations, when the war came to an end. To have the Armistice fall on his birthday, a day of personal meaning, was a sign from the gods, a good omen.

A later story, unfortunately untrue, had Patton and one of his company commanders, Harry Semmes, breaking out of the hospital to rejoin the fighting and reaching Verdun on November 11.

Patton could with good reason be satisfied with his achievements during the most exciting and fruitful of his life to that time. The former Master of the Sword had become the foremost American tank expert. He had founded a new branch of service, pioneered, like his Grandfather Wilson in another context, a new technique of warfare. At his tank school and center, he had established tank training. He had led his men in combat and proved the soundness of his teaching. He had shaped soldiers in the mold that would ever be his trademark, and they had contributed to victory in the two major American campaigns of the war. He had exhibited gallantry in the face of enemy fire, and his wound attested to his courage. For his devoted efforts and success, he had been promoted three times, rising to the grade of colonel. Most important, his leadership had worked.

Service in France provided him the chance to know the best officers of the time, those who would be influential in the post-war Army—Pershing, ever his model, Charles Summerall, Malin Craig, and George C. Marshall, future Army Chiefs of Staff; Fox Conner, a power behind the scenes; Hugh Drum, eventually the senior Army officer on active duty; Adna R. Chaffee, father of the tanks in World War II; and more. All admired his military professionalism, dedication to duty, and driving personality. He had attracted their favorable attention, one of his cardinal aims.

Rockenbach put Patton in for the Distinguished Service Cross. Under a hail of gunfire, he had motivated and directed men digging out tanks bogged down in trenches, then had moved them forward. By personal pressure, he had kept up the momentum of the attack. He had shown poise in great danger. Although wounded, he had continued to command.

The commandant of schools in Langres recommended Patton for the Distinguished Service Medal, as he said, "for having had the finest spirit and discipline in your command that I have ever seen." Patton literally prayed to God for both decorations. He wanted tangible reward for his exertions.

Rockenbach's paperwork was hurried and somewhat incomplete, and Pershing's headquarters twice returned the recommendation. Patton insisted that Rockenbach resubmit the papers with better documentation, with fuller descriptions by eyewitnesses of his battlefield exploits, and he lobbied subtly among his friends on Pershing's staff. Had he not believed he deserved the recognition, he would not have pushed for it. The fact was, he merited the award. And he wished to have the visible sign of the ribbon for his self-esteem, record, and future career.

In the end, he secured both decorations, the one for high achievement in a post of great responsibility, the other for his personal bravery on the field of battle, "conspicuous courage, coolness, energy, and intelligence," the citation read. He had truly distinguished himself in the Great War and nourished his legend.

5

BETWEEN THE WARS

Although the glow of Patton's wartime achievements remained to cheer him, the interwar years for him were a time of frustration, capped by a glimmer of returning hope. Rapid postwar demobilization destroyed the Army, and public apathy and congressional frugality prevented rebuilding. Pacifism, economic depression, and the natural protection of the Atlantic and Pacific oceans promoted a spirit of isolationism. The military establishment remained small and stagnant. Equipment rusted and became obsolete, units fell below authorized strengths. Lacking funds for research, development, and experimentation, even for realistic exercises, the Army atrophied during twenty years of peace. Toward the end of the period, when aggression overseas threatened international stability, government officials looking at the American warmaking capacity found it feeble and began, but haltingly, to modernize the military forces. Over the course of the twenty years, Patton would enter middle age and put on some weight, lose his youthful appearance and most of his hair, and pass through a midlife crisis. Despite his external ebullience, he despaired. Was he growing too old to participate in another war adventure? Many of his heroes like Alexander the Great and Napoleon had won immortality as young men. Patton wanted his chance, his war, and just as he thought he saw his opportunity appearing on the horizon, he was struck down by an injury that almost closed out his career. Fortunately, miraculously, perhaps prodded by his own driving willpower, he recovered in time to take part in changes prompted by armed conflict.

Throughout the period he played polo savagely, working off his discouragement and excess energy, practicing the teamwork he believed to be important in combat, keeping his body in shape, trying to dissipate his gloom, and exhibiting a profanity of virtuosic proportions. He read extensively, wrote military treatises almost constantly, and thought profoundly about the profession of arms. He stayed abreast of new military techniques and hoped to be ready for what everyone called "the next war," although he feared that it would come too late, after his Army retirement.

On four separate occasions he sought a position he wanted with all his might, to be commandant of cadets at West Point. If he was to be denied another war, he could at least pass his lessons to the younger generation. Although he obtained powerful support from friends, including Pershing, he failed. The last time, in a letter to Pershing, he cited his wartime experiences as his prime qualification to transmit "blood and guts" to the aspiring officers at the Academy. He remembered his words, and later, on the eve of World War II, he used them when describing his methods to newspaper reporters. They made the phrase so widely known that it entered the language. "Old Blood and Guts Patton" became his sobriquet for all time.

As he performed his duties faithfully and impeccably during these difficult years, always doing more than required, striving to be the best and to win the approval of his superiors, he wondered whether his destiny had deserted him. Had he already achieved, on the Western Front, everything intended for him? If so, no greater glory, no great fame awaited him. He was apparently not even to become a general officer. Although he fought the disappointing prospect, his melancholic view of being merely an ordinary rather than an outstanding officer possessed him.

Much of the time he served in staff positions, "a place," he said, "for which God never intended me." A staff officer serves the commander, tries to anticipate his wishes, and can direct others only in the commander's name. A good staff officer takes detail off the commander's mind and allows him the time to think and to plan. A staff officer is expected to be tactful, patient, and reticent, as well as diplomatic. He should be industrious, self-effacing, and unselfish, as well as happy to subordinate himself to the man in charge. These qualities were hardly Patton's strengths. Temperamentally, he was fitted for command, to be the forceful boss himself. In addition, he required strenuous physical activity for his own well-being, and he far preferred being with troops in the field to sedentary deskwork. Yet he persisted and persevered as a staff officer, giving his all, willing to endure the confining duty because of his devotion to the Army, his loyalty to his superiors, and his own habit.

The high pitch of wartime tension in France dissolved at once after the Armistice. It was "not as easy to get up in the morning" as before. His "laziness which ever pursued me" was troubling him again. He was in "a hellish and stupid world now and life has lost its zest." There was "nothing much to do now," and he was "getting worthless the same as I got in Mexico. I hate to feel this way."

Although he trained his men as usual—as always, he maintained an iron discipline—it was difficult to interest and occupy them. Braine had brought two American-built tanks to France too late for the war, and Patton tested them. He experimented with equipment and formations and installed in tanks radios capable of working when the vehicles were in motion. He glimpsed the future when he tried to free tanks from the pace of foot soldiers by advocating tank exploitation in enemy rear areas to paralyze enemy command centers, a vision made a reality by the Germans early in World War II. But he was unable to achieve a theoretical concept in the manner of a J.F.C. Fuller or a Basil Liddell Hart.

He pondered the lessons of the war and wrote papers to clarify his thoughts and to deliver as lectures, to his officers and men and to the students at the General Staff College. He collected British and French training notes, after-action reports, and operational histories and studied them to expand his understanding of tanks in battle. He read all the citations for bravery he could find, seeking to learn what impelled men to perform heroic acts.

His soldiers, he wrote Bea, thought a lot of him for having walked across the bridge into Essey ahead of the tanks in order to see whether the structure was mined and would blow up. He himself had forgotten the incident, for he had been pretty sure the bridge was not wired for demolition. Bea's reply was more than he anticipated: "You are the fulfillment of all the ideals of manliness and high courage and bravery I have always held for you . . . I have expected more of you than any one else in the world ever has or will."

Pershing's long separation from Nita, together with new romantic interests, had cooled his ardor. "It is possible," Patton told Bea, "that the game is up." Nita was about to break the unofficial engagement, but Pershing wanted to see her and wished her to come to France. Papa came under consideration for appointment as ambassador to Italy, and if Nita accompanied Papa and Mama to Rome, she could see him there. The ambassadorial post fell through. Patton then suggested that Nita travel to England, "as that will finally settle the matter one way or another." Nita stayed with Bea's sister Katharine in London, and Pershing came to call. They decided to go their separate ways. Nita would never marry, nor would Pershing again.

Patton and his brigade started their journey home in February 1919, entraining for Marseilles and staying in a camp while waiting to board ships. The base commander judged the men to be "the best disciplined unit he had seen pass through." Aboard the vessel, Patton was very solicitous over the men's accommodations and food. In New York in mid-March, Patton recorded in his diary, "The end of a perfect war. Fini."

After newspaper reporters interviewed him, he and Beatrice slipped away to Mitchel Field for a brief reunion. The troops were taken to Camp Meade, Maryland, located between Baltimore and Washington, D.C., and many men were discharged. Tankers who had trained at Camp Colt, Pennsylvania, near Gettysburg, under Lieutenant Colonel Dwight D. Eisenhower, joined those who had come from France.

Patton passed through the usual uncomfortable readjustment of many returning veterans. He found the "United

States in general and the army in particular . . . in a hell of a mess." He disliked the recruiting and reenlistment themes, which held out the promise of travel, fun, and vocational skills for civilian life, for he believed in national compulsory service. Americans "disreguard the lessons of history." At a theater showing a war play, the noise of shells and machine guns made him homesick. "War is the only place where a man realy lives." He bought an expensive Pierce Arrow automobile—"I can afford it," he said, "and believe in enjoying myself between wars"—and drove to Camden, New Jersey, for a visit with Joe Angelo, who had won the Distinguished Service Cross for saving Patton's life.

Member of a board in Washington writing a manual for tankers, Patton applied himself assiduously. Later he served on a committee examining how to improve tank equipment— tedious work but important, in Patton's view, in order to bring tanks out of their primitive infancy. An inventor named Walter Christie, of Hoboken, New Jersey, presented a gun-mount model, actually a tank chassis, able to run on interchangeable tracks and wheels and with a superior power plant and suspension system. The tankers were enthusiastic, but lack of funds prevented the Army from adopting it as a standard vehicle. Patton kept in touch with Christie and encouraged him to develop innovative armored models; he may even have privately subsidized Christie's work.

In California to see his parents, Patton received flattering coverage in the newspapers. Mama called him "my hero son," and he was touched by her approval. Papa was again being considered for a government appointment, this time as Secretary of Commerce, but he failed to get the post.

"The Obligation of Being an Officer," one of eleven lectures Patton delivered to his subordinates during the fall of 1919, showed the depth of his feeling for the military man, his identification with history, and the elegance of his language. He said, "We, as officers of the army, are not only members of the oldest of honorable professions, but are also the modern representatives of the demi-gods and heroes of antiquity. Back of us stretches a line of men whose acts of valor, of self-sacrifice and of service have been the theme of song and story since long before recorded history began . . . In the days of chivalry . . . knights-officers were noted as well for courtesy and gentleness of behavior, as for death-defying courage. . . . From their acts of courtesy and benevolence was derived the word, now pronounced as one, Gentle Man. . . . Let us be gentle. This is, courteous and considerate of the rights of others. Let us be Men. That is, fearless and untiring in doing our duty. . . . Our calling is most ancient and like all other old things it has amassed through the ages certain customs and traditions which decorate and ennoble it, which render beautiful the otherwise prosaic occupation of being professional men-at-arms: killers."

The National Defense Act of June 1920 prescribed the size and the shape of the postwar Army. Of the 280,000 men authorized by the Congress, less than half that number filled the ranks two years later. In that skeleton force, the military routines of peacetime were uninspiring, trivial, and ultimately irritating. Patton would suffer and sometimes exhibit petulance.

Of prime importance to Patton was the provision abolishing the tanks as an independent entity. Although Patton hoped for tanks to continue as a separate arm, unattached to infantry, cavalry, artillery, or engineers, he was pragmatic enough to foresee their probable connection to a traditional body. In that case, he preferred the cavalry, in which the tanks could, with relatively few inhibitions, extend their mobility and potential for shock. Instead, the law placed the tanks in the infantry. To Patton, the result was clear. The infantry was sure to turn the tanks into auxiliary units, armored infantry. They would accompany guns, or, worst of all, would serve as stationary pillboxes rendering fire support to foot soldiers.

This distasteful prospect led him back to the intention casually expressed to Beatrice during the war: to return to the cavalry. But there were other reasons prompting his request for transfer. The loss of autonomy diminished, if not entirely removed, his chances of promotion to general officer rank. He knew few infantrymen well; his friends, including Pershing, who was soon to be the Army Chief of Staff, were cavalrymen. He enjoyed the normal cavalry pastimes, polo, racing, horse shows, and hunting. No doubt he anticipated the budgetary restraints and cutbacks hampering the Army as a whole and the tanks in particular. He expected a war with Mexico, where the primitive road net made tanks useless, whereas horses could operate anywhere, unrestricted by terrain and weather.

He and Eisenhower, who had become close friends as a result of their warm discussions of the art of war at Camp Meade, certainly talked about the pros and cons of remaining with the tanks. Eisenhower also chose to sever his tank ties.

Leaving the tankers was a wrench for Patton. Their creator, he had gained triumphs with them and believed strongly in their future. He really hated to go, and his feelings were evident in his emotional and tearful speech of farewell to the assembled men. They were sad to see him depart, for his presence gave them purpose and order and, most of all, excitement. To Rockenbach, now a brigadier general and chief of the Tank Service, Patton wrote a goodbye letter and added, perhaps sincerely, "What ever I have learned has been due to the . . . councils and example you have given me."

Discharged as a colonel in the Tank Corps of the wartime National Army, reverting to his Regular Army grade of captain of cavalry, Patton was soon promoted to major and transferred to Fort Myer. In command of a battalion—squadron in the cavalry—he imparted the love of soldiering with his normal enthusiasm and flair. He stimulated initiative by personal example, devised exercises to test proficiency. He was teaching officers the art of the military, he told Nita ruefully, but he was the only one who was profiting.

He played a great deal of polo, a game then considered ideal for commanders, for the sport demanded speed, split-second decision, teamwork, concentration, judgment, and physical fitness—all in the context of danger. He also participated in horse shows, raced, and hunted. In the process he accumulated assorted lacerations, blows on the head, and jarring shocks, all of which could have aggravated the subdural hematoma or cranial damage that may have prompted the excessive swings between moodiness and euphoria.

He and Beatrice led an extensive social life in official Washington. Once when they were going to a formal dinner party at a private home on Dupont Circle, he dropped her at the door and parked the car. When he entered the foyer resplendent in his dress uniform and medals and joined Bea, an inebriated man sitting nearby mumbled an offensive remark about fake war heroes. Beatrice flung herself on him, knocked him out of his chair, rolled to the floor with him, and beat his face with her fists until Patton pulled her away.

In his speaking and writing, Patton attracted attention by his aphoristic statements. A general, he thought, should not live to explain a defeat. An imperfect decision executed at once was worth more than a perfect solution later. Success in war depended on speed, simplicity, and boldness. A com-

Patton (on leading horse) as major of cavalry, squadron commander, at Fort Myer, Virginia, in 1921.

mander was never defeated until he admitted it. The fog of war covered the enemy too.

Early in 1923, he attended the Advanced or Field Officers Course at the Cavalry School, Fort Riley. Working extremely hard, he earned good grades. He delivered a lecture to his classmates on Napoleon's marshals, "lest we forget that in war the personal element is most important."

Next he became a student at the Command and General Staff College at Fort Leavenworth, Kansas. He sent Bea, who was in Massachusetts, a photo of himself and explained, "Sad to say it is not as fierce as I had hoped though it has a more or less Prussian expression." On Christmas Eve she gave birth to a son and named him after his thirty-eight-year-old father.

An honor graduate of the class of 1924, in the top 25 percent, Patton was temporarily detailed to the General Staff Corps, where the brightest and most promising officers were placed. Assigned to the corps headquarters in Boston as G-1, director of personnel, he lived in comfort on the North Shore and served under an old friend from France. He spent eight pleasant months with his family.

Still a General Staff Corps officer, he was transferred to Schofield Barracks and the Hawaiian Division. Assigned again as G-1, but also as G-2, director of intelligence, he compensated by spending as much time as he could with the troops and by exercising violently. He also sailed and fished, and, as always, read history, studied warfare, and lectured.

Patton loved Hawaii for the climate and the year-round outdoor weather, as well as for the rigidly structured society with wealthy Americans at the top. He quickly came to know the best and oldest families, the rich and aristocratic households, where he felt at home. Walter Dillingham, who had a fortune founded on land and manufacturing, was a member of the royalty in the islands. A handsome and charming man who loved the ladies, he also played polo well. As Patton joined the hard-riding bluebloods in their polo matches, he and Dillingham became close friends.

When Patton heard that Eisenhower was attending the Command and General Staff College, he sent him his Leavenworth notes. Eisenhower graduated first in his class, and Patton was sure that his papers were responsible. In correspondence with Eisenhower, Patton asked what made "the Poor S.O.B." whose name usually appeared on the casualty lists fight—and then answered his own question: leadership.

From his experience, he told Eisenhower, "the solitary son of a bitch alone with God" was going to "skulk as he always has." Left to their own inclinations, he said, the "advancing waves" of infantry would move forward only if sufficiently superior artillery permitted the men to walk ahead in relative safety. A pessimistic view of soldiers' courage, it was a realistic and prophetic observation expressed privately to his friend. What turned men into fighters was, of course, superior leadership, which compelled troops to be warriors. This was Patton's central and constant problem, how to make soldiers aggressive and how to spur them in battle.

Bea was talking of buying a house, and he was sympathetic. He had always hoped, he said, only half joking, to gain supreme command in a great war and to attain such fame as to become President by ballot or dictator by force. A grateful people would then build them a palace at Fort Myer. But as he approached his forty-first birthday with no war in sight, he expected to be retired as "a useless soldier." Therefore, a home in the hunt country would be nice and no extravagance, for despite their owning polo ponies, boats, and squash courts, Bea spent hardly one-quarter of her income.

Papa and Mama visited, and Patton complained that "wars were getting scarce and that all the time I had spent getting ready would be wasted for lack of opportunity." Papa predicted that his son would be in the greatest war in history. Patton was reassured. He felt the same thing himself, and he certainly hoped so. For that was what gave meaning and direction to his life and professional preparation.

Ill for some time, Papa died in 1927. His son arrived in California too late for the funeral, where Aunt Nannie lost her self-control and carried on, crying out her unrequited love for her sister's husband. Patton went to the burial plot in the churchyard at San Gabriel for a solitary and final farewell. In Papa's study afterward, he composed a moving letter of tribute to him. "Oh! darling Papa," he wrote, "you were and are my darling."

Mama passed away in the following year, and her son left no immediate record of his grief. Her estate was extensive. Most was in undivided shares of land held with Aunt Nannie and difficult to appraise. The rest, aside from personal property, consisted of $200,000 of securities computed at par value and grossly undervalued, left by Papa. Patton signed a legal document renouncing his claim in favor of Nita.

Three years later, upon Aunt Nannie's death, Patton wrote a letter to his deceased "Darling Mama." She was "very near. I never showed you in life the love I really felt nor my admiration for your courage. . . . Forgive me, I had always prayed to show my love by doing something famous for you, to justify what you called me. . . 'My hero son.' Perhaps I still may but time grows short. I am 46." He had, he was sure, disappointed all three whom he loved and who had loved him, Papa, Mama, and Aunt Nannie, who were now gone without having seen him measure up to their high expectations.

In Hawaii, finally appointed division G-3, director of plans and training, a post he had pined for, Patton was overeager, too direct and savage in his denunciation of errors committed by senior officers during maneuvers, too outspoken and abrasive. After several months, he was relieved and placed as G-2. The demotion reminded him of his reduction from second to sixth corporal at West Point for being "too d— military."

He continued to coin memorable statements. The purpose of his memos, he warned, was "to stimulate thought; not to stifle it with dogma." Death in war "is incidental: loss of time is criminal." Battle was "an orgy of disorder" where "groups of weary wandering men seek gropingly" how "to kill their foe." The purpose of attack was to inflict "death, wounds, and destruction on the enemy troops" in order to obtain "both physical and moral ascendancy over them." "The gaining of ground . . . is simply an incident; not an object."

As always he believed in heredity as the ultimate shaper of leadership. Great military leaders resulted from two occurrences: a fortuitous blending of blood lines, and a situation allowing scope for abilities. A man's class showed in his behavior and sacrifice, and he recalled the wounded gentlemen in the hospital in France who concealed their pain whereas the others made no effort to do so. The lower classes had to be drilled to unquestioning obedience to authority. Success in battle was due to "indomitable will and tremendous energy in execution," together with commanders who held the hearts of their troops by displaying personal valor.

Patton's first division commander in Hawaii rated him unfavorably as "invaluable in war . . . but a disturbing element in time of peace," a judgment Patton considered extremely complimentary. When Patton's tour ended, Fox Conner was then the division commander, and he rated him as a good staff officer but better fitted for command.

Transferred in 1928 to Washington, D.C., and to the office of the chief of cavalry as a staff member, Patton became involved intimately in a burning question of the day: To what extent should machines replace horses in the Army? The issue was widely debated in and out of the military. Patton's assignment and his loyalty to his chief committed him to be a spokesman for the horse. He loved horses, but how could he renounce the tank achievements in the Great War? Trying to remain in the center of the argument, he was uncomfortable.

Mechanization spurred a rivalry between the infantry and cavalry branches. Because tanks belonged to the infantry by law, the cavalry experimented with armored cars instead—on a very small scale. The Secretary of War visited England in 1927 and, after observing a British armored force in training, instructed the U.S. Army to create a similar body. The War Department complied by assembling at Camp Meade a force composed of small units from the infantry, including tanks, and cavalry, along with cars, artillery pieces, Air Corps planes, and other detachments. Obsolete equipment and insufficient funds hampered development, and little was accomplished.

By 1930, Patton was advising the cavalry to be at least sympathetic to fighting machines. If the branch was still alert and adaptable rather than dying or dead, cavalrymen would show an open mind on the value of mechanization. The fourteenth-century knight had adapted to gunpowder, and the twentieth-century cavalryman, he believed, should have no fear of oil, grease, and motors.

The Army Chief of Staff, Charles Summerall, directed the Army to establish at Fort Eustis, Virginia, a mechanized force, with tanks operating together with teams of combined arms, that is, with infantry, cavalry, and artillery. A cavalry officer headed the organization; Sereno Brett, the infantryman who had succeeded Patton in command during the Meuse-Argonne campaign, was the executive officer, second in command. An embryo of the Armored Force created in 1940, the Mechanized Force, less than a battalion in size, died stillborn. Late in 1931, Douglas MacArthur, the new Army Chief of Staff, was compelled to exercise strict economy, and he abolished the formation. But he instructed every arm and service to develop mechanization and motorization as best it could, given the limited appropriations, understrength units, and worn-out equipment on hand. The infantry continued to maintain a few tanks at Camp Meade, the cavalry a few armored cars at Fort Knox. Two years later, partly because of Patton's urging, the cavalry tested combat vehicles, and the 1st Cavalry Division swapped some horses for armored cars. Further progress had to await the coming of World War II.

The high-level contact-making went on. He often talked with Eisenhower, MacArthur's assistant. He became reacquainted with Henry Stimson, Secretary of State. He had Vice-President Charles G. Dawes to dinner. Meanwhile Beatrice bought Green Meadows in the country at South Hamilton, Massachusetts, as the family home. Its generous acreage sloped to the Ipswich River, where a boathouse accommodated canoes. On the property were an unpretentious, comfortable New England clapboard house built early in the nineteenth century, a stable for a dozen horses, a corral and a barn, two large paddocks, and a garage. Patton constructed a hurdle consisting of a split-rail fence with brush and evergreens mounded on both sides. The average height of a jump in a horse show or steeplechase was just under four feet. Patton's was just over five. He was, of course, once again preparing to test his nerve, to qualify himself for danger.

He was dressed for polo one day when Beatrice saw him kneel by the bed and say a prayer.

"What are you praying for?" she asked. "To win the game?"

"Hell, no," he replied. "I'm praying to do my best."

In his military papers and lectures, Patton formulated one of his most unforgettable phrases. The best method to fight the enemy, he said, was to "grab him by the nose and kick him in the pants." This was, of course, the traditional American way of combat by fire and movement; pin down the enemy by fire with part of the force, enabling the rest to outflank and attack from the rear. Patton's figure of speech said it better.

After a visit to Fort Riley, he recommended improving the noncommissioned officers' quarters, "to facilitate their comfort and self-respect." This too was consistent with Patton's belief that the officer's first duty was to care for his men. Unfortunately, there was no money for repair.

Sorely tried over the enfeeblement of the military, Patton tried to act as though all were well in the world. Yet the butts and kicks and falls from horses, together with his discouragement over the state of the Army and his fading hopes of attaining fame, took their toll on him, inducing fits of depression and unexplainable outbursts of rage. During a hunt, a member of the Spanish embassy inadvertently came close to colliding with Patton's daughter Ruth Ellen, who barely escaped serious injury. Patton, who was nearby, rode up and gave the man an uncontrolled, severe, and profane tongue-lashing. Later, himself surprised by the ferocity of his verbal attack, Patton apologized by letter.

His tour ended in the summer of 1931, and the chief of cavalry, rating his performance, stressed Patton's drive. "He will accomplish what he sets out to do."

After a vacation with Beatrice in their new home, Patton returned to Washington to attend the Army War College, its highest educational institution. His old nervousness and apprehension seized him. "I have hay fever," he wrote Bea.

Applying himself zealously to his course work, he also wrote an ambitious study entitled "The Probable Characteristics of the Next War and the Organization, Tactics, and Equipment Necessary to Meet Them." From a survey of warfare through the ages, he tried to deduce the nature of the conflict he hoped was approaching. Cogent and learned, the paper was one of several sent to the War Department General Staff for reading. The commandant called Patton a superior officer with a special aptitude for command.

His eight confining years as a staff officer came to a temporary end when he moved in July 1932 to Fort Myer as the executive officer of the cavalry regiment stationed there. Three weeks later, as luck would have it, the Bonus March came to a head.

In the previous year, as the Depression spread despair and heartbreak, Joe Angelo, who was married and had a child and was out of work, walked from Camden, New Jersey, to Washington, D.C., to testify before a congressional committee investigating unemployment and the bonus claims of veterans. Like many ex-soldiers, Angelo wanted a job. If work was unavailable, he wished at least part of the $1,424 due him for his war service. But the Congress refused to authorize an immediate cash bonus.

Now, in July 1932, about 20,000 veterans flocked to Washington to press the Congress to distribute at once the cash bonus voted for disbursement in 1952. Camped on the Anacostia flats and in abandoned and partly dismantled buildings at the foot of the Capitol, they were neither disorderly nor unruly, but as a large, restless, and sometimes surly group of men, they had the potential of turning into a mob. President Herbert Hoover, Secretary of War Patrick J. Hurley, and

The passionate horseman, 1931.

★

Army Chief of Staff Douglas MacArthur regarded them as subversives and revolutionaries, and there were undoubtedly a few among them. Patton thought them all to be Bolsheviks.

When the Congress adjourned without voting the bonus, many marchers left the city. Many others remained. The government decided to clear them out.

The cavalry regiment across the Potomac at Fort Myer and the infantry brigade at Fort Washington about twelve miles downriver were poised and ready to respond in case they were needed to suppress a rebellion. Men and horses were trained in riot duty, and gas grenades and masks were handed out.

Early in the afternoon of July 28, the 3d Cavalry was turned out and assembled. The troopers rode down the Fort Myer hill, crossed the Memorial Bridge, and headed for the Ellipse behind the White House, there to await the 16th Infantry. There was no need for Patton, the executive officer, to accompany the cavalry contingent of fourteen officers, 217 enlisted men, and 213 horses, but the excitement and the chance of action were too attractive to resist. From the Ellipse, Patton reconnoitered the situation by trotting stonily along Pennsylvania Avenue. Several thousand veterans along the route greeted him with mixed cheers and jeers. Returning, he waited until the infantry arrived.

About 4:00 P.M., with the cavalry in the lead, the troops started down the avenue. The cavalrymen were wearing steel helmets, carrying gas masks, guarding carbines at the sling, and holding drawn sabers; the infantrymen were wearing gas masks and carrying rifles with bayonets. They advanced as far as 3rd Street, clearing the route. Some force became necessary, and Patton himself used the flat of his saber to strike the backsides of several men. Soldiers charged and dispersed veterans throwing stones and bricks. Quiet was restored in half an hour.

Orders then came to cross the Anacostia River and clear the encampment. MacArthur came up and issued explicit instructions. After the troops were fed, they crossed the bridge at the Navy Yard and cleared the flats. In the process, some huts and tents caught fire and burned. On the following morning, most of the marchers departed Washington, but the memory of the episode haunted the Army for nearly a decade.

Patton was deeply affected by the incident—marching against former American soldiers—and to clear his mind, he wrote half a dozen papers on what he called this "most distasteful form of service." Putting down what he saw as insurrection required quick reaction, the appearance of ruthless force, and abstention from unnecessary violence. The troops had to be highly trained and disciplined, strictly controlled. Officers had to identify ringleaders and deal with them harshly.

Staying at Fort Myer for three years, Patton tended to his duty and played energetically. He especially loved the excitement of the fox hunts. Riding to the hounds was rough, jolting, and perilous. The rider drove his horse with his muscles and balance and had constantly to measure the quickness of his own reactions to dangers in the form of rocks, trees, holes, and fences. Patton appeared to be reckless as he avoided low places in the fences and chose the high jumps with unknown landing sites on the other side.

Promoted to lieutenant colonel, he made patriotic speeches at American Legion halls, in which he termed perpetual peace a futile dream and disarmament a folly. He excoriated pacifists. Citizens who mocked courage, made a joke of patriotism, and tried to persuade the United States to become physically helpless and morally unworthy were mentally deluded. The thought of his country as both unready and unwilling to defend its honor outraged him. Wars, he proclaimed, were fought by weapons but won by men. The successful fighting man was a killer.

Posted in Hawaii, Patton designed another hurdle to test his mettle. In May 1935, with an amateur crew, including Beatrice, he voluntarily took the risk of sailing his yacht from California. Both captain and navigator, he brought the ship safely to Honolulu.

He was now fifty years old; he went into his midlife crisis, and turned sour. Angry, often bitter over his professional frustrations, he thought seriously of resigning his commission or retiring. He joined what was then called fast company, men and women interested in liquor and sex, and he drank too much and engaged in casual affairs. Temperamental and mean, he was often cruel, making life difficult for Bea and the children. His house was hardly a happy place.

Although he was delighted to be in the islands again, pleased to serve under Hugh Drum, an old friend from France, glad to be reunited with Dillingham and other swells, his assignment as G-2, director of intelligence, for the Hawaiian Department at Fort Shafter put him again in the unhappy position of a staff officer confined to an office, destined, he believed, to a military dead end.

At Drum's direction, he drew a plan to "maintain internal security and censorship" against potential subversion by the Japanese community in the event of a war with Japan. He devised a brutal scheme to "arrest and intern certain persons of the Orange [Japanese] race who are . . . inimical to American interests" and "to retain [them in custody] as hostages" rather than as prisoners, and he listed by name and address those to be seized. An unorthodox paper, it reflected Patton's frame of mind and his rage over his personal condition, as well as his suspicion of Japanese ambitions, particularly after the recent conquest of Manchuria. Certainly Hawaii was vulnerable to Japanese air and sea power; Billy Mitchell had warned of a surprise air attack. In an exercise several years earlier, the Navy carried out a successful carrier raid on Pearl Harbor. But Patton's paper also displayed the prejudice of his milieu. To the Caucasian elite, the Japanese inhabitants of Hawaii would always be an alien presence, never red-blooded Americans, and the wealthy whites regarded them with amused condescension and suspicion, an attitude applying generally to all minority groups of lesser social rank.

His compensation for the torpor of staff work was, of course, mayhem on the polo field, where he played with abandon and with loud, joyful curses. Polo was a wild sport for young men, but Patton at fifty was an exuberant exception. There was nothing genteel about the game—men riding fast horses each weighing 1,000 to 1,300 pounds, running at top speed, just under forty miles an hour, and often colliding with bone-bruising force.

During the Inter-Island Championship matches held in August 1935, the Oahu team, captained by Dillingham, was playing against the Army team, captained by Patton. The field was hot, tempers were high, when Dillingham's horse crashed into Patton's. "Goddammit, Walter, you old son of a bitch," Patton cried in his high-pitched voice that carried into the stands packed with spectators, including Drum, "I'll run you right down Front Street." When the period ended, Drum relieved Patton of his captaincy and forbade his return to the field.

After a long delay, Dillingham and Frank Baldwin, captain of the Maui team, approached Drum and asked whether Patton had really been banished. Yes, Drum said, because of his swearing. "Well, General," one of them said, "we didn't hear any unseemly language. If George doesn't play, neither will we, and we'll cancel the tournament." Faced with this ultimatum, Drum retracted and rescinded his order.

During another game, Patton had a very bad fall. Everyone was certain that he had suffered a serious injury. But he arose, mounted his horse, and continued to play. He seemed quite normal, but several days afterward, while sailing with Bea and the children, he said, "How in hell did I get here?" At the doctor's, he learned that he had suffered a brain concussion. After that, even mild drinking had a pronounced effect on him. He quickly became maudlin, sobbing openly as he recited verse with slurred and slipshod diction.

While on his earlier tour, Patton had sometimes taken the overnight steamer to the large island of Hawaii to spend a week or so purchasing horses for the Army, as many as sixty-six on one occasion, from the Parker ranch of half a million acres run by Alfred Carter. His knowledge of horseflesh had earned him the respect of Carter, who had moved him from the guest quarters to the main house, as well as the admiration of his military colleagues.

Now he performed again what was to him a very pleasant function. One of these horse-buying trips was planned while a niece, Jean Gordon, daughter of one of Bea's older half sisters, was visiting. She was about the same age as Ruth Ellen Patton, a good friend of hers, and a vivacious and lovely brunette. Bea, Ruth Ellen, and Jean were to go along for a nice vacation trip of several days. But Bea took sick, Ruth Ellen stayed home to look after her, and only Jean, who adored her Uncle Georgie, accompanied Patton to the Parker ranch. How could they resist falling in love? Jean never married, and she would turn up again in Patton's life.

With Bea and his young son George as members of the crew, Patton sailed his yacht back to California in June 1937. After selling the boat, the Pattons traveled home to Massachusetts.

Just as the international situation seemed about to produce Patton's long-anticipated "next war"—the Japanese moving aggressively into China, the Germans under Adolf Hitler rearming and threatening the peace, the German-Japanese anti-Comintern pact concluded in 1936, the Italians engaged in Africa, civil war in Spain—Patton almost had his military service terminated. While on leave and riding with Bea, her horse suddenly bolted and kicked Patton, fracturing his leg in

Polo in Hawaii, 1933.

Polo 1933. Semenian

two places. He was hospitalized for more than three months, then confined for three more at home. Phlebitis, a blood clot or air bubble in his bloodstream, brought him close to death. Six months after the accident, he limped and was still wearing an iron brace on his leg, which swelled after walking.

Would he ever again be fit for active duty? The question tormented him. And his inability to exercise also drove him to despair and rage. He had lost precious time in what appeared to be the twilight of his career.

A medical examination at a military facility pronounced him capable of limited service. An appropriate assignment was found for him. Early in 1938 he departed for Fort Riley to be a member of the faculty and staff at the Cavalry School. By systematic exercise, he swiftly regained his health and his fit physical condition.

Several months later, at midyear, as war clouds gathered in Europe and funding for the U.S. Army started to increase, he was promoted to colonel and sent to command a regiment of the 1st Cavalry Division at Fort Clark, Texas. The assignment and the locality delighted him. His unit was a combat organization training for war. The area offered his favorite recreational distractions, riding and hunting, and reminded him of his youthful experiences on the frontier at Sierra Blanca. He made many friends among the nearby wealthy ranchers. Third Army maneuvers in the late summer and fall were exciting.

Patton was enjoying himself thoroughly when a telephone call from Washington, D.C., brought his paradise crashing down. He was to be transferred at once to replace Jonathan Wainwright in command of Fort Myer. Wainwright was in debt as a result of the social expenses connected with the post. Patton, with an independent income, could afford the position. Turning to Bea, with tears streaming down his cheeks, he cried, "You and your money have ruined my career." Just as the international situation was about to flare into armed conflict, he was to go from a combat unit to a showplace.

As it turned out, Patton was fortunate. In the spring of 1939, another Pershing man, George C. Marshall, who appreciated Patton's inimitable qualities and strengths, became the Acting Army Chief of Staff. Because Marshall's house at Fort Myer was being repainted and repaired, Patton, whose family was away, invited Marshall to stay temporarily with him. When Marshall accepted, Patton exultantly wrote Bea about his "pretty snappy move," which would permit him to work his "natural charm" on the senior officer.

Marshall was impervious to blandishment, but impressed by Patton's performance in the maneuvers in northern Virginia that summer. Patton was declared eligible for promotion to brigadier general. Perhaps he'd be a general at last! But what he needed was assignment to a position requiring that rank. Still he remained at Fort Myer.

The outbreak of World War II in Europe on September 1, 1939, coincided with Marshall's official elevation to Army Chief of Staff. The astonishing blitzkrieg in Poland, which Patton followed avidly in the press, set him to rework in his mind the old formula of tanks helping the infantry, a concept now as outmoded as the Polish cavalry, and to ponder the new formations and tactics of lightning war. The American military establishment stirred uneasily, and Patton, outwardly imperturbable and gracious, secretly fretted too as he continued to perform his largely social functions. Was he too old to participate in changes being talked about and beginning to be acted upon? Was he, who believed "the liberal Democrat" to be "the lowest type of politican" and whose friends were wealthy Republicans, to prove to be persona non grata with the Roosevelt administration? Was he too erratic, too eccentric for the new type of warfare?

Maneuvers in Texas in the spring of 1940 confronted units of horses and those of machines and showed clearly the need for drastic Army modernization. Patton served as an umpire during the games, and the experience was invaluable. It brought him up to date on the latest equipment, developments, and thinking of American tankers.

At the same time, the Germans overran western Europe, defeating France and ejecting the British forces from the Continent. The shock of these events, together with the obvious conclusions in Texas, prompted Marshall to establish in July the Armored Force, a composite organization, which was to learn how to match the power and mobility of the German blitzkrieg. Chaffee was in command, and his immediate task was to create two armored divisions, one at Fort Knox, Kentucky, the other at Fort Benning, Georgia. He placed Patton's name on his preferred list of officers, those he wanted to help him generate the new formations. Specifically, he wished Patton as a brigadier general to command an armored brigade. The appointment of Patton's old friend Stimson as Secretary

☆

The father of the brides: *At left,* Bea's wedding in 1934;
above, Ruth Ellen's in 1940.

of War, as well as Marshall's recollections of Patton's exploits abroad in the last war, would be favorable to his selection.

His daughters were now married to West Pointers, John Waters, a cavalryman, and James Totten, an artilleryman. His son George, who later recalled breakfast with his father as consisting of corn flakes and military history, was at prep school and trying to follow his father's advice: Raising hell was foolish and running with a gang showed a lack of self-confidence.

At the end of July 1940, Patton reported to the 2d Armored Division at Fort Benning. After twenty years, he was back with the tanks, instruments of his earlier success. Once again he would endeavor to promote a new method of waging war. He was in the mainstream of military activities. The Army was finally starting to prepare seriously for war and was about to expand explosively to unprecedented size. His prospects were excellent. Although he would soon be fifty-five years old, Pershing had been that age when he went to France. Perhaps it was not too late; perhaps he still had time to achieve a measure of fame.

His first thought, as he observed his new armored troops, was vintage Patton. His men were far from smart in appearance. Setting an example himself of military bearing and conduct, he hoped for imitation and planned strong measures if necessary. Once he fixed his troops in the Patton mold, he would train them to fight anywhere and make them sure of their prowess. What seemed particularly joyful in his new role was the apparent return of his destiny. All that he'd require, to go along with his knowledge, energy, and self-advertising, was luck.

THE CHALLENGE OF WORLD WAR II

During the two and a half years after Patton took command of the brigade at Fort Benning, he gained a great measure of his fame. His success in preparing troops for battle and leading them in combat made an enormous impact on the public consciousness. Seizing the news media's attention, he became well known and widely admired and climbed to national prominence.

He and Beatrice had resolved the personal difficulties that had troubled their marriage during his midlife crisis. She tried not to notice his extramarital sorties. He depended on her to sustain his fragile emotions. Though the youthful fires of passion were banked, the couple remained close and settled into a comfortable life together. They entertained graciously and were socially charming. During the Depression, their horses and polo ponies had provoked resentment among some officers whose families were barely getting by on reduced pay scales, but now, as the Army started its growth and transformation, the Patton wealth and style of living prompted no more than occasional envy.

Small in stature, vivacious in conversation, entirely at home in the conventions of military existence, Beatrice was quick to put people at ease. She complemented her husband's high spirits, although he was now somewhat more restrained. With his patrician look and air of command, he inspired awe. Quiet and brooding at times, yet capable of the unrestrained outburst and instant contrition, he cultivated aloofness yet sparked excitement. What he had in incomparable measure was immediate and strong rapport with groups of soldiers.

He was in his prime. Mature, seasoned by experience, sufficiently youthful to impart infectious enthusiasm, he was also flexible. Open to the strange and beguiling new ideas, he was eager to master the techniques of armored warfare. He studied the improved weapons and equipment, as well as the current generation of young Americans. Years of reading and analysis, as well as of working with troop units, had turned him into a complete professional. Confident of his abilities, at least externally, buoyed by his past successes, particularly in the Great War, he was ready to meet the challenge of war in the 1940s.

In his comportment he cultivated a mischievous bad-boy image and showed a decided exhibitionism. He constantly paraded his energy, strutting, shouting, moving without apparent rest. The pose served to project force and drive. If he sometimes appeared rough, even brutal, he thus indicated the need for hard and tough men in warfare.

His acting served another purpose. During the last war, some senior commanders had lacked endurance and stamina, and a surprising number failed simply because they were too old. Marshall therefore sought younger, more vigorous officers for responsible positions, men like Eisenhower, Omar Bradley, and Mark Clark. Patton, half a dozen years older and more, was uneasy, and in private he sarcastically referred to Marshall's efforts in this regard as his "youth movement." For at fifty-five, Patton worried about his potential exclusion on the ground of age alone. He sought to prove constantly and ostentatiously, especially to Marshall, his physical fitness, his top condition, his ability to measure up to the demands of war in the field. He ceased playing polo and hunting, however, in order to avoid an accidental injury that might disqualify him for active duty. He continued to ride for exercise and recreation.

Patton's immediate superior was Charles L. Scott, the commanding general of the 2d Armored Division. Directly above Scott, Adna Chaffee, as commander of the I Armored Corps, directed the 1st and 2d armored divisions in training and presumably would do so in future battle. Chaffee was also chief of the Armored Force. Much like Rockenbach in the earlier Tank Service, he was responsible for creating and sustaining a new and composite combat branch in which the combined arms—infantry, tanks, artillery, and other components working together—were to learn to fight in the modern manner. He established the Armored Warfare School with a Pattonesque motto, "Kill or be killed." He put pressure on automobile manufacturers to produce tanks and other military vehicles.

Chaffee was already suffering failing health, from cancer, in September 1940. Scott moved from Benning to Knox and relieved Chaffee as head of the I Armored Corps, thus giving Chaffee more time for his Armored Force concerns. With Scott gone, Patton, after more than thirty years of service, became the acting or temporary commander of the 2d Armored Division and finally a brigadier general. "All that is now needed," he wrote in elation to his old friend Terry Allen, "is a nice juicy war."

The structure of the armored division, composed of about 15,000 troops, presented problems. All the combat elements were in the brigade, which was likened to a fist, and the other units supported the brigade's punch. For better flexibility and balance, two brigades, now called combat commands, twin fists, came into existence in March 1942. Final form appeared in September 1943 with three combat commands. The fourteen additional armored divisions activated in the United States before the end of the war were each a trim and mobile force of about 12,000 men. Patton's influence on these modifications was indirect and stemmed from his advocacy of speed and mobility.

The nature of the men being drafted in the Army prompted much concern in high government circles. The country was still at peace, and most of the recruits had little taste for military life. Civilians at heart, indifferent to authority at best, they had no wish to be soldiers. Would they fight if necessary? Would they strive to attain physical and mental toughness and proficiency in the martial skills?

Patton proved that his troops would perform in superior fashion. He accomplished this end in a variety of ways. Mak-

Costume balls just before the war: *At left,* the Pattons as Rhett Butler and Scarlett O'Hara; *above,* as King Arthur and Guinevere.

ing himself highly visible throughout the division, he served as a role model. He imposed strict discipline and strenuous training. He set rigorous standards and personally assured their attainment. Above all, he sang the division's praises, thus stimulating pride, esprit, and morale, essential ingredients for outstanding soldiering.

In his first talk to his officers, he seemed to breathe vitality, competence, and confidence. His impeccable dress contrasted with his offhand manner. An experienced lecturer, he held his listeners' rapt attention. Magically he drew them into a charmed circle composed of privileged members of Patton's team.

His subject was the 1939 German campaign in Poland, but he touched on other matters before driving home his message. "People of our rank," he said, "have no choice as to the . . . higher strategy. . . . Our job is to [fight, and] . . . without successful combat, all plans are bunk." Citing Julius Caesar, who trained his soldiers so well during the winter that they needed no orders for their spring campaigning, he said, "This [is] . . . exactly the goal we are seeking in this division. I know that we shall attain it and when we do, may God have mercy on our enemies; they will need it."

Keeping his men busy, he improved their physical conditioning, acquainted them with military lore, taught them how to march and to shoot, made them familiar, then expert with weapons and equipment, formed them into cohesive groups, and finally had them understand how their individual functioning contributed to the whole. All the while he imbued them "with a desperate determination to get forward [in battle] and . . . not permit themselves to be stopped by any obstacle."

In the exercises he planned and directed, he seemed to be everywhere, correcting, cajoling, condemning, driving. His own tank—its turret ringed with stripes of red, white, and blue, and an additional one of yellow for the cavalry to symbolize mobility—always appeared in moments of urgency. The blast of the foghorn on his command car could be heard for miles and thus signified his whereabouts. By his personal presence, he galvanized action, showed what he wanted, and gave unstinting praise when deserved. When Patton was satisfied, his men were pleased. He spoke again of blood and guts, and the expression took hold.

Frequently and with conviction he repeated to newspaper

reporters, visitors, and his troops a theme with variations. Nothing could defeat the enemy as well as the armored division. An armored formation "can smash its way into the enemy with tremendous force." Armored units were "terribly powerful instruments of destruction." Everyone believed what he said.

In December 1940, he staged with impressive advance publicity a journey from Columbus, Georgia, to Panama City, Florida, and back, a distance of 400 miles. He wanted to test and practice march formations, procedures, and discipline, but he wished above all to capture the public attention, not only for his own glory but also for the benefit of the Armored Force. He advertised the round trip as the longest movement ever made by an armored division. More than 1,000 vehicles, including tanks and half-tracks, participated, and warplanes occasionally flew overhead.

As promised, Patton put on a good show. Reaching its destination on the second day, the division turned around and roared home. Thousands of spectators along the route, among them wide-eyed children excused from school, gazed in wonder at the apparently endless column of new and formidable war machines. The newspaper coverage was extensive. Patton was content. The division, he was sure, "now has the popular imagination, and will go far."

Stories increasingly featured Patton. "His men swore by him," one reporter wrote, perhaps with intentional double entendre. "He would never order men to do anything . . . that he wouldn't do himself," said another. He "had the damnedest way of showing up when things went wrong." He started stalled tanks "by the power of his curses." Patton did have the uncanny ability, the intuitive sense to know exactly where and when things would break down or go wrong, and he was usually there to straighten matters out, to get events back on track. His legend was building.

In January 1941, he put on, again with appropriate advance publicity, a division parade. All of the 1,300 vehicles passed the reviewing stand smartly and without a hitch. Patton was immensely proud, and so were his troops. Beatrice contributed to morale by composing a march for the band. The music started with two shots fired by cannon.

Many of the tankers who had been with him in Bourg offered to return to the Army and serve under him. Unfortunately, most were too old. A notable exception was

Alexander C. Stiller, a former sergeant who was tough, fearless, and a weapons expert. He enlisted, then, at Patton's bidding, attended Officers Candidate School, received a commission, and became one of his two aides and unofficial bodyguard. The other aide was Richard N. Jenson, the son of family friends in California.

In April, after incessant exercises and maneuvers in bad weather, Patton pronounced judgment on eight months of work. "We have changed," he said, "from an idea to a powerful fighting force." Having impressed Marshall, the Army Chief of Staff, Stimson, the Secretary of War, and others with his energy and élan and with his ability to generate a strong spirit among his men, Patton gained his second star. He was promoted to major general and placed in actual, no longer temporary, command of the division.

Letters of congratulations poured in from Army friends. Patton replied to each with gusto and delight. He told every writer, always in different language, that he owed everything to the inspiration he had received from that particular person alone. For example, to one Patton said, "I am perfectly honest when I assure you that your influence upon me has done me more good than that of any other officer with whom I have ever served." To another, his promotion was solely the result of his having always tried to emulate that individual in all that he did. If this was high-powered flattery, perhaps as prescribed by Beatrice, it did Patton no harm.

He gave much thought to the task of operating an armored division. "On account of size," he said, such a force was "difficult to handle." How could he avoid having his horde of vehicles congest the roads and offer good targets to enemy aircraft? Seeking an answer, he bought a small plane, took flying lessons, got a license, and traveled over his columns to define and solve the problem. How could the commander overcome a timidity stemming naturally from the wish to safeguard rather than to expand so many costly machines? How far forward should he place himself to be able to react quickly to new information and to issue orders promptly? How could wounded men be removed from buttoned-up tanks? As in France, he worked out solutions by trial and error through exercises held in realistic conditions.

His thoughts on tactics were, as always, practical and pithy. Maintain radio silence before an attack. Make liberal use of tank firepower. Exercise leadership well forward. Refuel during darkness. Have many small gasoline dumps rather than a few large ones. The shorter the battle, the fewer men killed, hence greater self-confidence and enthusiasm among the troops. Advance rapidly but not hastily. Use mobile forces in large groups. "They must attempt the impossible and dare the unknown." If these points were less than altogether clear, if subtle distinctions like the difference between rapidity and haste were not quite spelled out, their meaning was apparent to him.

Experimenting with light planes, he found them valuable for many functions—to carry messages and information, to locate and identify units, to transport commanders and staff members, to serve as eyes for the artillery. His pioneering work contributed to the later adoption of small planes as adjuncts to ground forces.

He designed a new uniform for his elite tankers—of dark green gabardine to conceal grease spots. The double-breasted jacket had a row of white buttons down the side. Padded trousers cushioned the bruising jolts of tank travel. Pockets on the legs held first-aid packets, maps, and ammunition clips. The headgear was a football helmet of light plastic, furnished according to rumor by the Washington Redskins. Patton had a suit tailored, then modeled it for photographers. He looked ridiculous. He seemed to be clowning, but he was deadly serious. For a while he was known as the Green Hornet. The clothing was discarded.

Remaining interested in the cavalry "in spite of my gasoline affiliations," he stated his belief in the usefulness of soldiers on horseback and of horse-drawn artillery, especially in rugged terrain. He advised retaining the saber because it gave men the courage to charge the enemy. "Very few people," he explained, "have ever been killed with the bayonet or the saber, but the fear of having their guts explored with cold steel in the hands of battle-maddened men has won many a fight."

His chance to show what he could do came in the spring of 1941. Lesley J. McNair, in effect the chief of Army combat training, and Mark Clark, his principal assistant, announced a series of large-scale maneuvers, sham battles, to test the proficiency of units and commanders in simulated combat. Both armored divisions were to take part in the games.

Patton had two immediate reactions. Some of the standard and hallowed conventions governing maneuvers in the "old" Army might not apply to the new operating methods devel-

The Green Hornet: Patton modeling the ill-fated uniform he designed himself for his tankers.

oped by armored divisions. The main function of an armored force was to disrupt enemy command, communications, and supplies by imagination, surprise, and speed, attributes not normally associated with the conservative prewar Army. He was ready to break the rules if necessary to achieve his purposes. Combat was too serious, too important, too deadly to abide by artificial and outmoded regulations that might hamper his activities. If he had to play dirty pool to win, he would do so. Winning was the goal in war, and nothing could stand in the way.

His second reaction was his fear of being selected, because of his armored expertise, as an umpire for the maneuvers. He made known his wish to command his division in the war games. He staked his professional future on the results. If he showed influential observers successful action against his opponents, he would enhance his prospects for advancement.

He started preparing at once by speaking to the entire division assembled, the first time a division commander had ever addressed all of his troops. "An armored division," he said, "is the most powerful organization ever devised." Find the enemy, hold him, and get around him, "always moving, do not sit down, do not say 'I have done enough,' keep on, see what else you can do to raise the devil with the enemy. . . . You must have a desperate determination to go forward." He cautioned his listeners to obey the umpires. He congratulated every officer and man for his honest effort and enthusiastic support to date. He reminded them of the division doctrine: Attack weakness, not strength, and keep moving. Many senior officers doubted the value of tanks and armored forces, he pointed out, then issued his challenge: The maneuvers would settle that question.

By this time his soldiers were calling themselves "blitz troopers" or "trained blitzmen" capable of "terrifying strength." The division was the "juggernaut of the battlefield," and now it had a nickname, Hell on Wheels.

The maneuvering was held in Tennessee in June. At first Patton's division was unimpressive. But Patton quickly developed his feel of control and his sense of movement, and the division picked up momentum, demonstrating slashing and unorthodox tactics. Patton's speed and sureness brought the exercise to an end before the planned time. He completed in nine hours a problem scheduled for two days of action. Throughout the games, the aggressive behavior of the 2d Armored Division attracted favorable attention. Patton himself was at center stage. He had, there was no doubt, mastered the art of blitzkrieg.

Returned to Fort Benning, Patton started preparing for the next maneuvers. He told his troops what they enjoyed hearing: "The 2nd Armored Division is as good as they come." He stressed teamwork and energy. "If brevity is the soul of wit," he said, "repetition is the heart of instruction." His object was to make the division "utterly irresistible in maneuvers or in war."

A well-meaning friend advised him to curb his flamboyance. He refused. He was having too much fun. His color and profanity made good newspaper copy and were building his reputation. He had no intention of repressing his spirits.

An issue of *Life* magazine in July carried a feature story on Patton and the division. On the cover was Patton, standing in the turret of his tank, holding binoculars, wearing a shoulder holster and pistol, a helmet with chin strap, large rings on the third and fourth fingers of his left hand, and an appropriate scowl. The coverage stirred pride among the men. Their leader, they were sure, was someone special.

When Chaffee died in August 1941, Jacob L. Devers succeeded him as chief of the Armored Force. Devers was Patton's West Point classmate and former polo teammate, but they were hardly good friends. Nevertheless, in much the same manner as with Rockenbach in France, Patton gave Devers his complete loyalty and worked to overcome the coolness between them.

War games held in Louisiana and Texas in August and September engaged 400,000 soldiers. Scott's I Armored Corps headquarters directed the 1st and 2d Armored Divisions, and Patton and his men were the stars. Scott displayed a lack of command control, Patton a sure touch. Again in November, in the Carolina maneuvers, the 2d Armored Division created a sensation by its obsession to win and its willingness to dare. Patton exhibited the certain grip of command and superbly managed control and coordination. Scott was again criticized for command deficiencies.

In December 1941 came the Japanese attack on Pearl Harbor and the German and Italian declarations of war. The United States was now a belligerent. Marshall sent Scott to the Middle East as an observer and appointed Patton to command

Left: On maneuvers in Louisiana in September 1941. *Above:* Patton (left) thrashing out tactics with Geoffrey Keyes and Harry Flint, two close aides who would accompany him on the path to glory.

the I Armored Corps. Patton's energetic application to duty was clearly paying off.

His son George received a nomination to West Point, and Patton did not shrink from offering advice. Work hard, he said. "Do your damndest in an ostentatious manner all the time." Always be the best-dressed cadet. Always be ahead of time. Never make excuses. Never knowingly break a regulation. Dispense with friends and be a lone wolf. Avoid "harmless larks," for they showed an unstable mind. Fix firmly on what you want and get it. These were his own guides, and he assumed the same aspirations for his son, advancement and fame.

To a youngster who was growing up in the shadow of his father's imposing figure, a man in the process of becoming a legend, Patton's final admonition was cruel and crushing: Forgetting how patient Papa had been with him, Patton wrote, "Well we are real proud of you for the first time in your life. See to it that we stay that way."

Now Patton's ambition was to go overseas and fight. Haunted by the fear of being judged too old, he soon worried about being forgotten. For in February 1942, he received instructions to create and run a desert training area far from the center of the Army's power structure.

Specifically, he was to duplicate the conditions of fighting in the desert. Erwin Rommel's German and Italian army in Libya was pressing the British forces in Egypt and threatening to overrun the Suez Canal. From there, Rommel could drive eastward to the Caucasus and join the Germans who had been fighting the Russians since June 1941, then go even farther to a meeting with the Japanese in India. If Americans had to bolster the British in North Africa or the Middle East, they needed realistic preparation and hard conditioning.

Patton flew to Riverside, California, in March and reconnoitered from the air a vast wasteland about the size of Pennsylvania and including parts of California, Nevada, and Arizona. Desolate and uninhabited except by rattlesnakes, rabbits, and coyotes, the ground offered diverse terrain of sand, rock, and mountain. The climate and geography resembled North Africa. There was plenty of room for large units to deploy and maneuver and to fire live ammunition without endangering or annoying civilians. The troops, Patton decided, would take shelter in tents without electric lights, heat, and hot water, have cots without sheets, survive on a canteen of water per day, daily run a mile in ten minutes, march eight miles in two hours, and dispense with sleep from time to time.

With incredible speed he opened the center in April. "I believe the only way to start things is to start," he said, "so next week we start." As he had at Bourg and Benning, he put troops and units through a series of exhausting field exercises, driving, teaching, cursing, complimenting, and explaining why such arduous work was necessary. If every man did his best, victory was certain. In one period of twenty-three days, he conducted thirteen major tactical movements of extended duration in daylight and in darkness. He participated in every problem, appearing everywhere in his jeep, sedan, tank, half-track, or small plane. From a hill dubbed the King's Throne, he scrutinized marches and shouted instructions into his radio. "I'm a hell of a guy," he said. "I'm giving the men hell one minute and crying over them the next."

Patton had other concerns. His I Armored Corps headquarters remained in the Armored Force chain of command, in which Devers was his boss. But his function of training all troop components for combat came under McNair. Deciding to keep both officers satisfied, Patton inundated them with a steady stream of reports, memoranda, and letters, describing his activities, detailing his discoveries, and recommending new and proved techniques. All the while he made certain that they knew how healthy and energetic he was. He impressed them.

For the first time ever, he commanded units from the air by voice radio. He proved the usefulness of a tank retriever—a vehicle that could rescue damaged tanks on the battlefield. He experimented with formations. And always he gave enthusiasm and morale to his men.

To his friends at McNair's and Devers's headquarters, he sent confidential memos to get interesting ideas into circulation for discussion, warning them not necessarily to ascribe the notions to him. He reiterated his desire to avoid politics. He had no wish to play off Devers against McNair or the reverse. He wrote frequently to persons who mattered, informed them what he was doing, and asked them not to overlook him for a combat assignment. He told Devers frankly that he wanted to fight instead of being relegated to a training mission. He let McNair know candidly that when serious fighting started, he wanted the chance "to prove in blood what I have learned in sweat."

With Lesley McNair (left) at the Desert Training Center in California.

Eisenhower, now Marshall's right-hand man, sent Patton a letter to express admiration of his work. He wished he could get out of Washington and join Patton, who would probably be the Black Jack Pershing of this war.

Patton, who had urged Eisenhower to request transfer to the 2d Armored Division in 1940, was quick to reply. He would like nothing better than to be together with Eisenhower. He wanted very much, he admitted, to be the Black Jack of this conflict and to have Eisenhower as his assistant. Or, with prescience, he said he would be content if Eisenhower turned out to be the Black Jack and Patton his helper. "Sometimes I think your life and mine are under the protection of some supreme being or fate, because, after many years of parallel thought . . . my fate depends on you, because in this distant locality, one can very easily be forgotten."

He was not forgotten. In June 1942, soon after Eisenhower and Clark traveled to England to establish the European Theater of Operations, Marshall called Patton to Washington. Britain's Prime Minister, Winston Churchill, was conferring with President Roosevelt when news had arrived from North Africa. Rommel was attacking the British in Egypt, and he took Tobruk, a symbolic strongpoint. With Roosevelt's approval, Marshall offered to send an American armored division to help the British. Selecting Patton to exercise command, Marshall asked him to suggest how this could best be done. After a few days of study, Patton recommended dispatching two armored divisions instead of one. A single organization, he thought, couldn't decisively influence the battle. But by the time Patton made this report, Marshall had concluded that committing American troops in Egypt would take too long. They would arrive too late to affect the action. A quicker solution was to supply the British with 300 tanks and 100 howitzers. Churchill gratefully accepted. Patton was no longer needed.

Returning to his Desert Training Center, unaware of what had happened, Patton agonized over the possibility that he had committed a grave error. Could Marshall have misconstrued Patton's recommendation to send two divisions as a disguised plea to have his I Armored Corps headquarters participate? Had he angered Marshall by his seeming refusal to step down to division command? Would Marshall ever pardon him? Would Marshall ever give him another chance? Through his friends, Patton quietly made known his willingness, he said, to "take anything to any place at any time" with no questions asked.

Actually, he was far from being in the doghouse. His suggestions had been logical. Marshall was hardly displeased. When the President decided, less than two months later, to invade French North Africa in concert with the British, McNair, with Marshall's approval and Devers's concurrence, selected Patton and his headquarters to lead the first Americans going overseas from the United States directly to combat on the European side of the war. Patton had made his choice inevitable.

Before departing the desert center, Patton hastily summarized for McNair and Devers his activities and findings. Combat formations and matériel were, he believed, secondary in importance to discipline, rapid and accurate shooting, and the irresistible desire to close with the enemy and destroy him: "Killing wins wars."

Summoned to the War Department in Washington on July 30, Patton became acquainted with the operation code-named Torch. Eisenhower in London headed the venture as the Supreme Allied Commander. Convoys of ships leaving the United Kingdom and the United States were to land American troops on the North African shore. How, in what numbers, and where had yet to be determined.

With a small staff of several key officers, Patton set up his headquarters in the Munitions Building on Constitution Avenue, then, on August 5, flew to London to define with Eisenhower his own role in the endeavor and to synchronize his effort with the overall enterprise. Arriving late on the following day, he slept at Claridge's Hotel and reported to Eisenhower in the morning. He brought with him a welcome breath of fresh air. Eisenhower was already swamped under the details of a highly complicated expedition in which widely separated forces at the outset were to concentrate at designated places and times, Patton on the Atlantic coast of French Morocco, others on the Mediterranean shore of Algeria. Few officers had experience with amphitious operations. The tentative date of the scheduled invasion gave only a few months for the tremendous task of preparation. Cheerful, optimistic, thrilled to be close to combat, happy to be reunited with his old friend, Patton expressed his intention "to succeed or die in the attempt."

Three days later, after long discussions uncovered immense problems, Eisenhower appointed Clark his deputy commander and asked him to be the principal Torch planner. Patton was dubious of Clark, who had graduated from West Point eight years after Patton, was still very young and junior in the "old" Army, and had two stars like Patton. He was envious of the close relationship that Clark enjoyed with Eisenhower. But then Patton was disappointed in Eisenhower too. He was "not as rugged mentally as I thought; he vacillates and is not a realist."

Keeping his reservations to himself, Patton, together with Eisenhower and Clark, worked to establish guidelines for an operation that gave every indication of having extremely slim odds for success. Patton was willing to gamble, but admitted the probability of succeeding only if they were lucky. Yet in the final analysis, "wars are only won by risking the impossible." And in any event, they had no choice, for the highest Anglo-American authorities had decided on Torch.

The aims of Torch were several. French Northwest Africa was a good place to introduce the inexperienced Americans to action, for only the armed forces of Vichy France, less formidable opponents than German troops, were there to offer resistance. Although the French had pledged in the 1940 armistice to defend North Africa against invasion, perhaps they were secretly hoping to join the Anglo-American Allies in the war. Descending on the North African littoral would threaten Rommel's Italo-German army in Libya. The landings would help the Russians, who, seemingly close to defeat in the second year of their conflict, were clamoring for a second front. Possession of French Morocco, Algeria, and Tunisia would give the Allies territory from which to launch further offensives.

Toward the end of August, after three weeks in London, with certain basic points of understanding settled, Patton left for Washington. Eisenhower informed Marshall of Patton's "businesslike, sane but enthusiastic" manner and of his own pleasure at having Patton on the team.

In Washington, working with the Navy was not always easy. Naval officers had never engineered an operation of Torch's magnitude, and their methods differed in many respects from the Army's. Some friction was undoubtedly inevitable, but occasional flare-ups of Patton's uncontrollable temper intensified normal difficulties. Cooler heads in both services eventually ironed it all out.

By September 24, Patton's plans for his part in the invasion were complete except for last-minute adjustments. He was "very calm and contented." He had "a sure feeling we will win." How and where to get ashore—these questions had been resolved. While he descended on French Morocco to capture Casablanca, two forces sailing from the United Kingdom were to land simultaneously in Algeria, one near Algiers, the other near Oran. Mark Clark's clandestine submarine voyage to North Africa and his meeting with pro-American French elements promised, but hardly guaranteed, a friendly French reception at the shoreline. Whether Spain would remain neutral or intervene on the Axis side and whether Germany and Italy would send troops from Sicily and elsewhere to block the Allies in Tunisia were questions having no sure answers. What was abundantly clear, Torch was risky.

As the time for embarking his troops approached, Patton attended to some personal matters. He traveled to West Point to say farewell to young George. He thanked Devers for giving him the chance for combat. He learned from Stimson why he had been chosen—no one could better ensure the leadership, courage, and fighting qualities required; and Stimson warned him to avoid sacrificing himself, for he was needed for what was bound to be a long war. Patton saw Marshall, who was "very friendly and helpful." He visited Pershing at his quarters in Walter Reed Hospital and received his blessing. With Admiral H. Kent Hewitt, the naval commander, he chatted with President Roosevelt.

To his brother-in-law Fred Ayer, he wrote, "In spite of my faults you have always treated me as a real brother and I have always felt that way towards you. . . . The job I am going on is about as desperate a venture as has ever been undertaken by any force in the world's history. We will have to meet and defeat superior numbers"—at least 60,000 French soldiers were in Morocco—"on a coast where one can land 60% of the time"—because of high waves and other adverse sea conditions. "So my proverbial luck will have to be working all out. However, I have a convinced belief that I will succeed. If I don't, I shall not survive a second Donquerque (if that is how you spell it). . . . All my life I have wanted to lead a lot of men in a desperate battle. . . . At fifty-six, one can go with equanimity. . . . Thanks to you and Bea, I have had an exceptionally happy life."

Bea flew with him to Norfolk, where men and equipment were going aboard. On Hewitt's flagship, the *Augusta,* Patton immediately wrote Beatrice. Even though she would have no letters for some time, "I will be thinking of you and loving you." In his diary he set down a prayer: "God grant that I do my full duty to my men and my self."

Once the 100 ships transporting Patton's 24,000 troops sailed, Patton was in the captain's cabin with nothing to do. He was careful to refrain from overeating. He exercised on a rowing machine and ran in place in his room. He read the Koran. "I can't decide logically," he confided to his diary, "if I am a man of destiny or a lucky fool, but I think I am destined. . . . My claim to greatness hangs on an ability to lead and inspire. . . . I have no personal fear of death or failure."

The suspected presence of German submarines prompted him to "some extra praying," but what troubled him more was the possibility of bad weather at his landing beaches. A storm and a high surf might prevent his troops from going ashore. A heavy swell might swamp and overturn the small landing craft and drown many soldiers weighed down with weapons and equipment. A subsequent stormy period would deny him reinforcements and supplies from ships standing offshore. Forecasts were less than encouraging. Patton put these thoughts out of his mind. According to the Koran, all events were the will of God, and it was useless for men to worry.

Meditating, he wrote in his diary, "Almost inspite of my self my whole life has been pointed to this moment. When this job is done I presume I will be pointed to the next step in the ladder of destiny. Inspite of my over developed personal ambition, all I want to do right now is my full duty."

As the convoy neared the destination, Patton issued an order of the day to his force, a message of pride and exhortation. "We are to be congratulated," he said, "because we have been chosen." The troops were likely to meet "the gallant French" on the beaches and, although he regretted fighting these brave opponents, all resistance must be crushed. "Speed and vigor of action are the sure roads to success," he reminded. "A pint of sweat will save a gallon of blood."

Shortly before the early-morning hours of November 8, 1942, the scheduled date of Patton's landings, the weather miraculously cleared. The high winds dropped and the sea became smooth. Fate had smiled; Patton was lucky.

So was Eisenhower at Gibraltar. The convoys in the Mediterranean had passed undetected through the straits and were

on station. As Americans clambered down the sides of transport vessels into landing craft and headed to shore, the
French reacted instantly. At all the landing sites, French forces
opposed the invasion with coastal defense batteries, automatic
weapons, and small arms. In some places, naval shells added
their impact. Despite the response, spirited in some cases,
halfhearted in others, the Americans got to land, seized their
objectives, and established their positions.

In Algiers, which the Americans captured on the first day,
the forces concluded a truce, and the fighting stopped. Fresh
units, mainly British, followed the initial waves, and immediately headed eastward toward Tunisia, hoping to overrun
the country and to seize Bizerte and Tunis before Axis troops
could arrive to contest their advance. Mark Clark flew from
Gibraltar and entered into negotiations with Admiral Jean
Darlan, the single figure who commanded the allegiance of
the French military, and sought to reach an armistice extending through North Africa. Near Oran, fierce fighting lasted
two days before the Americans overwhelmed the French. In
Morocco, Patton met strong opposition directed by Auguste
Noguès, the Governor-General, and Admiral François
Michelier, head of the Casablanca defenses.

Patton's force made three separate landings. In the south, at
Safi, about 150 miles below Casablanca, Ernest Harmon held
off a substantial French garrison from nearby Marrakech,
which might otherwise have interfered with American action
against Casablanca. Fifty miles north of Casablanca, at
Mehdia, Lucian Truscott, Jr., moved five miles inland and
seized the Port Lyautey airport, which had the only concrete
runways in Morocco and could accommodate planes from an
aircraft carrier and others flying from Gibraltar to support the
attack on Casablanca.

Patton was with the main landing at Fédala fifteen miles
north of Casablanca. There substantial French forces with artillery and a strong naval contingent offered resistance. Fédala
was in American hands by 8:00 in the morning, when Patton
was scheduled to go ashore. His belongings were stowed in a
landing craft hanging from davits when, for some uncanny
reason, he asked his orderly, Sergeant George Meeks, to re-
trieve from it his cherished ivory-handled pistol. As he
strapped on the weapon, seven French cruisers burst from a
smoke screen and opened fire on the American fleet. Hewitt's
ships replied, and on the first salvo fired by the *Augusta* the

muzzle blast from the rear turret blew Patton's landing craft to bits. With Patton an interested spectator, a naval battle took place, ending when the French vessels withdrew.

Unable to leave ship until shortly after noon, Patton arrived at the beach around 1:30, very wet and in a bad mood. Desultory fire was coming in, and most of the men, instead of setting up medical aid stations and signal posts, instead of saving landing craft being swept out to sea, instead of performing the normal duties of beach parties, were digging foxholes. A disquieting inertia prevailed. Storming into action, Patton stirred groups of soldiers into activity. As he moved along, shouting, cursing, kicking one soldier who was crouching in a fetal position in the sand and who immediately jumped up and went to work, Patton restored order and purpose.

The combat troops were doing well. No messages arrived from Eisenhower, and Patton was unaware of the failure of his own periodic radio reports to get through to Gibraltar. His most troublesome condition at Fédala was that less than 20 percent of his weapons and equipment had been unloaded and hardly any supplies. This he would remedy the following day.

Up before dawn, he appeared at daybreak on the beaches and docks like the wrath of God. Taking charge of one party after another, he galvanized everyone into action. By afternoon, the unloading was going smoothly, landing craft were being salvaged, supply dumps were operating. According to the single British liaison officer present, Patton's personal effort had "a touch of magic."

Patton returned to the *Augusta,* persuaded Hewitt to move his transport ships closer to the coast to facilitate ship-to-shore traffic, and sent his staff to Fédala to set up his headquarters. The troops advanced toward Casablanca. No sign of surrender came from Noguès and Michelier.

As his units began to encircle the city on November 10, Patton decided to resolve the issue. He would attack Casablanca the next day. He set the time at 7:30 A.M. instead of at dawn, the normal hour, for he wanted no mistakes in the early-morning darkness. Although he was loath to hammer Casablanca, he ordered naval shelling and air bombardment. His plans were set by midnight, and his men were in their battle positions.

His intelligence officer awakened Patton at 4:30 A.M. on November 11. The French, he said, were preparing to surrender.

Should the attack on Casablanca be canceled? No, Patton said, not until they actually capitulated. Two hours later, less than an hour before the scheduled action was to start, the French ordered their troops to cease firing. Patton called off the operation. The end of hostilities was, he said, "a nice birthday present." He was fifty-seven years old.

He directed the troops to enter the city and to attack if anyone tried to stop them. There was no opposition, and the Casablanca garrison surrendered, agreeing to let the Americans occupy key points and to keep their own troops in their barracks.

The struggle in Morocco had cost the U.S. Army and Navy almost 530 killed; almost 650 had been wounded, and more than 100 were missing. The French losses were much higher.

Between 2:00 and 3:00 P.M., the ranking French officers came to Patton's headquarters at the Hotel Miramar in Fédala to terminate the conflict formally. Patton's deputy commander, Geoffrey Keyes, met them with a guard of honor, then escorted them to the smoking room where Patton and Hewitt waited. Patton received them with dignity and courtesy. He opened the meeting by complimenting the French on their gallantry, then moved quickly to the heart of the proceedings.

He had taken with him from Washington two approved versions of an armistice agreement, and he ordered both to be read. The first, assuming token French resistance, which was not the case, provided lenient treatment. The second, supposing protracted operations until a total French defeat, which hardly applied either, dictated the harsh terms of disarming and disbanding the French military forces.

Dissolving the French forces, Noguès pointed out, would remove law and order and lead to unrest among the Arabs, Jews, and Berbers. It would also leave the frontier with Spanish Morocco and the Allied lines of communication in North Africa undefended.

A number of points ran through Patton's mind. He was eager to reach a settlement. He didn't want to be responsible for an outbreak of civil violence. Uninterested in political issues, he saw no need for Americans to be involved in local problems. His foremost aim was to continue the war against the Axis. Admiring France and the French, comfortable with the officers with whom he was dealing, Patton proposed a gentlemen's agreement. The Americans were to have unrestricted access to whatever they needed to fight the Axis. French and American prisoners were to be exchanged. The French troops would retain their arms but remain in their barracks for the time being. All other matters would await resolution by Eisenhower in Algiers. The French promptly accepted.

Then Patton played what he called a "nasty trick" on the French. "Gentlemen," he said, "we have now settled everything, but there is one disagreeable formality which we should go through." The French officers were startled, but only for a moment. Producing champagne for all, Patton toasted the "happy termination of a fratricidal strife" and "the resumption of the age-old friendship between France and America."

On the following day when he left the *Augusta* for good, sailors spontaneously lined the rail and gave him an ovation, a gesture rarely accorded to a non-naval hero. As he moved his headquarters into the Shell Building in Casablanca and took rooms for himself at the Majestic Hotel, Americans at home were cheering him too. He had had the toughest job in North Africa, and victory made him a hero. His name was fast becoming known in every household.

WAR IN THE MEDITERRANEAN

The invasion of Morocco confirmed Patton's military brilliance. His zeal and unerring intuition had assured victory in the landings. His quick organization of a major attack on Casablanca was masterful. His selection of good men as his key subordinates, in this case Harmon and Truscott, was an important element of generalship. His spirit pervaded his entire force.

Elated by his triumph, he gave credit to his men, who "had achieved the impossible," and to his "proverbial luck or more probably the direct intervention of the Lord." He told his troops to be proud, to be neat and clean, to wear the uniform properly, and to salute French and American officers flawlessly.

"Your deeds have proven that you are fine soldiers. Look the part."

The next ten months held both despair and joy. Frustrated

by inactivity, he twice reached the heights of accomplishment, gained applause, and expanded his fame. Then dashed to the depths of disgrace and gloom, he faced a future uncertain and clouded.

Instead of being rewarded for his performance in Morocco, he was sick at heart to learn of Mark Clark's promotion—and on Patton's birthday. For his contributions to Torch, the planning in London, the secret submarine trip, the negotiations with Darlan, Clark received his third star and became a lieutenant general. Patton was bitter, frankly jealous. A new headquarters was being formed and would soon be activated as the Fifth Army. Patton was eligible to head the organization, which called for a lieutenant general, and Stimson had intimated that he would probably get both, the army and the promotion. Yet the younger Clark now had that grade ahead of Patton, would probably obtain the Fifth Army, and no doubt take control of Lloyd Fredendall's II Corps in Algeria and Patton's I Armored Corps in Morocco. Clark as Patton's direct superior was an unpleasant thought. Yet Patton manfully sent Clark a message: "Please accept my sincere congratulations on your promotion and also on the magnificent work you have been doing in connection with this operation."

Equally difficult for Patton was to endure his distance from the combat taking place in Tunisia. He had no immediate prospect of fighting. "I want to be Top Dog and only battle can give me that. . . . I have a mission, and . . . nothing can stop me. But the waiting is hard. Perhaps I am being made perfect through suffering. . . . I am pretty low today." To Beatrice, "Nothing seems to be happening and I just sit."

Concealing his unhappiness, showing an untroubled exterior, he bolstered his flagging ego by frequently reminding himself that he had yet to gain his destiny. He also wrote to old friends like Stimson, ostensibly to pass along observations—soldiers in the early landing waves were encumbered with too much equipment, the light tank was too light and its gun too weak—but actually to inform them of his regret to be so far from the action.

Two tasks occupied him, one military, the other diplomatic. He oversaw work to turn Casablanca into a first-class base, to renew the airfields, to improve supply. He received additional soldiers from the United States, and finding them slipshod, used his regular means to bring them to his standards.

Patton also maintained excellent relations with the French

and native rulers. Easy and graceful in ceremonial and social events, he impeccably represented the power of the United States at the Sultan's palace and at Noguès's residency, at formal dinners, lavish entertainments, and hunting parties. Above all, he sought to uphold what he called the "mythical supremacy" of the French. He termed both Noguès and Darlan "crooks," but he had no wish to disturb their traditional methods of dealing with the population. When Noguès reported unrest among Jews, who were trying to remove the anti-Jewish laws in force throughout North Africa, Patton advised him to handle the situation as he thought best. The Darlan Deal, no responsibility of Patton's, preserved the status quo and the Pétainist officials in their jobs. Only after the assassination of Darlan in December, which Patton judged "a distinct loss" to stability, and the appointment of Darlan's successor, Henri Girard, would the Americans seek reform of the French administration and an end to the racial statutes.

What was important to Patton was to have the country calm and the French cooperative. He was satisfied on both counts. As he had requested, French soldiers guarded all road and railway bridges, manned antiaircraft defenses, and stood ready to repel invasion from Spanish Morocco. All this freed the Americans for whatever military action might be necessary against the Axis.

Summoned to a conference in Algiers with Eisenhower and Clark, Patton had a premonition of bad news. "However," he wrote in his diary, "the Lord has helped me a lot and I think He will let me fulfill my destiny." In Algiers, word came from Washington of Clark's appointment to command the Fifth Army. Patton had to keep close rein on his emotions as he congratulated Clark. "I sat on for half an hour and left," he wrote Bea. In the privacy of his journal, he wished for "a nice clean death" in an airplane crash. On the following day he consoled himself, "I decided that my disappointment was but an additional act of God to temper me" and prepare him for his ultimate mission, whatever it might be.

A news magazine quoted him accurately as comparing troop leadership to moving spaghetti—pushing from behind buckled the pasta, whereas pulling from the front made it go. But the story, in what was sheer nonsense, went on to say that Patton had challenged Rommel to a duel, the weapons to be tanks. They would meet in a field with their armies drawn up as in a feudal tournament, the encounter to decide the outcome of the war. Just like Patton, the public said, enchanted. Beatrice subscribed to a clipping service, and less than a month after Torch had more than 1,300 articles about her husband. Patton made a great effort, as he always had, to publicize the exploits of individual soldiers in their hometown newspapers.

He became bored with his duties—"I get fed up sitting here"—so he visited the front in Tunisia. Officially his purpose was to observe how the Germans and Italians operated and to discover why they were destroying so many American tanks. Actually he was eager to be close to the fighting. What he saw disturbed him. Kenneth Anderson's First British Army, composed mainly of British units but with some American and French troops, opposed Germans and Italians who had come from Sicily and Italy into the northeastern corner of Tunisia and held Bizerte and Tunis. Many problems hampered the Allies—long distances, congested supply lines, a paucity of airfields, no modern weapons and equipment among the French, an absence of unity, and poor tactical procedures. The Americans were glad to see him, for he was the only general officer, they said, who had appeared in the area for more than three weeks, "a sad commentary," wrote Patton in his diary, "on our idea of leadership." The Allies, he concluded, had much to learn. In contrast, the Axis army was strong and efficient. How he wished he could enter the fray.

Increasingly, Patton lost respect for Eisenhower and Clark, the two senior American officers in North Africa. Eisenhower lacked decision and a sense of reality. He and Clark "certainly need to know the facts of life." Their instructions were "the most foolish" he had ever read. Their headquarters was "a mess and gets out contradictory orders almost daily." The "glamour boys have no knowledge of men or war. Too damned slick, especially Clark." Eisenhower was pro-British in outlook and "spoke of lunch as 'tiffin,' of gasoline as 'petrol,' and of antiaircraft as 'flack.' I truly fear that London has conquered Abilene." In no way did Eisenhower resemble Pershing, who had firmly upheld American interests. Permitting political and economic problems to divert his attention from the battlefield, "Ike is not commanding." Worst of all, there was a great deal of intrigue in Algiers, throat-cutting and "much back-bighting." He later told Beatrice privately: "It always takes me about three days to get over a trip to Alger.

One should wear chain mail to avoid the knife thrusts. It would be amusing if it were not serious."

Yet Patton was careful not to publicize these thoughts. His future depended on Eisenhower, and outwardly he was friendly, loyal, and responsive. In his letters to Beatrice, in order to confound the censors, he referred to Eisenhower by his first two initials, calling him Divine Destiny, a term of symbolic meaning. If Patton's destiny lay in the hands of God or fate, Eisenhower was clearly the executive instrument.

Concern in Washington over whether Eisenhower was equal to his immense tasks led Marshall to dispatch John Lucas, later Omar Bradley, to help Eisenhower. He named them his representatives to the combat elements, their function to act as his eyes and ears, to report on problems in the field.

The Fifth Army headquarters came into existence under Clark early in January 1943 and took Patton's corps under command. Fredendall's II Corps headquarters and several American divisions moved to southern Tunisia and augmented Anderson's First Army, for although the northern front remained quiet, a new danger arose in the south. Sir Bernard L. Montgomery and his British Eighth Army had defeated Rommel at El Alamein late in October and compelled him to retreat 1,500 miles across Libya. Rommel headed for the Mareth Line, just beyond the border with Tunisia, and settled his Italo-German troops into those defenses.

In mid-January, Patton was a busy host for the Casablanca Conference, where President Roosevelt, Prime Minister Churchill, and their principal military advisers gathered to discuss Allied strategy. Patton requisitioned the affluent suburb of Anfa, reserved a large hotel there for the meetings, took over luxurious villas for the notables, and had the whole area wired in and closely guarded. Although he participated in none of the deliberations, he spoke with all the celebrities and dined with most. Roosevelt was cordial, Marshall friendly. Everyone complimented him on the appearance and discipline of his troops and thanked him for his hospitality and entertainment. He responded by stating his hope for a combat role soon again.

Among the decisions reached at Casablanca, one shocked him. The next attack in Tunisia was to be made by Anderson's and Montgomery's British armies directed by Sir Harold Alexander, who was to be the Allied ground forces commander.

Patton as host of the Casablanca Conference in January 1943: *at top* with Churchill and at *right* with President Roosevelt.

The II Corps was to be under the British. "Shades of J. J. Pershing," he exploded. "We have sold our birthright." Eisenhower was to be elevated into the stratosphere while the British ran the war, "the result of clever politics by the British."

The Allies intended to invade Sicily, after the conquest of Tunisia, with British and American forces of equal size and with Patton in command of the Americans. Action at last! He was exhilarated to follow where the Athenians, Carthaginians, Romans, and Byzantines, the armies of Nicias, Hannibal, Scipio, and Belisarius had fought. Sizing up the difficulties, he wrote, "My luck will have to be pretty good and the Lord on the job to put it across."

Before attacking Rommel in Tunisia, Montgomery organized a seminar on his battle techniques for senior officers, with a series of lectures and demonstrations. Patton flew to Tripoli and attended some of the sessions. He met many distinguished British generals. Montgomery struck him as being "small, very alert, wonderfully conceited, and the best soldier—or so it seems—I have met in this war." (It was a view he would later modify.) The assembly gave Patton his first real contact with his British colleagues. Virtually unknown in England, Patton impressed all with his eccentricity and color. After attending a lecture titled "How to Make War," he fell in with Brian Horrocks, who had a certain flamboyance of his own and who asked Patton what he thought of the proceedings. With a sly grin, Patton replied, "I may be old, I may be slow, I may be stupid, but it just don't mean a thing to me." Patton's instant transformation from a polished Southern gentleman to a frontier-town cowboy startled Horrocks. The British began to notice his pistols, mannerisms, and speech. They loved his description of a particular unit as being like a bunch of bananas—some green, some yellow, some rotten—and spread it widely.

In Tunisia, bedlam had broken out. With an army in the north and another under Rommel in the south, the Axis forces acted to make the coastal plain and the 250-mile north-south Tunis-Gabès road secure by driving the Allies out of the mountain passes of the Eastern Dorsale range. The first blow came at Faid on January 30, the crushing attack on February 14. Seriously damaging Orlando Ward's 1st Armored Division, they drove the Americans and French fifty miles westward to the Western Dorsale, then seized the opportunity to throw the

Allies altogether out of Tunisia. Rommel pursued the fleeing units and buffeted the Allies at the Sbiba and Kasserine passes, but he was unable to break through. Calling off his offensive, Rommel withdrew to the Mareth Line to await Montgomery.

The engagement, known as the battle of Kasserine Pass, was a disaster for the Americans. Fredendall had directed the operations poorly and had lost control of his corps. In eight days, more than 3,000 Americans were killed and wounded, 3,700 were captured, and about 200 tanks were lost. What the encounter seemed to indicate was the inability of the inexperienced Americans to stand up to the skilled Axis troops. Much alarm appeared in press reports in the United States.

Alexander had arrived from Cairo at the climax of the action and assumed command. His observations persuaded him that the American soldier was of poor fighting quality. To Eisenhower he suggested replacing Fredendall with the best American corps commander available.

Far from the scene in Casablanca, Patton agonized. Not only had his beloved son-in-law John Waters been taken prisoner but the image of the American fighting man had suffered. Why were his own talents being wasted? "I trust the Lord, who has always looked after me, will see that I eventually get into it again."

On March 4, while Patton was out riding for exercise, Eisenhower telephoned and left a message. Patton was to leave on the following day for extended field duty. Entrusting the planning for Sicily to his deputy Geoffrey Keyes, taking Hugh Gaffey and Oscar Koch to serve on the staff, Patton flew to Algiers on March 5. Eisenhower met him at the airfield and gave him instructions. Patton was to take command and get the II Corps on its feet. He was to restore American prestige. He was to give the soldiers back their self-respect and prove their ability to defeat the Germans. He was to be "perfectly cold-blooded" about removing ineffective leaders. He had no need to prove his personal courage. "I want you as a corps commander, not as a casualty."

At Constantine, Alexander acquainted Patton with the current plans. In about two weeks, when Montgomery attacked Rommel in the Mareth Line, Patton was to launch a supporting effort to attract Axis forces away from Montgomery and thus facilitate his advance across the Gabès plain. In order to avoid a repetition of the Kasserine catastrophe, Alexander cautiously proscribed Patton's mission. He was to move from the Western to the Eastern Dorsale, seize Gafsa, a town on the road leading to Gabès, and take the Maknassy defile. He was merely to threaten the Axis flank on the coastal plain and not to go beyond the Eastern Dorsale.

According to these instructions, Patton had about ten days for remedial action to stiffen the corps, very little time. He resented Alexander's prudence, an implied slur on American capabilities. He hated to be restrained from smashing into the Axis flank. But he made no comment. Eisenhower regarded Anglo-American cooperation as sacred and saw nothing wrong in subordinating Americans to the British.

At the II Corps command post on March 6, Patton formally relieved Fredendall, who would go to the United States, be promoted to lieutenant general, and take command of an army in training. Noticing immediately the poor discipline and military courtesy around the headquarters, Patton issued orders to improve dress and saluting. Up at 6:30 on the following morning, entering the mess tent for breakfast at 7:00, finding only Gaffey there, Patton instructed the cooks to close in an hour. "Tomorrow people will be on time."

Bradley was at the headquarters as Eisenhower's representative, his eyes and ears, and Patton was uncomfortable with Bradley's apparent status as a spy. With Eisenhower's approval, Patton made Bradley his deputy commander. At some appropriate time later, Bradley was to take over the corps and allow Patton to return to planning for Sicily.

He had his four division commanders, his field artillery commanders, and the heads of the corps staff sections in for supper and a discussion of their plans. Terry Allen's 1st Infantry Division and Orlando Ward's 1st Armored Division were to attack, the former to Gafsa and beyond, the latter to seize Maknassy. The two other divisions were to be in reserve in case Rommel attacked the Americans first.

Unbeknownst to the Allies, Rommel had departed. He had flown to Italy, then to Germany, to urge Mussolini and Hitler to withdraw their troops from North Africa, thereby saving instead of sacrificing 200,000 men. Both dictators refused, and Hitler, because of Rommel's poor health, forbade him to return to Tunisia. There would be no personal encounter between Rommel and Patton.

Patton set about to galvanize his troops and to improve discipline, dress, and the condition of weapons. For a week, surrounded by motorcycle outriders and armored cars, he traveled like a whirlwind throughout his area with sirens screaming to pep up his men and infect them with "an adequate hatred of Germans." He visited every battalion in his four divisions, prodding commanders, making mandatory the wearing of neckties, leggings, and helmets, insisting on military courtesy and saluting, personally fining officers and men for infractions. He enforced speed limits, road intervals, and vehicle maintenance. Exhorting the troops to be vicious and aggressive, he urged them to kill rather than to die for freedom's cause. "We must utterly defeat the enemy. . . . I know you will be worthy."

He tried to dissipate what he considered to be an exaggerated concern with digging in, the antithesis of an aggressive attitude. At Allen's division he committed an unfortunate act that was misinterpreted and resented. Patton asked his old friend Allen, "Terry, where is your foxhole?" Allen pointed. Patton marched over and contemptuously urinated in the hole. He wanted only to show his disdain for passive defense. The men, who had great affection for Allen, interpreted Patton's action as an insult.

If he shocked and unsettled some soldiers, if he stirred others to detest him, if he gave rise to the heartfelt expression "Our blood, his guts," he generated excitement as well as discipline and order. He had to be ruthless, for he had only eleven days to shake his troops out of slovenly habits and into a state of alertness. At the same time, he expedited the arrival of new equipment, clothing, and mail. He improved living conditions by insisting on better food and well-cooked meals. Everywhere he went he assured everyone of winning the next time. His electric quality communicated itself to all and instilled energy and sense of purpose.

On March 12, to his great but brief satisfaction, he received his third star. "When I was a little boy," he wrote in his diary, referring to when he called himself George S. Patton, Jr., Lieutenant General, "I did not know there were full generals. Now I want, and will get, four stars."

As the day of attack approached, Patton, as always, was "a little short of breath before a match." During the night of March 16, Allen's division made a forty-five-mile approach march in a downpour, drove off the opposition and seized Gafsa on the following morning, then advanced ten miles down the road toward Gabès and took El Guettar. The action won wide publicity in the United States, counteracting the dismay over Kasserine. Patton benefited; his fame increased.

Pleased with Allen, Patton was disappointed in Ward at the Maknassy pass. Ward's vehicles were marooned in a sea of mud, but Ward nevertheless should have attacked, Patton felt, with infantry and half-tracks. As Ward made little headway, Patton fretted. Eventually he relieved Ward because he believed him to be an unlucky general and because he thought the division needed new leadership.

If the tanks broke through at Maknassy, how could Alexander deny Patton the chance to drive across the plain to the sea and cut off a large enemy force? Yet Alexander's low estimate of American capabilities and his wish to prevent a rash act leading to another American setback prompted him to remind Patton of his limited role. He was not to descend to the plain, where he might interfere with Montgomery's progress. What Patton saw was a British plot to make the battle an exclusive British victory.

At El Guettar, Allen stopped a strong thrust by two panzer divisions, one Italian, the other German. The Americans fought well; there was no panic. The Axis forces withdrew, leaving thirty tanks burning on the field. Another attempt later that day failed. The Americans held their ground. Patton was heartened, Alexander pleased. Patton had attracted two powerful divisions from Montgomery's front.

"I wish I could do more personally," he wrote in his diary. Because his forces at Maknassy and El Guettar were widely separated, he had to spend much time at his headquarters on the telephone, a practice displeasing to him. "It is awful to have to confide every thing to others, but there is no other way, and if you trust people, they seem to perform."

When he left his command post for inspections of forward areas and to make himself visible to the combat troops, he came under fire regularly. "I still get scared," he confessed, contradicting his earlier claims that he had no fear. "I guess I will never get used to it." Close fire was all right, but "I hate shells and bombs." He disliked strafing airplanes most of all, and was nervous about the profusion of mines laid by the Axis, "a distinct mental hazard." When he was exposed, he felt depressed for about half an hour. The palms of his hands became moist. When an incoming round came close, it broke the spell, and Patton thought no more of the danger. The sensation was much like his experience at the New York horse show. The first time he rode the jumps, he was frightened, but by the end of the week, the performance was routine.

He visited the hospitals often, and the sight of the wounded hurt him badly. But the men enjoyed seeing and talking with him. "I suppose I do some good," he wrote Bea, "but it always makes me choke up. . . . I hate to look at them."

When the Axis, under Montgomery's pressure, began to pull out of the Mareth positions, Alexander ordered Patton to suspend operations at Maknassy and to attack down the Gabès road to hasten the Axis withdrawal. Still lacking confidence in the Americans, Alexander gave detailed instructions.

After protesting respectfully Alexander's overly specific orders—in the U.S. Army superiors told subordinates what to do but not how to do it—Patton set about to gain a great victory on the Gabès plain. He moved tanks to Gafsa for a drive to Gabès. C. C. Benson, who had been with Patton at Bourg, commanded the assault. He made little headway against strong Axis forces protecting the flank of the main body now abandoning the Mareth Line.

On April 1, to Patton's grief, his young aide Jenson, whom he had attached temporarily to Benson's staff, was killed when twelve German planes bombed the headquarters. In his situation report for that date, Patton blamed the Allied air forces. "Total lack of air cover for our units," he said, "has allowed German air force to operate at will." Alexander's air officer rejected the criticism and struck back. The II Corps, he declared, was not battleworthy and was using the air force as an alibi for its lack of success. An enraged Patton demanded public apology.

Three air force generals came to mollify Patton. While they were talking, four German aircraft flew over, firing machine guns and dropping bombs. Part of the ceiling in the room where the officers were meeting came down and the door jammed shut. No one was hurt, but the appearance of the enemy planes seemed to prove Patton's contention.

"How in hell did you manage to stage that?" someone asked.

"I'll be damned if I know," Patton shouted, "but if I could find the sons of bitches who flew those planes, I'd mail each one of them a medal." Eventually, both parties to the dispute retracted their statements and restored surface harmony.

Benson was getting nowhere, and Patton told him to press on until he found "a fight or hit the ocean." Displeased with Benson's progress, still hoping for a great victory, Patton

Wearing his long-desired third star, Patton surveys his forces at El Guettar, Tunisia.

hounded Benson on the radio and eventually drove to Benson's headquarters to put more pressure on. He told him again to keep pushing "for a fight or a bath" in the sea. When Patton saw Benson's leading units stopped at a mine field, a cold fury came over him. Preceded by nothing more than a jeep and a scout car, he drove through the mines and led Benson's force down the road. "My luck in being at the right place at the right time held," he later said. With everyone worrying about his safety, knowing his behavior to be reckless, Patton turned back after a few miles. Shortly thereafter, Benson's men came into contact with a British patrol. The Axis troops had escaped Patton's thrust.

With the battle of what was sometimes called El Guettar over, Patton complimented his troops. "Due to your united efforts and to the manifest assistance of Almighty God, the splendid record of the American Army has attained added luster." He praised Bradley and Allen.

Now another and probably final engagement in Tunisia was necessary, and Alexander's plans excluded the American divisions from a major role. Patton protested vigorously to Eisenhower and Alexander. All the Americans, he maintained, should have a sector of their own and fight together for the sake of national prestige. He eventually won his point. Privately he was bitter. Eisenhower, he felt, rather than Patton, should have insisted on equal access to battle honors for the Americans. "Ike," he said in his diary, "is more British than the British and is putty in their hands." Distinctly irritated, he wrote, "God damn all British and all so-called Americans." With the II Corps assured a specific place in the forthcoming action, Patton turned over the command to Bradley and went back to Casablanca to prepare for Sicily.

Like Hanson Ely, whom he had seen in the last war turn the demoralized 5th Division around in three days, like Matthew B. Ridgway, who later in Korea was to restore an offensive attitude in the Eighth Army, Patton rehabilitated the four divisions of the II Corps in ten days, a great personal achievement by a master of the art of command. Having infused a fighting spirit among his men, he led them to a victory of sorts and gave them back their pride and self-esteem. Though he resented Alexander's tight rein, which prevented a glorious American triumph, he followed his orders to the letter. As he said in his diary, "I have been gone 43 days, fought several successful battles . . . lost about ten pounds, gained a third star and a hell of a lot of poise and confidence, and am otherwise the same." A message from Marshall capped his satisfaction. "You have done a fine job and have justified our confidence in you." Explaining his success, Patton noted, "War is very simple, direct, and ruthless. It takes a simple, direct, and ruthless man to wage war." As he turned to prepare for the invasion of Sicily, he regretted having departed Tunisia before the end of the campaign there. But he saw himself as being "in the hands of fate, who is forging me for some future bigger role."

If that was to happen in Sicily, uncertainty, confusion, and bickering would make it difficult. The initial plan, drawn in Washington and London, was plain and logical. Montgomery was to land around Catania on the eastern shore, Patton around Palermo on the northern shore. With both in possession of major ports and receiving buildup and supplies to sustain their operations, they were to drive along the eastern and northern coastal roads to a meeting at Messina in the northeastern corner of the island. But Montgomery was averse to having the two ground forces separated. He wished both to come ashore aside by side and be mutually supporting. With Montgomery and Alexander occupied in the final battle in Tunisia and able to devote little time and energy to Sicily, with Eisenhower reluctant to interfere, no final decision came until May, after the Axis surrendered 250,000 troops in Tunisia. Then Montgomery bullied and dominated Alexander and had his way. Montgomery would land on the eastern face of Sicily, Patton adjacent to him on the southern face, where no large harbors existed. Although Alexander enunciated initial objectives beyond the beaches, what was to happen afterward, how the campaign was to unfold, remained unsettled and vague.

To Patton, the war, it seemed, was being fought for the benefit of the British Empire. Eisenhower was weak, but "I owe him a lot and must stay in with him." Patton needed to retain his self-confidence, always difficult. "I have greater ability than these other people," he said, trying to bolster his spirits, "and it comes from, for lack of a better word, what we must call greatness of soul based on belief—an unshakable belief—in my destiny."

Lacking seaports, he hoped that a new amphibious truck called a DUKW or duck, still unproved, would make over-the-beach supply feasible. As for the subsequent campaigning, Patton conjectured, while Montgomery drove up the eastern

With the boss, General George C. Marshall.

With his key subordinates: aides Alexander Stiller and Charles Codman (far left and far right) and his chief of staff, Hobart Gay (to Patton's right).

shore to Messina, Patton would advance inland, go around the left or western side of Mt. Etna, and head for Messina too.

He was pleased to obtain Bradley's II Corps headquarters and Allen's 1st Division, both experienced in combat, instead of the green and untried organizations originally scheduled. With his usual uncanny prescience, Patton put Allen in the center to land at Gela, where he expected the Axis to attack in strength. On the left, Truscott's 3d Division was to come ashore at Licata; on the right, at Scoglitti, Troy Middleton, a solid commander, was to land his 45th Division, which had recently come from the United States. Patton and Bradley, who "grows on me as a sound and extremely loyal soldier," both felt the chances of surviving to be no more than 50-50, "but God, or luck, will tip the beam to us." In a letter to Marshall, Patton promised to leave the beaches only as "a conqueror or a corpse."

Leading a healthy and well-regulated life, Patton was up at 6:00, had toast for breakfast, soup for lunch, hiked a mile and a half at a rapid pace up a steep hill in the evening, had a single drink and a good dinner before going to bed at 10:00. Despite newspaper reports of his profanity and lack of godliness, he attended Episcopal services every Sunday. He chose Charles Codman, an aviator decorated in World War I and a cultivated and mature gentleman, to be his new aide. To the War Department, he stated disingenuously, "I do not deserve or desire publicity"; he preferred, he said again, that the newspapers feature soldiers.

In mid-May he learned of a decision to upgrade his I Armored Corps. In order to put the Americans on an equal footing with the British, Patton during the voyage to Sicily was to rename his headquarters the Seventh Army, thus gaining the same status as Montgomery's Eighth Army. This made it unneccessary for Patton any longer to be envious of Mark Clark, who had the Fifth.

Marshall was in Algiers early in June to discuss with Churchill and Eisenhower whether to invade the Italian mainland after Sicily, and he visited Clark and Patton. The discipline and combat readiness of Patton's troops pleased Marshall. In Clark's presence, although Patton still distrusted Clark and was uncomfortable with him, Patton told Marshall how helpful Clark had been, which was true and "tactful as hell." He added in his diary, "If you treat a skunk nicely, he will not piss on you—as often."

His son George, like his father, was turned back to repeat his first year at West Point. Sympathetically, he wrote to tell George how proud of him he was, no matter what happened. If young George continued to follow his father so accurately, he said, he was bound to be at least a lieutenant general.

Lecturing to the inexperienced 45th Division, he reassured the men on their forthcoming entrance into combat. Battle, he said, was "the most magnificent competition in which a human being can indulge. It brings out all that is best; it removes all that is base." Everyone was afraid but only the coward let his fear overcome his sense of duty. "We must not only die gallantly; we must kill devastatingly." Victory was the prize and worth everything.

As the time of invasion approached, Patton had alternating emotions. He sought to retain his self-confidence, yet was troubled, as always, by apprehensions about doing less than he could, less than his best. He needed God's help to win, yet he often wondered whether he deserved it. He tried to figure out how the campaign was to proceed after the troops were solidly ashore. Having originally liked and admired Alexander, now mystified by his apparent lack of decision, Patton noticed Alexander's "exceptionally small head. That may explain things."

Boarding the *Monrovia*, Admiral Hewitt's new flagship, Patton was happy to be sailing to battle in command of 90,000 men in the initial assault. Eventually his Seventh Army would have more than 200,000 troops. His message to the soldiers at sea stressed the pride of "having been selected" for the invasion, the "privilege to attack and destroy" the enemy. In their hands lay the "glory of American arms, the honor of the U.S. Army, and the future of the world. See to it that you are worthy of this great trust." As for himself, he told his diary, "I have the usual shortness of breath I always have before a polo game."

In the early-morning darkness on July 10, more than seven Allied divisions started landing along 100 miles of shoreline. Montgomery's men had little difficulty on the eastern side, took Syracuse, but were stopped before Augusta. Patton's troops, hampered by high winds and waves, descended along seventy miles of coast. As naval shelling silenced enemy coastal batteries, Keyes, Patton's deputy, and Lucas, dispatched by Eisenhower, organized beach parties and directed men and units inland. German and Italian divisions moved toward

With his rival Mark Clark, who infuriated Patton by getting his third star first.

Gela, and, after being driven back by heavy naval and ground fires, prepared to assault in strength on the morrow.

That was when Patton, accompanied by his chief of staff, Hobart Gay, along with his aide Stiller, and several soldiers, came ashore. Landing about 9:30 A.M., he drove into Gela, intending to go down the coastal road to see Allen. On impulse—or was it intuition?—he stopped in town and visited William Darby's Rangers just as an Italian infantry division and a German armored division renewed their attack on Gela. Had Patton continued on his route, he would have run into seven German tanks.

A fierce battle erupted with Patton in the front line. Excited to be so close to the combat, he displayed himself prominently, shouted encouragement—"Kill every one of the goddamn bastards"—helped a party lay in their mortars, and by his presence undoubtedly stiffened the defense. Once again he was in the right place at the proper time. Axis tanks and infantry came close to entering Gela, but in the afternoon, with sixteen German tanks destroyed, they withdrew. Only a battle-experienced division like the 1st could have withstood and turned back the Axis blow.

After arranging with Allen, his assistant division commander, Theodore Roosevelt, Jr., and Gaffey, formerly his chief of staff, who now commanded part of the 2nd Armored Division, to attack on the next day, he returned to Gela and the beach, where he came under air bombardment. He maintained his composure and walked around for the benefit of the men working on the shore. He was back on the *Monrovia* at 7:00 P.M. after a strenuous day. He had, he felt, earned his pay. Well satisfied, he recorded, "God certainly watched over me today." To Beatrice, "I was right in the middle of it and had a swell time."

Montgomery took Augusta, but finding the coastal highway leading to Catania and eventually to Messina blocked by strong opposition, he decided to drive up the inland road as well. The route was in the American zone and reserved for Patton's use. Ignoring the boundary between the Seventh and Eighth Armies, Montgomery high-handedly, without informing Alexander or Patton, usurped the road and sent one of his two corps to advance along it.

Alexander, flying from Tunisia, visited Montgomery, who told him what he had done. Accepting the fait accompli, Alexander came to Patton and passed along the information.

Montgomery, not Patton, now had access to the road. The decision reflected Alexander's continuing doubts about American competence. Without the road in question, the 45th Division had nowhere to go and Patton had no chance to get to Messina. The mission now devolving on the Seventh Army, protecting Montgomery's flank and rear, was a humiliation.

Remembering Eisenhower's instructions in Tunisia, Patton kept his temper. If he was to be denied Messina, he would strike for Palermo. But he said nothing and asked permission merely to take Agrigento, twenty-five miles west of Licata, and its satellite Porto Empidocle, which would give Patton a harbor for his supplies. Still concerned about overextending the Americans, Alexander approved if Patton could do so with a limited effort.

Patton told Truscott to reconnoiter in force to Agrigento and to take the port. He instructed Bradley, who was angry over Montgomery's action and Alexander's acquiescence, to relinquish the road meekly and to sideslip the 45th to the left across the rear of the 1st, a tedious and time-consuming movement, then to advance with both divisions to the northern shore of Sicily.

Shifting the road to Montgomery wasted at least two days. As it turned out, Montgomery soon bogged down on both routes, and he lacked the flexibility to reinforce either advance. Patton's retention of the inland road would undoubtedly have shortened the campaign.

With Truscott in possession of Agrigento and Bradley attacking to the north, Patton flew to North Africa on July 17 to protest Alexander's explicit order, now published, of Patton's mission to protect the Eighth Army rear, an indignity to the Americans and to the Seventh Army. Patton revealed what he wanted, and an embarrassed Alexander approved his drive to Palermo.

As Bradley's II Corps headquarters supervised the two divisions heading for the northern shore, Patton formed a Provisional Corps under his deputy Seventh Army commander, Keyes, gave him the 3d Infantry and 2d Armored divisions, and told him to take chances and go all-out for Palermo. Showing tactical skill, good staff work, and excellent initiative, Keyes covered the 100 miles in several days, taking 300 casualties, capturing more than 50,000 Axis prisoners, and seizing the city on July 22. The fall of Palermo created a sensation in the newspapers at home and brought Patton much praise. At

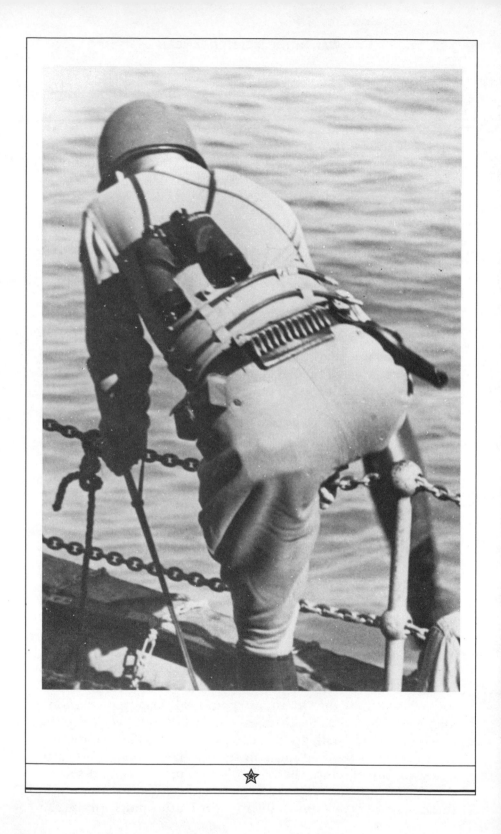

☆

Left, Over the rail for Sicily; *above* striding up the
invasion beach at Gela with his staff. (Patton is at left.)

the same time, Bradley reached his destination, the northern shore of Sicily. Both triumphs put Patton's Seventh Army on the coastal road running eastward to Messina, while Montgomery was stalled near Catania.

Patton's reaction was typical. "I really feel like a great general today—all my plans have so far worked. I hope God stays with me." The attack to Palermo was, he thought, "a classic example of the proper use of armor." He himself had contributed a personal act. Traveling to visit the forward troops, he came to a narrow bridge where a balky mule hauling a cart was holding up the tanks. Breaking his walking stick over the mule driver, he had the animal killed and, together with the cart, pushed off the structure, allowing the tanks to cross.

On July 25, a day before Mussolini was deposed from power in Rome, Patton met with Alexander and Montgomery to reach agreement on the final dispositions. With the British blocked on the Catania plain and on the western side of Mt. Etna, Patton received the northern coastal road and a parallel route inland, both leading to Messina. Looking ahead to possible amphibious end runs on the northern shore, Patton asked for landing craft, and the Navy reluctantly made some available to him.

Now Patton was determined to reach Messina ahead of Montgomery. Resenting the condescending British attitude toward the Americans, Patton became obsessed with proving the skill and strength and spirit of his troops by getting to Messina first. He put pressure on his subordinates to keep moving forward as fast as possible in order to arrive in Messina before the Eighth Army. "This is a horse race in which the prestige of the U.S. Army is at stake. We must take Messina before the British."

Unfortunately, progress was slow. The Axis forces had all the advantages. Having decided to abandon Sicily but grudgingly, the Germans and Italians were withdrawing methodically and with great skill, using the rugged mountains to the utmost. As the Axis forces pulled back into the northeastern corner of the island, they successively decreased the length of the front and could thus take units out of the line. These troops marched to ferries near Messina for transportation to the mainland across the few miles of the straight, which was defended by a formidable concentration of guns.

Patton constantly looked for a suitable place to launch an amphibious operation to get around the mountains and bottle up or otherwise interfere with the Axis withdrawal. The problem was that he had only enough landing craft to transport a reinforced battalion of men, about 1,500 troops, and so small a force lacked the power to survive the strong Axis reaction to be anticipated. Impatient and insistent, Patton finally put on a seaborne assault in the early hours of August 8. The men came ashore and found the Axis troops gone.

Two days later he directed another landing to be made. Bradley and Truscott objected. Seeing no need for such an extraordinary measure when ground attack would eventually get them to Messina, failing to understand Patton's driving need for haste to prove beyond doubt the mettle of American troops, wondering whether Patton's motive was a desire for personal prominence, they wanted to call off the landing because the 3d division seemed to be too far away to join quickly the men coming ashore from the sea. The operation in their eyes was risky and unwarranted, and they tried to change his mind. Patton refused to budge. He categorically ordered the landing over the telephone, then went forward to reassure Truscott. There, several naval officers also recommended postponing the operation. Patton was adamant. This time, he knew, he would hurt the enemy.

The troops came ashore at Brolo early on August 11 behind the Axis forces, scurried across the beach and the coastal road, set up defensive positions on high ground, and, supported by naval gunfire and aerial bombardment, battled all day long as the Germans and Italians tried to dislodge and eliminate them, for they were a threat to the withdrawal. Truscott launched a heavy attack and made contact with the men out front that evening. The Americans took high casualties but compelled the Axis to move back ahead of schedule.

Had Patton had more landing craft and been able to send more troops by sea, he would undoubtedly have trapped a large enemy body. Had he listened to his subordinates, the battalion would have come ashore too late. "I have a sixth sense in war," Patton wrote in his diary, ". . . and also I am willing to take chances." Later he noted, trying to enhance his self-confidence, "I may have been bull-headed, but I truly feel that I did my exact and full duty . . . and demonstrated that I am a great leader."

Over the reluctance of Bradley and Truscott, he insisted on a third landing early on August 16. It turned out to be unnecessary. The 3d Division was already moving into Messina. The

A morning briefing in Sicily. Someone has gotten long-winded and Patton is bored.

city was in American hands at 10:00 P.M. The Axis forces had departed; 40,000 Germans and 70,000 Italians had escaped from Sicily with 10,000 vehicles, 200 guns, forty-seven tanks, ammunition, and supplies.

Truscott accepted the surrender of the municipal officials at 7:00 A.M., August 17. Three hours later, Patton, in high spirits, arrived at the ridge overlooking the city. To a party of photographers and newspapermen snapping his picture and writing notes, he said, "What in hell are you all standing around for?" Taking the lead of a column of vehicles, he drove into Messina while Axis artillery fired on the road from the Italian mainland.

Montgomery had planned and canceled two landing operations before sending a small force ashore just below Messina on August 16. Blocked by a destroyed bridge, the soldiers entered the city at daybreak, August 17, to find the Americans there. Several hours later, the senior officer came up to Patton, saluted, shook hands, and said, "It was a jolly good race. I congratulate you."

Patton was on top of the world. He had fought what he considered to be a perfect campaign. He had won a second Distinguished Service Cross for his actions at Gela. By reaching Messina first, he had presented dramatic proof of his ability to overcome obstacles. No longer would American troops be looked upon as second-rate or feel inferior to the British veterans. In a tribute to his men, he wrote, "Soldiers of the Seventh Army: Born at sea, baptized in blood, and crowned in victory in the course of 38 days of incessant battle and unceasing labor, you have added a glorious chapter to the history of war . . . Every man in the Army deserves equal credit. . . . You have destroyed the prestige of the enemy. . . . Your fame shall never die."

Conspicuous in forward areas, unmistakably himself in his smart uniform and looking cool and confident despite the almost unbearable heat and dust, Patton was the star of the press photographers and reporters, both American and British. He had created an army in his own image, skillful, hard, imbued with a lust to win. He had transformed American soldiers into a professional force second to none. As against Montgomery's casualties of close to 12,000 men, the Seventh Army sustained 7,000 losses while taking about 100,000 prisoners of war. The best and most experienced, as well as the most senior, American battle general, he now had the best claim to further advancement. Had he fulfilled his destiny? He hoped not. For he was, he believed, the best-qualified soldier "to win the war and also the peace."

And just as he stood at the height of his career, an invincible and heroic figure on his way to even greater glory and fame, he suffered a crippling indignity perpetrated on him not by his American rivals, not by the British, but by Patton himself.

8

THE WAR IN EUROPE

Patton knew that he was in trouble, in real hot water, four days after the fighting ended. A letter from Eisenhower expressed shock over a report of Patton's behavior, specifically his brutal abuse of sick men and his public exhibitions of uncontrolled temper. Although Patton's actions warranted a formal investigation and charges of conduct unbecoming an officer, Eisenhower preferred to avoid that course because of Patton's services of "incalculable value" during the Sicilian campaign. But he questioned Patton's judgment and self-discipline and wondered whether he could continue to exercise command and be useful in the future. Despite his long friendship, despite his admiration of Patton's military qualities, Eisenhower was unable to tolerate such deportment. He wanted Patton to explain his actions and to apologize to those who had witnessed the scenes.

He was referring to the two now-famous so-called slapping

incidents. They occurred a week apart in evacuation hospitals in Sicily. In each case there was a soldier suffering from combat fatigue, known in the First World War as shell shock. The medical authorities considered the condition a legitimate psychoneurosis.

The first incident took place early in August. Visiting the wounded, Patton started his usual practice of going down the row of cots, speaking to each man, commending him, showing sympathy, and pinning on Purple Heart medals. Bandages, to him, were badges of courage. He came upon one patient who had none, and Patton asked where he was hurt.

"I guess I can't take it," the soldier replied.

Bursting into a rage, Patton cursed him, slapped his face with his gloves, and left the tent. According to a later diagnosis, the patient additionally had chronic dysentery and malaria.

That evening Patton issued a memo to his subordinate commanders. A few soldiers, he said, were going to the hospital "on the pretext that they are nervously incapable of combat." They were cowards and a disgrace to their brave comrades, and they were to be dealt with in their units. It was shameful, he believed, to put skulkers and courageous men in the same hospital tents. In his diary, Patton noted that "one sometimes slaps a baby to bring it to."

The second incident happened in much the same manner. Accompanied by a medical officer, Patton was going down the line of cots, talking with each patient about where and how he was hurt. Coming to a man shivering in bed, Patton asked what the trouble was.

"It's my nerves," the soldier said and started to cry.

"Your nerves, hell," Patton shouted. "You are just a goddamned coward, you yellow son of a bitch. You're a disgrace to the Army and you are going back to the front to fight, although that's too good for you. You ought to be lined up against a wall and be shot. In fact, I ought to shoot you myself right now, goddamn you."

He pulled his pistol from the holster and waved it, then struck the man across the face with the gloves he held in the other hand. As the soldier trembled on his cot, Patton said to the physician, "I want you to get this man out of here right away. I won't have these other brave boys seeing such a bastard babied." He started to leave the tent, turned, rushed back, and hit the weeping soldier again.

The doctor then placed himself between Patton and the patient. "I meant what I said about getting that coward out of here," Patton exclaimed. "I won't have these cowardly bastards hanging around our hospitals. We'll probably have to shoot them some time anyway, or we'll raise a breed of morons."

At Bradley's command post, Patton apologized for being late. "I stopped off at a hospital on the way up," he explained. "I slapped one of them to make him mad and put some fight in him." Showing cowardice in the face of the enemy, he believed, was the ultimate dishonor. Saving an individual from that humiliation was, in Patton's view, justified and humane. Yet his actions made him subject to court-martial for striking an enlisted man. If charged and convicted, he would have to be dismissed from his command.

What had prompted Patton's suppressed hysteria to break into the open? It was never easy for him to see the wounded, yet visiting hospitals was a duty. He forced himself to carry out that burden, and he had to keep a tight grip on himself to avoid breaking into tears over men who had sacrificed for their country as well as for him. To some extent he felt guilty for having been spared himself. A few days earlier he had observed a man with the top of his head blown off and waiting to die. The scene unnerved him.

Other pressures hammered at him. He resented the need to submit to British command and bore a grudge for his subordinate role vis-à-vis Montgomery. He was obsessed by his desire to beat the British into Messina and disappointed because his subordinates failed to understand the need for speed. He was upset because the enemy, in possession of favorable defensive terrain, was dictating the course of the battle. He was angry because Allied aircraft had bombed American troops by mistake on several occasions. He was troubled because he had decided to relieve Allen and Roosevelt for letting the 1st Division become an undisciplined and private army contemptuous of other organizations. He was outraged by an unfortunate British Broadcasting Corporation report describing American troops as eating grapes and bathing in the sea while the British did most of the fighting.

Above all, he was tired as the result of what he called his "intense mental and physical activity." Driving himself savagely in the heat of a terribly hot summer despite his age, he was close to exhaustion. Additionally, the clash of his inner urges robbed him of balance. He teetered between his need, on the one hand, to be ruthless and to project force and his wish, on the other, to enjoy the beautiful views and vistas of the landscape and the sea and to examine the ruins of antiquity, the fragmentary columns, the medieval architecture, all of which he described rapturously in his letters to Beatrice. The battle within himself, the conflict between his opposing inclinations, wore him down and loosened his grasp on himself.

The medical authorities sent Bradley a report of the slappings. Motivated by his loyalty to his boss, Patton, Bradley locked the paper in his safe and said nothing. The only other choice was to bypass Patton and send the paper to Eisenhower, and that would have been a breach of military courtesy.

The physicians had no such qualms, and they sent their report through medical channels to Eisenhower, who got the details on August 16, the last day of the Sicilian campaign. When Patton read Eisenhower's letter four days later, he was thoroughly chastened. His motive, he decided, was correct because malingering was an infectious disease and could hardly be condoned. Only his method was wrong.

When some newspaper correspondents learned of the incidents, a delegation called on Eisenhower for the facts. He frankly disclosed what had happened and asked them to withhold publication. Press coverage was likely to result in violent condemnation of Patton and make it necessary to fire the best American fighting general. The journalists agreed to bury the story in the interest of winning the war.

To make amends, Patton summoned all the doctors, nurses, and medical specialists of the two hospitals to his headquarters in the Royal Palace at Palermo. He expressed regret for his impulsive actions and told about a friend in World War I who had lost his nerve in battle and later committed suicide. "If someone had been rough with him and slapped some sense into him," Patton said, "his life might have been saved." He called the two soldiers he had slapped to his office, explained his attempt to restore their manhood, apologized, and shook hands. Then he toured all the divisions on the island and spoke to the men of their achievements. In his talks, he vaguely mentioned his regret for loud talking and criticism. He replied to Eisenhower's letter and spoke of his "chagrin and grief at having given you, a man to whom I owe everything and for whom I would gladly lay down my life, cause for displeasure with me." He disclaimed an intention to be harsh and cruel. He was trying merely to make the patients understand "their obligation as men and soldiers."

In correspondence with Marshall, Eisenhower reviewed his options. He could reduce Patton to his permanent grade—colonel—or send him home for a military trial. Instead, he chose to keep him because of his fighting ability, determination, unflagging aggressiveness, and refusal to be halted in battle. Eisenhower could ill afford to lose him. Yet because of his character flaws, Eisenhower would retain him as an army commander and permit him to go no higher.

Early in September, at a large open-air entertainment for the troops, Patton appeared on the stage. "I thought I would stand here," he announced, "and let you see what a son of a bitch looks like and whether I am as big a son of a bitch as you think I am." They howled and cheered, and everything seemed to be all right again. His statement was an attempt to keep up his courage. For he wondered where he was to go from Sicily. Before the slapping incidents, Eisenhower had mentioned several possible missions for the Seventh Army—a landing near Florence in Italy, perhaps transfer to the United Kingdom for the cross-Channel attack to Normandy in the spring. "You need have no fear," Eisenhower said, "of being left there in the backwater of the war."

Yet there he was, marooned on the island. As Mark Clark's Fifth Army invaded Salerno and fought the Italian campaign, Patton sadly broke up his victorious Seventh Army, an organization he had endowed with skill and spirit, and sent his units to Clark. When Eisenhower dispatched an officer to England to organize an army and an army group headquarters for the Normandy invasion, he chose Bradley, not Patton, who expected the selection. Remaining in Sicily with his Seventh Army headquarters, some antiaircraft units, and little else, a total of about 5,000 men, he was in evident disgrace, apparently without a future.

He was to suffer an excruciating wait of five months before learning his next assignment, then another six before entering combat. Once committed to battle, he gained a great triumph and became the darling of the American and British people. And then, as he seemed about to win the war, he was denied the opportunity.

Meanwhile, he was in torment. He was "completely in the dark" on the future of the Seventh Army, but he hoped to have "another chance to fight somebody somewhere." Anywhere, he meant, and in any capacity. Once more he felt jealousy toward Clark, who was actively engaged. Was Patton being kept in Sicily to replace Clark if Clark failed as a commander or became a casualty? "I have to keep working on my belief in destiny, and poor old destiny may have to put in some extra time to get me out of my present slump."

To his son George, who was repeating his plebe year at West Point, he advised, "Self-confidence is the surest way of obtaining what you want. If you know in your own heart you are going to be something, you will be it. . . . Do not permit your mind to think otherwise. It is fatal." He was, of course, lecturing himself.

As Lucas in command of the VI Corps and Keyes at the head of the II Corps moved to the Italian mainland, Patton kept his staff busy planning ephemeral invasions of northern Italy and southern France. He exercised, read military history, and accepted occasional invitations to dine with well-to-do Italian families, noting in his letters to Beatrice the abundance of the food and the attractions, dubious and otherwise, of the ladies. The social conversations, he remarked, were quite the same as in Boston.

Because of his combat reputation among the Germans, Patton served as a decoy to deceive them on nonexistent invasions. He traveled ostentatiously to Algiers, Tunis, Corsica, Cairo, Jerusalem, and Malta, officially inspecting docks and airfields and visiting for his own pleasure places of interest to him, castles, Napoleon's birthplace, the pyramids. The Maltese knights, he told Beatrice, "had to vow poverty, chastity, and obedience. They only kept the last vow."

He dropped out of the news except for press speculation as to his whereabouts. Friends told him of rumors placing him everywhere, even in Burma and India. They, like him, wondered where he would turn up next.

On Armistice Day, he attended a memorial service at the cemetery where his soldiers were buried and spoke a few words. "I consider it no sacrifice," he said, "to die for my country. In my mind we came here to thank God that men like these have lived rather than to regret that they have died." That evening, his staff had a cocktail party to celebrate the taking of Casablanca. There was a birthday cake for him. He was fifty-eight.

Later that month, in a Sunday-evening national radio

broadcast from Washington, D.C., the columnist Drew Pearson revealed the slapping incidents. The furor throughout the country was immediate and violent. Many citizens called for Patton's dismissal. To his friend Stimson, Patton explained, "I love and admire good soldiers and brave men. I hate and despise slackers and cowards. I am quite tender-hearted and emotional in my dealings with wounded men." To Bea, "Personally I have complete confidence that this is not my end. . . . I have a mission which is far from completed."

Eventually the clamor for Patton's removal subsided. When President Roosevelt and his party, returning from the strategic conferences in Cairo and Tehran, stopped in Sicily in December, everyone was nice to Patton. Eisenhower, who had just been appointed to be the Supreme Allied Commander of Overlord, the invasion of Normandy, told Patton of his probable transfer to command an army in England, but nothing was yet certain. "Send me some more pink medecin," he wrote Beatrice. "This worry and inactivity has raised hell with my insides."

On Christmas Day, to bolster his spirits, he wrote in his diary, "My destiny is sure and I am a fool and a coward even to have doubted it. I don't any more. Some people are needed to do things, and they have to be tempered by adversity as well as thrilled by success. I have had both. Now for some more success." On New Year's Eve, he wrote, "I hope I do bigger and better fighting in 1944." To reassure himself, he added, "Destiny will keep on floating me down the stream of fate."

He was shattered when his orderly George Meeks informed him of an announcement on the radio: Bradley was to command all the American troops in the United Kingdom. Bradley, Patton speculated, would then no doubt be elevated to command the U.S. army group. "I had thought that possibly I might get this command. It is another disappointment, but so far in my life all the disappointments . . . have finally worked out to my advantage. . . . If I am predestined, as I feel I am, this too will eventually be to my advantage."

In his bitterness, he characterized Bradley as a man of great mediocrity. "At Benning . . . he failed to get discipline. At Gafsa . . . he suggested that we withdraw. . . . In Sicily . . . he bolted . . . in fear. . . . He tried to stop the landing operation [near Messina]." Then he remembered their cooperation at Fort Benning, where he had enjoyed their association, as he had said in a letter to Bradley, more than any other. He thought of Bradley's perfect loyalty. "He wears glasses, has a strong jaw, talks profoundly and says little." And he concluded, "I consider him among our better generals." If Patton obtained an army, he would serve under the younger Bradley, the reverse of their previous relationship. "The news about Omar was most disconcerting," he wrote Beatrice. "I felt so low that I just stayed in bed."

Months before, Eisenhower had corresponded with Marshall on the choice of the leader of the American part of Overlord. Patton certainly deserved consideration. His rehabilitation of the II Corps in Tunisia had been "quickly and magnificently done," and his leadership in Sicily was "close to the best of our classic examples." Patton thought "only in terms of attack" and had a "native shrewdness" about logistics. He was a "truly aggressive commander" with brains. Yet if Patton was sure to press for victory, he gave intimations of instability. He was moody, sometimes childish, quick to be elated, perhaps too ready to gamble, too close to "ill-advised action." To keep him under control, Eisenhower treated him "much more roughly" than any other senior commander. In contrast, Bradley was balanced. Bradley was safer. Bradley would prevent disaster. Yet Eisenhower very much wanted Patton to be one of his army commanders.

Eisenhower laid out his organizational structure. He wanted Bradley to lead the initial or assault army across the Channel. When Bradley had gained enough space on the Continent to allow another army, "probably under Patton," to come ashore, Bradley was to turn over his army to Courtney Hodges and move up to the army group command, with Hodges and Patton under him. Bradley and Hodges would ensure stability, Patton drive.

Word of his future finally reached Patton on January 22. He was finally delivered from Sicily—and from disgrace.

Four days later he was in London, where he learned of his selection to command the Third Army. The headquarters and all the subordinate components were inexperienced in combat. He would have to start again from the very beginning to shape the organization into a competent and spirited force.

The army headquarters, about 1,500 officers and men, including staff members, signal specialists, engineers, military police, and others, was in Knutsford, about five hours' drive from London, near Chester in Cheshire. Most people were billeted in a camp at Toft Hall; his close staff assistants were in

Peover Hall, the mansion where he lived. Devers, who had replaced Eisenhower in Algiers as the senior American and was deputy to Sir Henry Maitland Wilson, the Mediterranean theater commander, was obliging and honored Patton's request to transfer his principal staff officers from the Seventh Army to him. Gaffey and Gay were his chief and assistant chiefs of staff. Koch, his G-2, directed intelligence and set up an elaborate war room with maps and charts. Walter J. Muller, the G-4 or supply officer, functioned with such efficiency that Patton rarely inquired into his methods.

Patton trusted, supported, rewarded, and dominated his staff. When they were in combat, he ordered, at least one officer from each staff section was to visit the fighting elements every day, "to observe, not to meddle," and this practice would later enhance understanding of conditions at the front.

His "family" consisted of Gaffey and Gay, his aides Codman and Stiller, his orderly Meeks, and his chief medical officer Charles B. Odom. Later he acquired a bull terrier he named Willie. On the continent, Willie would be afraid of shellfire and bombardment, and the noise would send him cowering under a chair of Patton's bed. He snored during the night. He was disgusting around women, pushing his nose up their dresses, clasping their legs, and rubbing his belly against them. Yet Patton loved him because, as he said, Willie adored him. As he told Bea, to Willie, Patton was always right.

Every organization had a code name—for example, Liberty, Master, Eagle, Danger. Understanding the need for good fortune in war as an essential requisite for success, Patton chose Lucky for his Third Army headquarters. His small command group, the key officers who advised him, was called Lucky Forward. The larger administrative group was known as Lucky Rear. He himself was Lucky 6.

Under him and his headquarters was his army, anywhere from 100,000 to 300,000 men, depending on the number of corps and divisions assigned to him. Originally he had four corps headquarters, Middleton's VIII, Wade Haislip's XV, Walton Walker's XX, and Gilbert Cook's XII. Under them were the infantry and armored divisions, twelve in all.

As he set about to transform his men into a superb fighting force, he began, as always, with discipline and dress. He quickly went on to combat training. Traveling to his subordinate units, he personally inspected, taught, and advised. He shaped their attitudes, habits, and practices, stirring morale

G.S.P., Jr., with his ever-faithful bull terrier, Willie.

and achieving cohesion. Having brought the Seventh Army to a high level of competence, he displayed a sure touch with the Third. Busy again, serving a definite purpose, pleased with his job of forming his army, he looked more benignly on the slapping incidents. But for them he would have had Bradley's position, which would be too distant from the fighting.

Soon after Lucas and his VI Corps made the Anzio landings, Patton almost became involved in Italy. Alexander judged Lucas to be unequal to the occasion, and he cabled London to ask for "a thruster like George Patton." Eisenhower summoned Patton to London, where he waited in great excitement for a decision. Whether he was to replace Lucas or Clark was unclear, but it made no difference to Patton. After several days, Alexander and Clark sent Lucas home and elevated Truscott to command the VI Corps—to Patton's intense disappointment.

Returning to his training program, he instructed commanders to "lead in person." Praise, he said, motivated men better than blame. The farther forward command posts were established, the less time was wasted traveling to the front and back. The best plans were "simple and flexible." Information was "like eggs: the fresher the better." Discipline, cleanliness, and neatness guaranteed alertness. "Do not take counsel of your fears." Everywhere he went he made two types of talks, one full of profanity to the enlisted men, the other quiet and thoughtful to the officers. He found everyone too complacent, "willing to die but not anxious to kill. I tell them that it is fine to be willing to die for their country but a damned sight better to make the German die for his."

A young soldier lined up with others before Peover Hall wrote to his family: "General Patton walked out on the little terrace, three steps above us . . . most of us had never seen him in the flesh, and when the drum, ruffles, and bugles sounded the General's march, we stood transfixed upon his appearance. Not one square inch of flesh [was] not covered with goose pimples. It was one of the greatest thrills I shall ever know. You stood at rigid attention . . . that towering figure impeccably attired froze you in place and electrified the air. . . . In a somewhat boyish, shrill yet quiet voice, he said . . . 'I can assure you that the Third United States Army will be the greatest army in American history. We shall be in Berlin ahead of everyone. To gain that end, we must have perfect discipline. I shall drive you until hell won't have it. . . .

We are going to kill German bastards—I would prefer to skin them alive—but, gentlemen, I fear some of our people at home would accuse me of being too rough.' At that point General Patton slyly smiled. Everyone chuckled enjoyably. He talked on to us for half an hour, literally hypnotizing us with his incomparable, if profane eloquence. When he had finished, you felt as if you had been given a supercharge from some divine source. Here was the man for whom you would go to hell and back."

The Germans were aware of a coming invasion but ignorant of the time and place. A systematic Allied effort, including dummy headquarters, bogus camps, false radio traffic, even the pattern of continental bombing, sought to deceive the Germans and to fix their attention on the most obvious landing area across the narrowest part of the Channel, from Dover to the Pas de Calais, which led most directly to Germany. There the substantial German Fifteenth Army awaited the Allied landings. Patton's role in the deception was to serve as the commanding general of a fictitious organization that the Germans called Army Group Patton. In order to enhance German suspicion of Patton's nonexistent force, his name never appeared in the press. Wherever he traveled, whenever he spoke, he constantly cautioned his listeners of his status—he was incognito, a ghost, a myth, not to be mentioned in public.

Late in April, women volunteers opened a welcome club in Knutsford for the American soldiers, who were always so clean and neat and so polite to the civilians. They asked Patton to say a few words. Reluctantly he agreed but warned against revealing his presence. He found several press photographers, but apparently no reporters, waiting for him, and they knew about keeping him secret. Patton spoke briefly and graciously to about sixty people. He thanked the ladies for furthering the understanding between British and Americans, who, together with the Russians, were bound to rule the world after the war. On the following day, the story of what was called Patton's first public address in Great Britain appeared in the newspapers. Was British intelligence or the Ministry of Information responsible for placing Patton firmly in England for the benefit of German spies?

The news was trivial, but in America the account created a sensation. Castigating Patton for intruding in the political sphere by speaking of ruling the world, government officials seized upon his innocuous comment to embarrass the Roosevelt administration. Although the matter was inconsequential, even silly, Eisenhower became enraged. Bearing responsibility for the invasion, now little more than a month away, and under great pressures, Eisenhower found Patton's remarks and the outburst against them adding to his burdens. Despite Eisenhower's repeated advice, Patton had again stirred controversy by talking out of turn. He weighed seriously whether to remove Patton from his command. Thoroughly worried, Patton reiterated to himself and in his diary, "I am sure that I am needed, for no one else can do the things which must be done." Eisenhower finally decided to retain Patton for the approaching campaign, for Patton was indispensable to victory.

During the course of his residence in Knutsford, Patton, as was his custom, became acquainted with some of the prominent families in the area. He enjoyed their company, rode their horses, attended their dinners and entertainments, and came to know several intimately. An officer of the day on duty at Peover Hall, sitting at his desk near the front door, was astonished at 2:00 one morning to see his beaming commanding general graciously escorting a lovely lady down the staircase and out to his car, which was waiting to take her home. Perhaps Patton was making a point of conforming with his dictum to his soldiers: "A man who does not screw will not fight."

Satisfied with his troops' mastery of the Patton combat methods, he toured his units to whip up their spirits. "As in all my talks, I stressed fighting and killing," as well as doing one's duty. A speech he made several times shortly before the invasion tickled the soldiers. "Men," he said, "you've been bitching about what you call 'chicken-shit drill.' That, like everything else in the Army, has a definite purpose. . . . A man must be alert all the time if he expects to stay alive. If not, some German son of a bitch will sneak up behind him with a sock full of shit! . . . An army is a team, lives, sleeps, fights, and eats as a team. This individual hero stuff is a lot of horseshit. The bilious bastards who write that kind of stuff for the *Saturday Evening Post* don't know any more about real fighting under fire than they know about fucking! Every single man in the Army plays a vital role. . . . Every last man on KP has a job to do, even the guy who boils the water to keep us from getting the GI shits! Remember, men, you don't know I'm here. . . . Let the first bastards to find out be the goddam Germans. I want them to look up and howl, 'Ach, it's the goddam Third

Army and that son of a bitch Patton again!' We want to get . . . the hell out of here, and get at those purple-pissin' Japs! . . . When it's all over and you're home once more, you can thank God that twenty years from now, when you're sitting around the fireside with your grandson on your knee and he asks you what you did in the war, you won't have to shift him to the other knee, cough, and say, 'I shoveled shit in Louisiana.'"

According to the Overlord plan, Montgomery was to command the Allied ground units on the continent until Eisenhower, the Supreme Allied Commander, arrived and additionally assumed command of the land forces. Preceded by a drop of parachutists and troop landings by glider, Bradley's First U.S. Army was to come ashore on two beaches in Normandy, Sir Miles Dempsey's Second British Army was to land on three. Dempsey was to take Caen, head for the Falaise plain, and obtain enough space for Henry Crerar's First Canadian Army. Bradley was to seize Cherbourg and drive to Avranches. There, at the entrance to Brittany, Patton's Third Army was to become active and subdue the province. How Patton ached to lead the Normandy assault instead of coming later "without the necessity of wetting my pants," as he told McNair, to conquer Brittany.

Montgomery invited the four army commanders to spend the night with him near Portsmouth so that all would know each other better. They had a pleasant dinner, made some bets about the duration of the war, and gambled moderately. Patton, the oldest, reflected on the changes since Sicily. There he had been Montgomery's equal and Bradley's superior. Now both were over him.

During the first days of the invasion, time dragged for Patton. In England, he felt like a slacker. He packed in case he was needed on instant notice, but there was no such luck. To get into the fighting mood, he wore his shoulder holster. He worried whether the war would end before he got there. Trying to convince himself that opportunity still awaited him, he wrote in his diary, "I have always hoped to be a hero, and now may be the time to attain my ambition."

Everett Hughes was a West Point classmate of Patton's. They had served together in Mexico and France and were good friends. Now Hughes was Eisenhower's eyes and ears for logistics. A shrewd and observant officer who was good company, he delighted in gossip and girls. Though inclined to be somewhat malicious, he admired Patton immensely. Patton

Old friends, Patton and Eisenhower shifted back and forth
between affection for each other and ire.

★

Left: Patton in Normandy in July 1944 with one of his top officers, Hugh Gaffey. *Above:* Patton (left) with two more occasional thorns in the Patton side, Omar Bradley (center) and Bernard Montgomery.

liked and humored him, and, knowing his propensities, occasionally titillated him. For Hughes was a source of entertaining information on backstairs feuding and dealing, on what was going on unofficially in the theater of operations behind the scenes.

According to Hughes's diary, Jean Gordon breathlessly telephoned Patton from London early in July. She was assigned to the Third Army as a Red Cross doughnut server, one of about twenty-five young ladies who would dispense coffee and doughnuts, along with small talk, to the GIs on the continent and remind them of home and raise their spirits. Patton apparently drove to the city, and was glad to see her, to speak a little French with her as they always did, to get caught up on news of the family. She lifted his spirits. Hughes wondered about their relationship, and Patton told him, with some exaggeration, "She's been mine for twelve years."

Beatrice learned of Jean's trip overseas, and she let her husband know she knew. Her warning reached Patton early in August, when he was in the midst of complicated battle movements and extremely occupied. He replied briefly, in some annoyance. The first he had known about Jean's arrival, he said, was Bea's letter. But he was busy and had no spare time. "So don't worry."

A month to the day after the invasion, on July 6, he was summoned to France. Flying over the Channel, he landed near Omaha Beach. He visited Bradley, Montgomery, and other commanders to get the feel of the campaign. His Third Army headquarters set up. Nearby was O. P. Weyland's XIX Tactical Air Command headquarters, which would provide close air support to Patton's units and which Patton regarded and respected as a partner in his enterprise. The services provided by the XIX TAC were an important element in Patton's success. Patton's corps headquarters and divisions were crossing the Channel, and some were funneled temporarily into the First Army, which was engaged in the frustrating battle of the hedgerows, where gains were measured in yards. Bradley had captured Cherbourg, but Avranches, the entrance into Brittany, was still distant, forty miles away. Idle except for inspecting his units, impatient to start fighting, outwardly calm and smiling, Patton fretted and grumbled in the privacy of his diary. "Neither Ike or Brad has the stuff." "Bradley and Hodges are such nothings."

Dempsey's army was making little progress too. With the aid

of a heavy bombardment, the British took half of Caen, but were unable to get onto the Falaise plain. The Germans were tough and skillful. Persistent rain in July hampered the Allies. Prospects of quick advance were discouraging.

What changed the whole mood and tempo and set the stage for Patton was a plan devised by Bradley and called Cobra. Constant downpour delayed the operation until July 25, when, after an unimpressive start, the advance exploded. Using heavy bombers to blast a hole in the German defenses, sending infantry and armor through the gap, Bradley demolished the German left flank. Two days later he asked Patton to take charge unofficially of Middleton's VIII Corps, which was heading toward Avranches.

Joyously, Patton took hold. Moving two armored divisions into the lead and running them side by side, Patton pointed them to Avranches. Three days later, Americans were in the town. A day afterward, they had the Pontaubault bridge. There, three main roads gave access to three directions, west into Brittany, south to the Loire River, and east toward the Seine River and Paris.

At noon on August 1, almost two months after the Normandy landings, Bradley stepped up to command the 12th Army Group, Hodges assumed command of the First Army, and Patton's Third Army became active. Patton, Lucky 6, was fortunate on several counts. The rainy weather vanished, and August was dry and clear. The theater of operations was well organized to support the combat elements. Bradley's and Dempsey's armies had ground down the German forces for seven weeks. With a passage through Avranches open to his units, though just barely, Patton could deal with each of his corps successively, inserting them into the battle one at a time. He knew the countryside well from his travels with Beatrice when he had worked with Adjutant Cléry.

Finally, he appeared just at the right place and time in the campaign, on the open German flank, as the static warfare of June and July dissolved into exciting mobile operations exactly suited to his unique talent of driving forward with outright abandon, with seeming recklessness, to far-off targets. Fighting, he commented, "always scares and lures me like steeple-chasing." He was in the saddle again.

One condition bothered him slightly. In the interest of continuing the deception and keeping the German Fifteenth Army pinned to the Pas de Calais, Eisenhower retained Patton's secrecy. Newspaper reporters were unable to mention his name.

Despite the destruction of their left flank, the Germans continued to hold resolutely before the other Allied armies, Hodges's First U.S., Dempsey's Second British, and Crerar's First Canadian. In Brittany there were relatively few German troops. Most had come to Normandy to meet the invasion. The rest took refuge in the port cities of St. Malo, Brest, Lorient, Nantes, and St. Nazaire, as about 20,000 French Resistance fighters surfaced in the province. With Patton showing great flair in getting thousands of men and vehicles through the narrow Avranches corridor, Eisenhower, Montgomery, and Bradley came to an immediate and momentous decision. Instead of sending the entire Third Army into Brittany, a single corps would suffice. While Middleton's VIII Corps swept into Brittany, Patton was to turn his three other corps eastward and southeastward from Avranches and head for the Seine and Loire rivers.

With Middleton's units through the congested Avranches passageway and into the open, Patton sent one armored division to Rennes, then Lorient, more than 100 miles away, and the other to seize Brest, 200 miles distant. These organizations set off at a run. Middleton, conditioned by the slow and meticulous warfare in the hedgerows and concerned about a concentration of German forces in St. Malo, diverted the division racing for Brest. By good fortune or intuition, Patton was following to check on compliance with his orders. Discovering the units deploying to attack St. Malo, Patton quickly rescinded Middleton's instruction and sent the division on its way. He dispatched an infantry division to besiege St. Malo, which fell after three weeks of difficult battle.

Delayed at least a day at St. Malo, the armored division reached Brest to find the city strongly garrisoned and unwilling to surrender. Arrival a day earlier might have gained the fortress. Now all the division could do was to bottle up the defenders. It would take three infantry divisions three weeks of hard fighting late in August and early in September to capture the place.

The other armored division sped to Rennes, then to Lorient, where a substantial German force had barricaded themselves. The Americans could do no more than to ring the city and hold the defenders at bay. Lorient would remain in

German hands and guarded by American infantry until the end of the war.

As Brittany declined in importance, Patton sent Haislip's XV Corps, his next formations, through the corridor, to the southeast and east around the German open end, then Walton Walker's XX Corps to the Loire River. Both slashed forward against little opposition, bowling over and scattering German rear-area installations and units. In less than a week, Haislip advanced seventy-five miles and was at Le Mans.

At this point occurred three significant events. First, although the German field commanders believed that their open left flank required them to start to withdraw from Normandy, perhaps from France, Hitler decided to restore the situation by a counterattack. A blow through Mortain westward to Avranches would secure the flank and cut off Patton's army. This he ordered in a series of communications to his commanders. Intercepted, decoded, translated, and disseminated to the top Allied commanders by a high-powered intelligence group in Bletchley, England, these messages, known as Ultra Secret, alerted Bradley and Patton to the German plan.

Since early in the war, Ultra had supplied the top Allied civilian and military officials with German transmissions. No one below the army commanders was privy to this information. Patton had received Ultra in Sicily, but it had been of little value to him. In France, although he occasionally listened to briefings by his Ultra representative, Melvin Helfers, he preferred to trust his intuition. Nevertheless, out of caution, Patton halted one of his divisions near Avranches for movement to Mortain in case the Germans attacked. When they did so, as Ultra had predicted, Patton changed his mind about Ultra. He saw his Ultra man every day, listened closely to what he said, and instructed him to come to Patton at any hour of the day or night if he had startling news. It made good sense to check his remarkable intuition against Ultra.

The German thrust started in the early-morning hours of August 8 and struck Hodges's First Army at Mortain. A magnificent defense on the ground and the quick commitment of nearby American units, together with devastating Allied air attacks after daylight, brought the effort to a quick halt. The German field commanders wished to break off the operation and pull back, but Hitler insisted on continuing the attempt to get through Mortain to Avranches. This, in effect, pushed the leading German combat units into a noose that the Allies would try to close.

The second event was a strong Canadian attack to the south from Caen to Falaise, sixteen miles away, on the morning of August 8. If the Canadians reached Falaise, they would threaten to cut off the Germans at Mortain.

The third occurrence was a significant decision by Eisenhower, Montgomery, and Bradley, who ordered Patton to turn Haislip from an easterly orientation at Le Mans to the north. If Haislip drove through Alençon to Argentan and if the Canadians were at Falaise, the two Allied forces would be fifteen miles apart. Through this extremely narrow gap, the Germans, if they sought to escape, would have to pass at least 150,000 troops of their two field armies in Normandy. In the process, Allied artillery and air could destroy them. For the Allies, the opportunity was present to trap all the German forces in a giant double envelopment reminiscent of and rivaling the classic envelopments of Cannae and Tannenberg.

Patton argued for a deeper envelopment. Instead of striving for a relatively shallow encirclement of the Germans by heading for Argentan and Falaise, why not let Haislip's and Walker's corps go to Dreux and Chartres or even to the Seine River before turning north to trap all the Germans? His superiors demurred. Haislip's short hook was risky enough, for on his left yawned fifty miles of uncovered ground between Hodges's and Patton's armies. According to military logic, the Germans had to start pulling back soon. A quick Allied reaction and Canadian-American juncture near Falaise and Argentan would hurt at least a good part of the German units.

Bowing to the decision, Patton turned Haislip to the north. The XV Corps bounded forward, took Alençon, and on August 13 was just short of Argentan, but across the boundary traced on the map by Montgomery to keep the two army groups, his and Bradley's, from intermingling. Although there was every reason to believe that Haislip could have continued to Falaise and a meeting with the Canadians, thereby enclosing the Germans in a pocket where they could be destroyed, Bradley instructed Patton to halt Haislip along the boundary. Patton of course complied.

Bradley's decision was one of the most controversial of the war. His motivation stemmed from prudence. Ultra had cautioned about a German intention to attack in the territory between Patton and Hodges and against Haislip's open flank.

Bradley waited for Montgomery to invite him across the army group boundary. The Canadians had bogged down as a result of several unfortunate accidents, including a bombing by Allied aircraft, and were only halfway to Falaise, still eight miles short. Misled by his own intelligence information, Bradley mistakenly believed the Germans to be stampeding out of the pocket through the Argentan-Falaise gap. Actually, although they pulled back from Mortain, the Germans were desperately holding the sides of the pocket to prevent them from caving in as they awaited Hitler's permission to withdraw.

Believing Bradley's halt of Haislip to be wrong, Patton persuaded Bradley to let Patton keep moving. Why stand still when undefended territory beckoned to the east? If the shallow envelopment was halted, why not try for the deeper? With Bradley's permission, Patton left three divisions along the Argentan line and sent Haislip's XV Corps with two divisions eastward on August 14. Patton directed Haislip to Dreux, Walker's XX Corps to Chartres, Manton Eddy, who had replaced an ailing Cook, and his XII Corps to Orléans. Two days later, all were at their destinations. Patton modestly called the advance "probably the fastest and biggest pursuit in history," and indeed it was so: No army had ever moved with such speed and dash.

On that day Eisenhower released Patton's name to the press. The newspapers could now reveal Patton's movements and achievements, and the headlines and columns were full of excitement and praise. He had once again become, he said, "public property," and the people in America and Britain thrilled to Patton's running wild. To Bea he wrote, "Well I am delighted and know that your long and loving loyal confidence in me is justified."

In the south of France, the Seventh Army, now under Alexander Patch, together with forces eventually formed into the First French Army under Jean de Lattre de Tassigny, both ultimately coming under Devers and his 6th Army Group headquarters, invaded the Riviera on August 15. On the following day Hitler finally permitted his forces in Normandy to withdraw from the partially closed Argentan-Falaise pocket. On that day too, the Canadians reached Falaise. Montgomery then asked Bradley to move Patton's forces to the north beyond Argentan and to meet the Canadians coming south from Falaise, thereby closing the pocket.

Unfortunately, no corps headquarters was present near Ar-

Packing his famous pearl-handled revolver, Patton awards a Silver Star after the capture of Chateaudun, France, in mid-August 1944.

gentan to handle the American endeavor. Patton immediately formed a provisional headquarters with Gaffey and several key officers and instructed Gaffey to attack on the morning of August 17. Bradley sent Leonard Gerow's V Corps headquarters, which had been pinched out of the fighting, from the First Army to take over the Argentan front. Arriving there as Gaffey was ready to launch his operation, Gerow found he disliked Gaffey's plan and canceled the action. Gerow drew his own maneuver and started his effort on August 18, thereby giving the Germans another day to escape.

Americans and Canadians made tenuous contact on August 19, but were unable to close the pocket firmly until August 21. The Germans lost about 50,000 men, but around 100,000 other soldiers, perhaps more, traveling in small groups and taking little heavy equipment with them, fled eastward. Without Bradley's imposition of delay, which gave the Germans five days, from August 13 to 18, to withdraw, the Allies might have captured or destroyed them all.

Instead of pulling off a Cannae and bringing the end of the war close at hand, the Allies had botched the encirclement. Eisenhower, Montgomery, and Bradley had been incapable of the flat-out determination, the acceptance of great risks, and the cohesion to bag two German field armies. Patton might have accomplished the feat by the shallow or deeper envelopment, but he was, unfortunately, too far down the chain of command to have the required clout.

From Dreux, Haislip, guided by Patton, skipped to the Seine River at Mantes, thirty miles from Paris. Patton wished to send both of Haislip's divisions across the river and to turn them downstream on the far bank to prevent the fleeing Germans from crossing. His superiors deemed that course too dangerous. They permitted him to get one division across the Seine during the night of August 19. The other drove down the left or near bank and was less than effective in stopping the German crossings. What was, in fact, a great Allied victory in Normandy was, in long-range terms, inconclusive. Substantial remnants of the Germans defeated at Argentan and Falaise and harassed at the Seine River would reappear and again face the Allied armies.

The press announced the liberation of Paris permanently, and the stories named Patton's Third Army as the liberating force, poetic justice, Patton thought, for keeping his name in the dark for so long. Actually, Hodges's First Army, with

Jacques Leclerc's French armored division and an American infantry division, both under Gerow's corps headquarters, had the honor of entering the city on August 25. Patton would have loved to free Paris from the German occupation. The city knew how to welcome conquerors, and Patton's presence would have enhanced the festivities. Unlike most Allied officers, his love for France was real, his use of the language was fluent, his relations with the French leaders, Charles de Gaulle, Alphonse Juin, Pierre Koenig, and Leclerc, were excellent.

Instead, following Bradley's instructions, Patton turned over Haislip's corps to Hodges and, with Walker and Eddy traveling seventy miles in a single day, crossed the Seine River at Melun and Fontainebleau and the Yonne River at Montereau and Sens before the Germans could demolish the bridges. Giving the Mantes and Melun crossing sites to Hodges, who was to drive north toward Liége, Belgium, Patton headed eastward toward the World War I battlefields, which he knew well. Troyes, Reims, and Chalons fell quickly. The German resistance in France appeared to have collapsed. Patton was hoping to get across the Moselle River between Nancy and Metz, less than 100 miles from the Rhine River, when the ax fell.

In their swift pursuit, the combat troops had outrun their supplies. Plenty of gasoline existed in rear-area depots near the original landing beaches, but there was no way, not even by the Red Ball Express, to get sufficient amounts to the front to keep the armies moving. Patton's lightning march sputtered to a halt. He was unable to go farther than the Meuse River, and Walker and Eddy crossed at Verdun and Commercy on August 31.

The German West Wall, what the Allies called the Siegfried Line, defenses protecting the western approaches to Germany, was then unmanned. Nothing could have stopped a thrust through the empty pillboxes. Patton pleaded with Bradley for 400,000 gallons of gasoline. He could, he promised, be in Germany in two days, then drive to Worms and Frankfurt and beyond. The prospect of ending the war was bright. The Russians on the eastern front, having started a massive offensive in mid-June, had driven Finland, Rumania, and Bulgaria out of the war, had overrun East Prussia, and were at the gates of Warsaw. Devers's 6th Army Group was driving up the Rhône Valley virtually unopposed. All the armies in France were speeding forward against practically no resistance, and Patton might have brought chaos to the heart of Germany, which seemed at the point of defeat and capitulation.

No fuel was available to Patton. Eisenhower had decided to sustain Montgomery's advance on the other flank, where objectives deemed more important lay—the Rhine River, the great port of Antwerp, and the launching sites of the German buzz bombs, the V-1 and V-2 rockets, which were terrorizing London.

On September 1, Eisenhower replaced Montgomery as the Allied ground forces commander, Montgomery was promoted to field marshal, and Eisenhower called him "one of the great soldiers of this or any other war." Patton retired to his headquarters, immersed himself in paperwork, and sulked all day long.

He was the outstanding soldier. He had gained the greatest success. His inexperienced Third Army had displayed instant efficiency and parlayed Bradley's Cobra, a local breakthrough, into a theater-wide breakout. Despite his superiors' timidity, he had taken risks and made them pay off. In a single month, his army had liberated most of France north of the Loire River. He had maintained control over his army while it sped off in three directions, west, south, and east, like the old cavalry story—"The soldier went out and charged in all directions at once, with a pistol in each hand and a saber in the other." Six hundred miles separated Middleton at Brest from Walker and Eddy at the Meuse. And now when Patton had an opportunity to enter Germany and bring the end of the war within sight, he was denied his supreme chance.

THE LAST YEARS

Had the war come to an end on August 31, 1944, Patton's sweep across France would have guaranteed him eternal fame as a great commander. He had demonstrated audacity in action and control of formation in achieving a masterful example of blitzkrieg at its best. No one else could have done so well. His personal qualities and his professional attainments had made him unique. He was worthy of the public adulation lavished on him. Had he then at long last gained his destiny? More was to come. During the Battle of the Bulge and at the Rhine River, he would again exhibit an incomparable battle leadership. And then, as the war wound down, ending in boredom instead of a cavalry charge, he would again find himself in the slough of despond, wondering what the world was coming to and what his place in it was to be.

Seriously troubled by the halt imposed on his Third Army at the end of August, Patton maintained his cheerful demeanor. "I will be stuck here for a few days for supplies," he wrote Bea. "I am impatient with my friends for not letting me go faster as I am sure . . . that the Boche has no power to resist." Several days later, "God deliver us from our friends. We can handle the enemy." Perhaps because of the recent arrival at the Third Army headquarters of Jean Gordon and the doughnut girls, he added, "I am delighted you know I love you."

The conditions of the campaign changed suddenly and profoundly. Rain and winter weather came early that fall. The Germans recovered with miraculous speed and manned their defenses along the approaches to the fatherland. Shortages of gasoline continued to plague the Allies, and deficiencies of ammunition could soon have an adverse effect on their operations.

When, after a few days, supply deliveries permitted Patton to resume his advance, it was too late to pick up the momentum. Beyond the Meuse, Patton's men ran into bitter resistance. Getting to and across the Moselle was extremely difficult. Because of what Patton called Eisenhower's "fatal decision" to stop Patton, the Germans were fighting hard. As Patton told newspaper correspondents at a press conference on September 7, "Whenever you slow anything down"— meaning his own progress beyond the Meuse—"you waste human lives." Four days earlier he could have crossed the Moselle with ease. Now he was locked in a grim struggle. Then with a flash of spirit and optimism, he said, "I hope to go through the Siegfried Line like shit through a goose." It was not to be. The sixteen weeks of the Lorraine campaign would be bloody and frustrating.

Regaining Haislip's XV Corps headquarters, Patton put the organization on the Third Army right and south, adjacent to Devers's 6th Army Group. Eddy's XII Corps seized Nancy, which fell on September 15. Metz, "the strongest fortress in the world," defended by a number of fortified works built mostly underground, held out against Walker's XX Corps until mid-November, the last fort capitulating in mid-December.

Meanwhile, Hodges's First Army entered Germany on September 12. "I fear I am off the first pages [of the newspapers] for the moment," Patton noted to Bea, "as we are not going fast." On the contrary, progress was downright slow. Yet he kept pushing his subordinates, hoping to open a hole somewhere in the German defenses so that he could streak to the Rhine.

The Allies wished to get across the Rhine because of its psychological importance to the German people. By crossing, by breaching this historic barrier, the Allies hoped to show the Germans, as perhaps nothing else could, the futility of continuing the struggle. In a dramatic strike to get across the lower Rhine in Holland, Montgomery on September 17 launched his Operation Market-Garden, a drop of several airborne divisions to gain bridges along a corridor in front of Dempsey's army, together with an armored thrust up that corridor. The attack partially succeeded, but the structure across the Rhine at Arnhem was the bridge too far.

In Patton's zone, the Rhine was distant, and the Third Army moved slowly toward the stream, fighting hard for every village and hill. The advance was dogged, grim, and dirty, lacking glamour. As supply deliveries declined, two blows fell on Patton. He had to turn over Haislip's corps to Devers—"May God rot his guts"—because Devers, based on the port of Marseilles, received more logistical support and could maintain Haislip better. The second was the imposition on Patton of what was called the October pause. Until the port of Antwerp opened and received ships for unloading, supply was extremely inadequate. For example, Patton's howitzers were limited to firing seven rounds daily. Montgomery, whom Patton called a "little fart," was to have priority in the allocations of fuel, shells, and other matériel necessary to keep the armies nourished. Patton had to go over on the defense. He "felt very low. Must trust to God and my destiny."

During the month he drove everywhere in his army area, addressing his troops and radiating optimism. He made certain that mail deliveries were fast and regular, that food was the best possible, that daily changes of socks were distributed to prevent trench foot. He saw to it that hot showers and clean clothing were available. He rotated units in the line and instituted liberal passes and leaves, providing transportation for troops to visit Nancy and other rear-area towns. Morale remained high despite the almost constant mud, rain, sleet, and snow. Yet the strain on him was heavy. "You had better send me a couple of bottles of pink medecin," he wrote Beatrice on October 31. "When I am not attacking, I get bilous."

Two days later, Bradley told him he could attack on Novem-

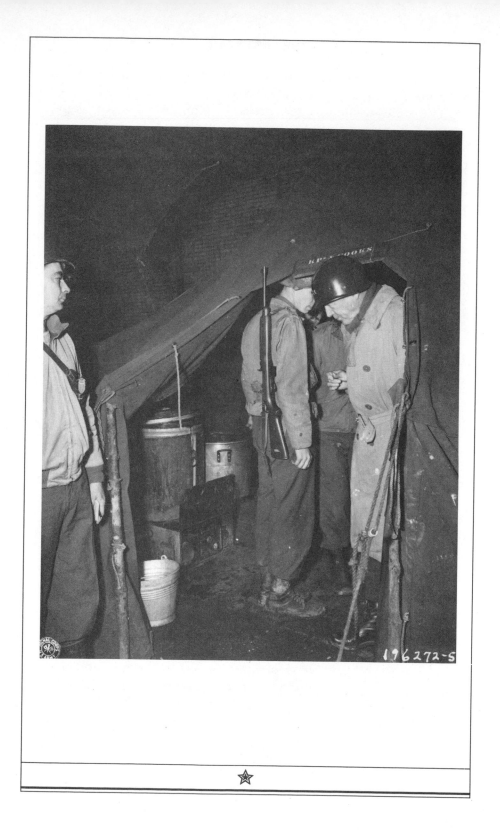

Patton, ever concerned about his troops' welfare and their equipment, inspecting a mess tent and an ordnance maintenance shop.

ber 8. "I feel 40 years younger," Patton wrote Bea. Three days afterward, as he prepared his effort: "Had a bad case of short breath this morning—my usual reaction to an impending fight or match." Two days before the operation, he confessed to Bea, "I am having indigestion and the heaves as I always do before a match. . . . It is not fear as to the result but simply the anxiety to get started."

Ten divisions were to attack on November 8, but the constant rain swelled the streams to flood stage and turned the roads into quagmire. Several of his commanders requested a postponement, but Patton refused to change his plans. The night before, he was unable to fall asleep because of nervous tension. Selecting Rommel's book on infantry attacks in the last war, he opened at random and began to read how the Germans had dealt with rain in September 1914. He was reassured, as though he had received a sign from heaven. He slept soundly until the preparatory bombardment of more than 400 guns awakened him. The rain had stopped, the stars were out. The weather was the best in two months. "Thank God," he noted in his diary. Progress along the front was better than expected. Then at 5:00 P.M., the rain started again. During the following five weeks in November and December, the Third Army fought in depressing conditions resembling the battle of the hedgerows in Normandy. There were, he told Bea, "about four inches of liquid mud over everything and it rains all the time, not hard but steadily."

On his fifty-ninth birthday, the heads of his staff sections had a party for him. Shortly thereafter, Devers "made a monkey of me" by ramming through the Belfort and Saverne gaps and reaching the Rhine at Mulhouse and Strasbourg. Patton was still distant from the magic stream.

The Red Cross Clubmobile girls invited Patton to dinner at their quarters in Nancy, and he went. They were glad to have him, for driving trucks to the combat units in order to serve doughnuts and coffee was a hard and dirty job, and now for an evening they could imagine themselves almost in civilian surroundings. Putting on their best clothes, wearing Class A uniforms, white scarves and gloves, dress shoes, and perfume, they had a lovely party. Some young ladies were overawed, intimidated by Patton. Jean called him Uncle Georgie and joked with him. He was charming to all, played a fatherly role, and thoroughly enjoyed the feminine company.

When he had important visitors to entertain, he sometimes

asked Jean to act as his hostess. Coming from the same social set as he, she was interested in horses, sailing, and history. She helped him forget for a while the cares of command.

In frightful weather and awful terrain, Patton continued to push forward, trying to force a breakthrough that never came. His ammunition supplies remained low. Because his units were short of riflemen and needed at least 9,000 replacement troops, which were unavailable, Patton combed his rear-area installations for physically fit men who could be trained to become infantry soldiers. Frustrated with logistical and personnel deficiencies, he remarked, "At the close of the war, I intend to remove my insignia and wristwatch, but will continue to wear my short coat so that everyone can kiss my ass." As though understanding Patton's frame of mind, Marshall wrote from Washington: "Since landing in France your Army has written a great page in history of which the American people will always be very proud."

"Every one but me has lost faith," Patton noted on December 15. The Third Army had advanced thirty-five to forty miles in heavy fighting, and he was preparing a final attack through the West Wall to the Rhine and Frankfurt. He was ready to move his headquarters out of Nancy and to the east, but a nagging intuition held him back. Late in November, writing in his diary, he remarked a mistake he thought Bradley and Hodges were making. They were keeping Middleton's VIII Corps front static, as a place to introduce newly arrived divisions to combat gently, a place where tired units could rest. Patton wondered whether the Germans were building up strength in the area, which was on his left and to the north.

The current feeling in the Allied camp was that the Germans were finished; they had already lost the war. Ultra indicated messages from German ground forces in transit calling for protective air cover. This should have made G-2s suspicious, but Allied intelligence had as good as written the Germans off; they were incapable of further offensive action. Yet Koch, who made it a practice to observe German activities in the zones adjacent to the Third Army, discovered ominous signs. At a staff briefing on December 9, he pointed to the VIII Corps front. The Germans were possibly, he said, concentrating forces opposite Middleton.

With Patton's disturbing premonition thus partially confirmed, he set his staff to plan to "be in position to meet whatever happens." Part of the preparations included surveying the roads and bridges, now snow-covered and icy, leading to the north.

On the fog-filled morning of December 16, the Germans struck the First Army and opened their Ardennes counteroffensive. It seemed at first to be what was called a spoiling attack, nothing serious. Bradley, unable to fly because of the weather, drove to Versailles to discuss plans with Eisenhower. By evening, he had received enough information from the front to be thoroughly concerned. The Germans were pushing a huge bulge or salient into Middleton's corps area. Telephoning Patton, Bradley asked him to send an armored division to help Middleton. Patton argued against weakening his own effort, but when Bradley insisted, Patton had a division moving within the hour.

Beginning to grasp the implications of the developments on the following day, Patton spoke with John Millikin, who had recently arrived with his III Corps headquarters. There was a coolness between them, perhaps dating from some inconsequential yet lasting disagreement at West Point—or had Millikin, Peyton March's son-in-law, disparaged archrival Pershing at some time? Patton alerted Millikin to a possible course of action. If Bradley ordered Patton to counterattack to the north against the German penetration, he would probably use Millikin's corps to direct the operation. He advised Millikin to become acquainted with the ground.

At 10:30 A.M. on December 18, Bradley, now returned to his army group headquarters in Luxembourg, telephoned and asked Patton to bring his G-2, G-3, and G-4 to a conference with him. Patton and his staff members left within ten minutes. When Bradley showed Patton and his officers a detailed map of the bulge, Patton was surprised by the size and extent of the German gains. The Germans threatened to reach the Meuse River, and if they continued, as they had in 1940, they would menace the port of Antwerp, which had recently opened to Allied shipping. Patton understood at once the need to call off his own attack.

What did Patton believe he could bring to bear against the bulge? Bradley asked. Having thought of the possibility, Patton replied at once. He could send three divisions to the north, the first starting at midnight, the second moving at first light of the next day, the third in twenty-four hours, all to go under Millikin. If Devers, to the south of Patton, could extend his front to the left and cover Eddy's XII Corps area, Patton thought of moving Eddy's troops north too, to fight alongside Millikin.

What he was about to do, if he received approval, was to turn a large part of his army quickly from an eastward orientation and swing units 90 degrees to the north. It was an extremely dangerous and delicate movement that only a seasoned professional could pull off with sureness and aplomb. To change the direction first of more than 50,000 men, later the same number, all traveling on unknown and slippery, snow-covered roads, and to redirect the flow of signals and supplies in their wake required a high degree of nerve and skill.

Bradley asked Patton to be in Verdun on the following day for a conference with Eisenhower at 11:00 A.M.

At 7:00 A.M. the next morning, Patton met with his key staff advisers, along with Millikin and Eddy, and discussed with them how to address several contingencies. He arranged a simple code with his chief of staff Gay—Gaffey was now commanding the 4th Armored Division—so that Patton could issue orders by telephone. At 8:00 A.M., the entire staff gathered as usual for the normal briefings. At 9:15 he left for Verdun, which he reached at 10:45. He found Eisenhower, Bradley, and Devers as well as many staff officers gathered.

Eisenhower's G-2 opened the meeting by describing the circumstances in terms of gloom. When he finished, Eisenhower said briskly, "The present situation is to be regarded as one of opportunity for us and not of disaster." Patton spoke up and said, "Hell, let's have the guts to let the bastards go all the way to Paris, then we'll really cut them off and chew them up." Everyone laughed, and the tension was broken.

Asked by Eisenhower to go to Luxembourg and take command of the southern shoulder of the bulge, Patton agreed. Devers consented to cover the corps area on his left so that Patton could send Eddy's corps headquarters and several divisions to Luxembourg.

Turning to Patton, Eisenhower asked, "When can you attack?"

Without hesitation, Patton answered, "On December 22, with three divisions."

Murmurs of astonishment broke out in the room. Patton's announcement sounded like bravado. How could one deploy with such speed?

French General Alphonse Juin bestows a ceremonial kiss upon Patton after making him a Grand Officer of the Legion of Honor. The two men shared a strong distrust of the Russians.

Making no comment on the timing, Eisenhower questioned the size of the force. He wanted a heavy blow against the Germans, and three divisions, he thought, were insufficient. Patton insisted he could beat the Germans with three; to wait for additional ones to come up would deny him the advantage of surprise and also give the Germans more time to push westward. Convinced, Eisenhower approved. Telephoning Gay, Patton transmitted his coded orders.

Thus without difficulty was fashioned one of the astonishing decisions of the war, and thus was started a no less astonishing movement to be characterized by dash and boldness. Because it was Patton, no one wondered overtly whether he could pull it off.

In Luxembourg at 9:00 A.M. on December 20, Patton conferred with Bradley. Patton wanted to put his main strength at once into a drive to the northeast in order to close the German entrance into the salient. But Bradley had his eyes fixed farther west on Bastogne. The Germans had surrounded the 101st Airborne Division and other American units in the town, and were heavily attacking in order to gain possession of this important road center. As long as the Americans held the place, they obstructed the German advance in that area. Bradley, together with Middleton, had decided to hang on to Bastogne. That, Bradley told Patton, was the decisive objective of the attack.

So Patton went to Arlon and talked with Middleton, Millikin, and Gaffey. Millikin was to launch the immediate attack with three divisions, including Gaffey's, to relieve the siege of Bastogne. After Eddy had some divisions up on Millikin's right and east, he was to drive to the northeast to cut the base of the German salient.

Patton spent the day and the next shifting his units and getting them moving to the north—battalions of tanks, tank destroyers, and artillery, infantry and armored divisions, hospitals, engineer units, ammunition depots—conducting the whole thing by telephone through Gay in Nancy. Within a week he had moved the bulk of his army of 250,000 men and thousands of tanks and trucks between fifty and seventy miles over treacherous roads. Even more remarkable, Millikin's III Corps was ready, as promised, to attack early on the morning of December 22, with three divisions pointed toward Bastogne.

On the day before, with Eisenhower still somewhat dubious

about attacking too soon with forces too weak, Patton called all the major staffs together for a conference. "As usual on the verge of an attack," he commented afterward in his diary, "they were full of doubt. I seemed always to be the ray of sunshine, and by God, I always am. We can and will win, God helping." To Beatrice that evening, "I am confident that a great success is possible and I hope certain. Yesterday I again earned my pay. I visited seven divisions and regrouped an Army alone. . . . Destiny [Eisenhower] sent for me in a hurry when things got tight. Perhaps God saved me for this effort."

Millikin's corps jumped off on a twenty-mile front. It snowed all day and the terrain was dreadful, but the troops advanced seven miles. Millikin's performance was better than Patton had expected. But then progress slowed on the snow-covered slopes and slick roads. The "battered bastards of Bastogne," as they would call themselves, held on grimly. Anthony McAuliffe, asked to surrender, replied with his incisive "Nuts!"

A small card, carrying Patton's Christmas wish on one side and a prayer on the other, went to everyone in the Third Army. The first: "I have full confidence in your courage, devotion to duty, and skill in battle. We march in our might to complete victory. May God's blessing rest upon each of you on this Christmas Day." The second echoed Achilles' prayer before the walls of Troy, when he asked Zeus for clear weather to disperse the fog: "Almighty and most merciful Father, we humbly beseech Thee, of Thy great goodness, to restrain these immoderate rains with which we have to contend. Grant us fair weather for Battle. Graciously harken to us soldiers who call upon Thee that armed with Thy power, we may advance from victory to victory, and crush the opposition and wickedness of our enemies, and establish Thy justice among men and nations. Amen."

After several days of intense fighting, just before darkness, on December 26, some of Gaffey's men made contact with the Americans holding Bastogne and lifted the siege. Patton wondered whether the Germans would bottle up Gaffey's soldiers too, but on the following day, troops broadened the passageway to the town and began to take out the wounded and to bring up supplies.

"The relief of Bastogne," he wrote Beatrice, "is the most brilliant operation we have thus far performed and is in my opinion the outstanding achievement of this war. Now the enemy must dance to our tune, not we to his." He had equaled, perhaps surpassed, his glorious achievement in August. If the earlier exploit showed his ardor in rolling forward against little opposition, his accomplishment in December exhibited his sureness of touch against heavy resistance. No one else could have moved so quickly and so far to grapple at close range with substantial enemy forces. As Patton later throught back to what the Third Army had done, he regarded the Bastogne operation as "the biggest and best . . . not excluding the battle of France, and I hope the troops get the credit for their great work."

Patton's New Year message to his troops read in part: "From the bloody corridor at Avranches, to Brest, thence across France to the Saar, over the Saar into Germany, and now on to Bastogne, your record had been one of continuous victory. Not only have you invariably defeated a cunning and ruthless enemy, but also you have overcome by your indomitable fortitude every aspect of terrain and weather. Neither heat nor dust nor floods and snow have stayed your progress. The speed and brilliancy of your achievements is unsurpassed in military history. My New Year wish and sure conviction for you is that . . . you will continue your victorious course to the end that tyranny and vice shall be eliminated, our dead comrades avenged, and peace restored to a war-weary world."

At a press conference on the first day of 1945, he said, "The purpose of this operation as far as the Third Army is concerned is to hit this son of a bitch—pardon me—in the flank, and we did it, with the result that he is damn well stopped and going back. . . . To me it is a never-ending marvel what our soldiers can do. . . . The people who actually did it were the younger officers and soldiers. . . . Marching all night in the cold, over roads they had never seen, and nobody getting lost, and everybody getting to the place in time—it is a very marvelous feat: I know of no equal to it in military history. . . . I take off my hat to them."

The battle was far from over. The Germans fought hard to extricate themselves from the bulge. Patton urged putting pressure on to the northeast to trap them, but timidity, he believed, on the part of Eisenhower and Montgomery allowed most to escape. "The only way you can win a war is to attack and keep on attacking, and after you have done that, keep attacking some more." But the weather remained awful, and the troops were tired. "We have to push people beyond endurance in order to bring this war to its end." Patton was already looking ahead to Berlin, which the Russians were nearing. Although he urged Bradley to keep the momentum going, no one seemed as concerned, as obsessed as Patton was to win quickly.

On the road in his jeep one day, he was enraged to see several trucks full of replacement soldiers stuck on a slippery hill. He stopped, yelled at the men to get out and push the vehicles up, then fell in with them and put his weight into the effort.

Another time he came upon a long column of vehicles closed up and halted, offering an excellent target for air attack. The problem was that a large howitzer had become stuck in an underpass of a railroad. The colonel in charge of the column did not know what to do. Patton told him incisively. "Colonel," he said, "you can blow up the goddam bridge. Or you can blow up the goddam gun. Or you can blow out your goddam brains, I don't care which."

Early in February, Eisenhower assigned the main effort to Montgomery to enable him to reach a long stretch of the Rhine River. Because of restricted supplies, lesser amounts were available to the armies under Bradley and Devers. With relatively little matériel support, they could maintain no more than a subsidiary and low-key attack. It was, Patton thought, "a foolish and ignoble way for the Americans to end the war." In his opinion, every division should attack, for the Germans, having shot their bolt in the Ardennes counteroffensive, lacked the resources to stop an all-out push. "I feel pretty low," he wrote Beatrice, "to be ending the war on the defensive."

The depression was momentary. Patton continued to press his commanders to advance. But the weather remained bad, thaws and military traffic destroyed the roads, and flooded rivers and defended pillboxes in the Siegfried Line slowed the Third Army.

As the momentum ran down, Patton and Codman departed for three days of leave in Paris. Everett Hughes reserved rooms for them in the Hotel George V. Patton hunted duck, pheasant, and hare at an old royal preserve, probably at Rambouillet, and went to the Folies Bergère, "which is perfectly naked, so much so that no one is interested." He received a standing ovation from the audience when he entered his box, later drank champagne backstage with the theater manager and his wife.

When the 1303rd Engineers built a bridge across the Sauer River, between Luxembourg and Germany, they named it after their favorite general.

☆

Returned to the war somewhat refreshed and relaxed, Patton noted the roads as "miles of cocoa colored goo." He received a batch of clippings—"I love to read about my self." After the war, he thought, "The scrap books will probably be my only literature." He was joking, for a few weeks earlier he had written to a friend, "Fortunately for my sanity, and possibly for my self-esteem, I do not see all the bullshit which is written in the home town papers about me."

When Patton visited Trier, he followed the road traveled by Julius Caesar. The entrance to the Roman amphitheater, he found, "still stands in its sturdy magnificence." So immersed in military history was he, so sure of his previous presence there, so vivid was it in his imagination, that he "could smell the sweat of the legions."

The Third Army reached the Rhine River near Coblenz on March 7, but the Germans had demolished all the bridges in Patton's zone, and no immediate crossing was possible. One of Hodges's armored divisions captured the Remagen bridge intact, and troops crossed the stream. Patton had mixed feelings on Hodges's triumph and luck, disappointed not to be the first army commander to cross, but pleased to have Americans cross ahead of everyone else.

When Eisenhower came for a visit in mid-March and stayed for dinner, Patton invited four Red Cross girls to his table. They stimulated Patton to be his most convivial and entertaining self. To Eisenhower he showed a tact and flattery that were very close to condescension. To all he was humorous and charming.

Eisenhower expressed surprise because a unit was disappointed when he had to cancel a review, then added, "Hell, George, I didn't think the American GI would give a damn even if the Lord Himself came to inspect them."

"Well," Patton said, "I hesitate to say which of you would rank, sir."

He and Eisenhower sat up talking to 2:30 in the morning. When they were together, just the two of them, the bond of friendship was close and firm. Yet in the bottom of Patton's soul rankled resentments over Eisenhower's failure to give him praise on repeated occasions, over Eisenhower's imposition of humiliation on Patton at the times of the slapping and Knutsford incidents, and over Eisenhower's timidity and lack of feel for battle. Eisenhower pleased him by saying that the

Third Army veterans "did not appreciate our own greatness and should be more cocky and boastful."

A few days later a telegram from Marshall to Eisenhower read, "Please pass on my personal and enthusiastic congratulations to Patton." Eisenhower added in longhand before forwarding the message, "Dear George: To this I add that I continue to have reason to cheer that you came with me to this war. Always, Ike."

As the Third Army closed to the Rhine River, Patton wrote to Bea, "We are the eighth wonder of the world." He had his fingers crossed. "I hope things keep smooth. It seems too good to be true." But there was no doubt. "This is a great show." During the night of March 22—a day before Montgomery, who had made elaborate, and as it turned out unnecessary, preparations for his crossings—Patton, using surprise, slipped a division across the Rhine. "God be praised," not only for success but also for the dry and clear weather. "I am realy scared by my good luck," he wrote Beatrice. "This operation is stupendous." Typical was his message to his troops. "Please accept my heartfelt admiration and thanks for what you have done, and remember that your assault crossing over the Rhine . . . assures you of even greater glory to come."

Two days afterward he drove across a pontoon bridge, stopped in the middle, got out, and pissed in the Rhine. It was a standard performance. Churchill would do the same later. On the far bank, imitating William the Conqueror as he stepped ashore in England, Patton deliberately stumbled, knelt, and picked up a handful of German soil. Did he actually compare himself to William of Normandy? Did he feel that he had been William in an earlier life? Or was he acting out and displaying, perhaps only to himself, his knowledge of military history? He never explained.

Since August 1, 1944, the Third Army had captured 300,000 prisoners of war, more than any other. Eisenhower wrote, "You have made your Army a fighting force that is not excelled in effectiveness by any other of equal size in the world." Patton had, in truth, raised his Third Army to the level of the greatest fighting armies in history, comparable to Hannibal's, Cromwell's, Napoleon's, and Lee's.

And now, as Patton rode the crest of a wave of popular admiration, he committed another controversial action. His son-in-law John Waters had been captured in Tunisia and was

Celebrating in his own way, Patton pisses in the Rhine, which his troops have recently crossed.

incarcerated in a prisoner of war camp for Allied officers in Poland. Early in 1945, as the Russians approached and threatened to overrun the camp and liberate the inmates, the Germans marched them westward. According to unsubstantiated Allied intelligence and fragmentary Red Cross reports, they were now confined at a place called Hammelburg, perhaps 5,000 in all, of whom about 1,500 were Americans. Many were sick, all were undernourished. Waters was probably among them, but his presence was not altogether certain. With American forces nearing the installation, would the Germans march the prisoners away again? If so, some would die, some would perhaps be murdered. Patton decided to rescue them.

On March 20, Patton flew to Eddy's XII Corps headquarters and revealed his intention. Eddy was reluctant to send a separate force on an independent foray into enemy territory because of the risk. Furthermore, Eddy was attacking north to join Hodges's First Army at the Ruhr, whereas Hammelburg lay to the east. An armored combat command of about 4,000 troops was large enough to take care of itself and might deceive the Germans on the direction of the XII Corps attack. But for a lightning hit-and-run affair, a smaller group might be better. Patton agreed, and later thought his assent was a mistake.

Captain Abraham Baum, big, rough, and red-haired, who had worked in New York's garment district before the war, took command of a little over 300 men in ten medium tanks, six light tanks, twenty-seven half-tracks, seven jeeps, and three motorized assault guns. His mission was to drive to Hammelburg, now forty miles away, liberate the prisoners, load as many Americans on his vehicles as he could, and bring them back. Shortly before he started, Patton's aide Stiller showed up. Patton had asked Stiller, who knew and could recognize Waters, whether he would like to accompany Baum. Stiller regarded the request as an order. Baum was suspicious of Major Stiller, who outranked him, but when Stiller assured him he wanted to go along "for the thrills and laughs," Baum invited him into his jeep.

Stiller's presence prompted later talk. Was Patton interested in liberating the prisoners and incidentally Waters, or the reverse?

Baum's men rushed toward Hammelburg, rudely dispersed a small German tank unit, destroyed railroad locomotives, smashed antitank guns on flatcars, set free 700 Russian prisoners who began to loot the area, fought off an assault gun battalion, and reached the camp. The German commander decided to surrender and sent four volunteers, among them Waters, to make contact with Baum. As they were proceeding, a guard shot and seriously wounded Waters. Baum's force then broke into the camp as thousands of joyous officers milled about.

Loading his vehicles with as many Americans as he could, Baum started back. The Germans were lying in wait for him. A light aircraft had verified the small size of Baum's group, and German units converged on Hammelburg to prevent his return. As a firefight broke out, most of the prisoners walked back to the prison camp. Surrounded and outnumbered, Baum's men fought well, tried to escape, and eventually were captured. Baum, hit three times, was sent to Hammelburg. Stiller was marched to Nuremberg.

A week later, several officers who had escaped and walked to the American lines confirmed the presence of Waters in Hammelburg, according to Gay's journal, for "the first time." Two days afterward, the Seventh Army overran Hammelburg and found about seventy prisoners, among them Waters, whose life had been saved by a Serbian surgeon. Odom, Patton's friend and a medical officer, flew there in a light plane and brought Waters to an American hospital in Frankfurt. When Patton came to visit, Waters's initial question was whether his father-in-law knew of his confinement at Hammelburg. Obeying the tradition that West Pointers never lied to each other, Patton answered, "Not for sure."

Waters recovered from his wound and after a distinguished military career retired as a full general. Baum got well and after the war returned to the business of manufacturing ladies' blouses. Stiller was liberated from a prisoner of war camp late in April and, having lost thirty pounds during his confinement, rejoined Patton.

What the newspapers featured was Patton's sacrifice of Baum's soldiers to rescue his son-in-law. "How I hate the press," Patton told Bea.

Beatrice was apprehensive of Jean Gordon's proximity to Patton and wrote to convey her concern. "Don't worry about Jean," Patton replied, perhaps with some guilt. He had seen her occasionally in the company of other Red Cross girls, "but I am not a fool, so quit worrying."

Beyond the Rhine, the Allies engaged in a triumphal march

☆

Left: Eisenhower visiting Third Army headquarters in Luxembourg in mid-March 1945. *Above:* Patton, Eisenhower, and Lieutenant General Jacob Devers plotting the endgame of the war in Europe.

against sporadic resistance. "It has gotten to the point where you can go where you damn well please." To give the appearance that both Western Allies, Americans and British, were winning the war together, and to keep them from rushing headlong into the Russian forces advancing westward, Eisenhower regulated the pace of the advance to keep the armies generally abreast. Whenever Eisenhower and Bradley "get together," Patton complained in his diary, "they get timid. . . . Had a bold policy throughout been used in this war, it would have long since been over."

Early in April, the Third Army processed its 400,000 prisoners of war, a total surpassing the numbers captured by any other army. At the end, the Third Army would round up almost a million captives.

Patton's men overran two places of interest, the German gold reserve as well as assorted treasures hidden in a mine shaft, and the infamous Ohrdruf Nord concentration camp, the first to be liberated. Eisenhower, Bradley, and Patton drove to both and inspected them. The first was a curiosity, but the second was shocking, in Patton's words, "one of the most appalling sights I have ever seen." The existence of what Patton called the "prison camp for slave labor" confirmed what had been until then rumors of the death camps. Sickened by the sight, Patton had the mayor and his wife brought there and conducted through, and upon their return home, they hanged themselves. The senior American officers agreed to have as many soldiers as possible visit what Eisenhower called the "evidence of inhuman treatment, starvation, beating, and killing of these prisoners."

Third Army troops liberated "a similar camp only much worse" near Weimar, this one Buchenwald. "I told the press to go up and . . . build up another page of the necessary evidence as to the brutality of the Germans." He threw up during his inspection. Later he wrote, to Bea, "Honestly, words are inadequate to express the horror of those institutions." Gay recorded in his journal, "The scenes witnessed there are beyond the normal mind to believe. No race except a people dominated by an ideology of sadism could have committed such gruesome crimes. . . . Inmates, all in a bad state of starvation. . . . Even those who lived, in my opinion, will never recover mentally."

A whole series of events and impressions depressed Patton in mid-April. The atrocities of the concentration camps were very much on his mind. The plight of thousands of impoverished and homeless displaced persons from Germany and eastern Europe traveling the highways bruised Patton's sensibilities. The destruction by "indiscriminate" and "cruel" bombing, Patton's words, of the cities forced women, children, and old men to live in cellars and basements underneath the rubble. Eisenhower revealed his intention to let the Russians take Berlin—a political mistake, Patton was certain—in favor of overrunning the so-called Redoubt area in the mountains along the Austro-German border, where thousands of fanatic Nazis were supposedly assembling for a last-ditch fight—a myth, Patton correctly believed. He had looked forward to getting to Berlin ahead of everyone, and to fighting the climactic battle of the war in the city; but now the war was just "petering out" and "very dull," without great and glorious excitement.

Jean Gordon had fallen in love with a young married officer who was resolved to return to his wife and children, and whether because of concern for her welfare or because of personal jealousy, Patton transferred Jean's friend from the army headquarters to a combat unit, then regretted his action.

"Some times," he wrote Beatrice, "I feel that I may be nearing the end of this life."

To shake his troubles, Patton flew with Codman to Paris and spent the night with Everett Hughes. They sat up talking into the late hours. On the following morning at breakfast, Hughes discovered that *Stars and Stripes* had announced Patton's promotion to full general. Without comment, Hughes casually passed the newspaper to Patton, who scanned the headlines and threw the paper down. Hughes picked it up and passed it back. Patton again put it down. Hughes gave it once more to Patton, this time saying, "Read that," and pointing. Patton did, then leaned back and said in a loud voice, "Well, I'll be goddamned." He was neither surprised nor particularly elated. He had expected his fourth star.

Returning to Germany that day, he had little to do. He flew in a light plane to see Walker, who was in the Schloss Weissenstein, "the most magnificent and most hideous building I have ever seen." Ever alert to architecture and art, he inspected the many murals, "a very fine art collection," and a lot of "very bad statutes." From there, he was proceeding to the III Corps headquarters when a British Spitfire with markings indicating it was being flown by a Polish pilot inexplicably made three

Patton wearing four stars for the first time (before his helmet could be altered), on April 19, 1945.

passes at Patton's small plane, firing its machine guns. Patton's pilot, taking evasive action, descended close to the ground. The Spitfire, pursuing, was unable to pull out of its dive and crashed, killing the pilot. The event was disturbing. Was someone trying to assassinate Patton?

Early in May he was "nearly killed by a bull cart coming out of a side street," he reported to Bea. "We missed the end of the pole by a few inches." Was this, together with the Spitfire incident, a sign from heaven of his coming death?

Noticing that the plants in a greenhouse attached to his mess were dry, Patton watered them personally. "I am not as hard as painted," he explained to Bea. Nor was he impervious to Nuremberg, almost entirely destroyed. "It is really rather pathetic to see such a historical monument so completely removed." The weather was clear, the countryside verdant. "I wish we could take a drive in this country in peace," he wrote with yearning to Bea. "It is full of beauty and ruins—not the ones I have made but old ones too."

The surrender of the Germans in Italy foreshadowed the end in Germany. Soon, he told Beatrice, "I will be out of a job." Peacetime "is going to be hell on me. I will probably be a great nusance." He wished he could be home for a few days. "I miss you." They had been separated two and a half years.

One last flurry occurred. Bradley phoned and ordered Patton to enter Czechoslovakia and to go no farther than Pilsen. Patton immediately sent Clarence Huebner's V Corps on the mission. Reaching Pilsen easily, Huebner asked permission to go on to Prague, where patriots had risen up against the Germans and were calling upon the Western Allies for help. The Russians were still distant. Patton desperately wanted to go on to Prague, but that meant disobeying his instructions. Wait, he told Huebner, until he checked with Bradley. Bradley consulted Eisenhower, who said no. Bradley transmitted Eisenhower's order, and Patton reluctantly directed Huebner to stay where he was. He felt rotten to be denied capture of one of the great capitals of Europe.

The German unconditional surrender, signed in Reims and later in Berlin, came into effect on the first minute of May 9, 1945. Remembering Armistice Day in the Great War, Patton predicted "a tremendous let down." He was reflecting his own gloominess. Was his destiny fulfilled?

As early as February he had volunteered to go to the Pacific, but MacArthur, jealously guarding the publicity for himself, preferred a less colorful subordinate, not a prima donna like Patton. Offered Hodges, MacArthur gladly accepted him and his First Army staff after the war in Europe came to an end. In March, Patton wrote to Marshall and asked to be considered for any command, from division up, in the fight against the Japanese. His combat methods, he was sure, would work against them. Besides, "I am also of such an age that this war is my last war, and I would like to see it through to the end." Marshall promised to send Patton to China at the head of an American force, but only if the Chinese wrested a major port from the Japanese and opened it for Patton's entry. This seemed unlikely, so Patton sent a letter to his classmate Robert Eichelberger, who commanded the Eighth Army in the Pacific, and offered to sit at his feet and learn to fight. Eichelberger could make no commitment.

Detesting the Russians, calling them Mongols, he believed an eventual American-Soviet confrontation and clash to be inevitable. The U.S. Army was clearly superior at the moment. Why not initiate hostilities at once? But he knew this to be out of the question. The war against Japan had yet to be won, the Russians were allied to the West in that struggle, and the American people were hardly willing to undertake the considerable task of extending the conflict into eastern Europe. All Patton could do of a positive nature was to look the other way as thousands of refugees fleeing the Russians illegally crossed the border into his territory.

Instead of engaging in further campaigning, he was to undertake the occupation of northern Germany, with Keyes, now commanding the Seventh Army, administering the western part, Patton the eastern part of Bavaria. It was hardly a glamorous job. Downcast, he wished he had been killed by the last bullet of the last battle.

Eisenhower invited the four American army commanders to lunch on May 10. He spoke "very confidentially" of the need for them all to maintain a united and solid front if called to testify before congressional committees that might later investigate the conduct of the war. To Patton, Eisenhower's talk sounded like "covering up probable criticism of strategical blunders which he unquestionably committed during the campaign." Whether the errors were Eisenhower's alone or the result of "too much cooperation with the British," Patton was "inclined to think that he over-cooperated."

It was a sad note on which to end the war. Victory was to have been the climax, the solution to all problems, the final glorious effort. While the Allied military triumph had led Hitler to suicide, Germany to capitulation, and the Nazi party to extinction, the world was hardly a perfect place. Germany was ruined, homeless people tramped the countryside searching for lost relatives, and the Allied armies had to attend to such matters as starting up the economy, keeping order, restoring normal conditions of life, and keeping the survivors alive. The Russians, who had emerged as American rivals, threatened postwar stability. "They are a scurvy race and simply savages. We could beat hell out of them." Gay's journal noted, "Everything they did impressed one with the idea of virility and cruelty."

In the political power vacuum of postwar Europe, according to Patton, with the Germans crushed, the British were untrustworthy, the French weak, and the Russians dangerous. Only the Germans, Patton thought, who had fought skillfully on the battlefield, were worthy allies in an inevitable war against the Russians. Harking back to the reconstruction after the American Civil War and the calls for binding up the nation's wounds, he argued that the same should apply in Europe. The Allies should forget the excesses of Nazism and be generous to the former foes and rehabilitate the country. The Nazi party, he said at a press conference, was like the Republican and Democratic parties. ("Nazis just like the Republicans and Democrats," read one American newspaper headline; another furor.) Not all Germans were Nazis, and those who joined the party had done so to get ahead in their jobs and professions. With the Germans as allies, Patton could engage in the excitement of battling the Russians and further fulfill his destiny.

His fame at home exceeded all his expectations. Everyone wanted to hear about Patton and his famous Third Army. In the movie houses, when newsreels were shown, Patton's appearance generated more applause than anyone else's.

In mid-May, Patton flew to Paris, then to London for several days of leave. He needed a vacation, and he intended to visit friends in the Knutsford area. According to Hughes, he took nine condoms with him. In London he attended the theater, had his picture taken everywhere, and was cheered wherever he showed up. Before he could depart on the following day for Knutsford, Eisenhower telephoned and asked him to return to Reims at once. He complied and learned that Tito was "raising hell" at the northern end of the Adriatic Sea. Marshall had recommended using Patton's prestige and five armored divisions to bluff Tito. Patton was excited by the prospect of further action, but Tito soon backed down, and Patton returned to England, where he spent four days. According to Hughes, Patton used four condoms in three days during his stay—unless, of course, Patton was trying to meet Hughes's expectations and fibbed to please him.

Early in June, Patton left Europe, the stage of his great final drama, and flew to Boston for what was supposed to be a triumphal tour, a victory celebration. He landed at the Bedford Airport, where Bea and his children greeted him. Bea's hair was now graying—and she looked smaller, almost frail. He rode in a car the twenty-five miles into the city, standing during the drive and acknowledging with salutes and waves the cheers of a million people lining the roads and streets. He was, no doubt, an authentic man of the hour to the American people, beloved and cherished, to whom gratitude was due.

Then, at the Hatch Shell on the Charles River Esplanade, he gave a speech that, once again, almost destroyed his image. A soldier killed in action, he said, was not automatically a hero but frequently a fool. Pointing to 400 wounded soldiers of the Third Army seated in a special section, he said, "These men are the heroes." He drew himself to his full height and dramatically saluted them, then sat down.

His words on heroes and fools, widely reported, prompted many Gold Star parents to write in protest to Marshall and Stimson. It was heartbreaking, they said, to have Patton expressing scorn for their sons who were buried in France and Luxembourg. The profane and pistol-packing Patton, to them, was hardly representative of the best American qualities. Rather he was the antithesis of the ideals of American life and culture. Marshall, Stimson, and the Army Public Relations Bureau released stories and answered letters trying to explain and correct Patton's meaning.

In Boston, at a state dinner for him at the Copley Plaza Hotel that evening, Patton was overwhelmed with emotion. On the following day he spoke to his neighbors at South Hamilton before flying to Denver, where he addressed an enthusiastic audience. He flew to Los Angeles, and at the Coliseum, 100,000 Americans turned out to hear and see him as he called for the defeat of Japan and swore and wept. Staying with Nita, he visited an Army hospital and appeared at the

June 1945: Boston hails the conquering hero.

★

These two pictures, taken at a welcome-home dinner in Boston, show Patton's susceptibility to rapid and extreme swings of emotion.

☆

Among the greeters were of course his family: *Left,* his son George, Beatrice, and the Patton daughters, Ruth Ellen and Beatrice. *Above,* a platoon of grandchildren.

Rose Bowl. He attended services at the Church of Our Savior and placed a wreath on his parents' graves. After a stopover at Fort Riley, he continued to Washington, where he saw his daughters and grandchildren. Visiting the double-amputation ward in the Walter Reed Hospital, he burst into tears. "God damn it," he said, "if I had been a better general, most of you wouldn't be here."

It was Patton on his customary roller coaster, up and down, savoring the applause, questioning his worthiness to receive it.

Before he left to return to Europe, he told his daughters of his premonition of death. Although he expected to see their mother again, he said, this was the last time that they would see him alive. He cut short their objections, for he was convinced of the truth of his prediction.

He was glad to leave the United States. He felt out of place. He had been away too long. He was out of touch with the civilians and their aspirations, their war-weariness, their glad acceptance of peace in Europe. He felt at home only among soldiers and in a military environment, where discipline and the pomp of ruffles-and-flourishes thrilled him. He was filled with bitterness over the wrongs, real and imagined, inflicted on him. He was infected with a mind-numbing fatigue.

10

⭐

BEHIND THE LEGEND

When he returned from the United States to Europe in July 1945, the welcome extended by his organization cheered him. As he was flying from Paris to Bavaria, three fighter groups of Weyland's XIX TAC met his plane in the air and escorted him playfully to the landing field, where a guard of honor and a band waited. In his car, preceded and followed by motorcycles, as aircraft buzzed overhead, he passed through files of tanks and soldiers stationed along the road and saluting him. At his headquarters, his corps commanders led him to a stand for a review. After he spoke a few words of greeting, they took him to cocktails and lunch. He was at home and comfortable, where he liked to be. The ceremonies were exactly what he would have arranged for himself.

He was now at Bad Tolz, his headquarters beside Lake Tegernsee. In that lush countryside, surrounded by landscapes of great beauty, the problems of the occupation seemed entirely remote. Instead of dealing with complicated matters such as government, banking, and education, Patton spent most of his time visiting his troops, addressing them before they departed for redeployment. "Show the world how great you are," he implored. "Look like soldiers!"

To his colleagues it seemed that the old fire was gone. Admired as a winning leader in war, he appeared to be out of touch with the postwar circumstances. He looked older, overtaken by events. His bounce was unconvincing, his message outmoded, his posturing somehow pathetic. Patton himself knew that something was wrong and couldn't figure out what.

When Japan surrended, he informed Bea: "Well the war is over. . . . Now the horrors of peace, pacafism, and unions will have unlimited sway." He wished he were young enough to fight in the coming war against "the Mongols." "It is hell to be old and passe and know it." Victory had terminated "my usefulness to the world. It is for me personally a very sad thought. Now all that is left to do is to sit around and," he added with foresight, "await the undertaker and posthumous immortality."

In his gloom he worried over questions looming large in his mind, and his thinking became poisoned. Why had he not been allowed to seize Berlin ahead of the Russians? Who was going to curb the power of the Bolsheviks? What was to be the future of Europe, the fate of Germany? How could he enforce denazification when he was out of sympathy with the concept? The authentic non-Nazis were those liberated from the internment camps, and they seemed to be labor leaders, Jews, and Communists. Unable to differentiate among them, he came to believe that they all formed an international conspiracy working for the downfall of the United States. It must be they who were setting detestable policies and ruining the prospects for a stable social order. He could no longer repress the more or less natural anti-Semitism endemic to his milieu, and he relapsed into the neurotic comfort of old and stereotyped attitudes.

He could not cope with massive issues so alien to his upbringing, interests, and social outlook.

Fatigue, not only physical but mental, robbed him of equilibrium. The effort he had expended all his life against his inner nature had absorbed enormous energy. His fabled drive was ebbing. "I think I was never so tired and stiff as I was yesterday," he wrote Beatrice.

He used his absence in the United States as an excuse to ignore Eisenhower's directive to remove and exclude Nazis from public office and important positions. "I had never heard," he wrote Bea, "that we fought to de-nazify Germany—live and learn. What are we doing is to utterly destroy the only semi-modern state in Europe so that Russia can swallow the whole." He missed the point of the war for most Americans, the need to do away with immoral regimes. Forgetting the extermination camps, he saw only the small and ordinary German, the man on the street, the soldier who had fought so well and so bravely. How could they be responsible for the evils of Nazism? "Actually the Germans are the only decent people in Europe." The troublemakers must be the Jews, who wanted revenge and whose newspapers were shaping public opinion to their ends. He made no secret of "my personal feelings against them."

To Patton, it was unfair to strip from their jobs qualified German managers who happened to have been Nazis. Removing them would lead to a breakdown of production and a lack of food and heating fuel for women and children and other innocents. Eisenhower explained the need to uproot "the whole Nazi organization" despite resulting "administrative inefficiency," for victory would be final only when all the Nazis were eliminated from responsible positions and properly punished. But Patton thought the pursuit of war criminals to be "not cricket." To him, "The virus started by Morganthau and Baruch of a Semitic nature against all Germans is still working."

When Eisenhower informed him of his intention to inspect the camps for displaced persons in Patton's area, Patton was disturbed. Everyone, he said in his diary, believed "that the Displaced Person is a human being, which he is not, and this applies particularly to the Jews who are lower than animals." As his earlier disgust and horror over the death camps receded, he concluded, "Either the Displaced Persons never had a sense of decency or else they lost it all during their period of internment by the Germans. My personal opinion is that no people could have sunk to the level of degradation these have reached in the short space of four years." Their troubles, he forgot, had endured for more than a decade, but he was unable to comprehend the Holocaust and its effects.

Eisenhower's arrival coincided with Yom Kippur, the Day of Atonement, and when he and Patton visited a Jewish camp, all

Back in Europe, the general expresses his thanks to a
Czechoslovakian girl for the cut-glass vase her town
presented him with. *Above,* Patton commandeers a horse
Hitler had taken from the riding school in Vienna to give to
Emperor Hirohito.

On September 7, Patton reviewed the 16th Armored Division in Czechoslovakia. The great career was coming to an end.

the inhabitants were in the synagogue. When the two Americans entered, the rabbi interrupted the worship service to let Eisenhower address the congregation. Patton almost fainted from the stench of human beings packed into an overheated, underventilated room. These people could hardly be members of the human race to which he belonged. They must be subhuman and inferior. They were poor, sometimes dirty, strange in appearance, speech, and manner, less than exquisite according to the standards of Anglo-Saxon drawing rooms, still struggling to reduce their suffering. Unable to understand their plight or their ways, he despised them.

Let Eisenhower visit the camps. Patton much preferred hunting deer with Harmon on a large estate in Czechoslovakia, or shooting chamois in the mountains of the French zone of occupation. He spent much time replying in detail to the new superintendent of West Point, who had asked for his recommendations on changing the curriculum. He agonized over the rapid dismemberment of his Third Army as soldiers went home for discharge and separation "while the displaced sons-of-bitches in the various camps are blooming like green trees."

His hysteria came also from worry over his future. Everyone except him had found a new place for himself. Bradley was heading the Veterans Administration. Clark was the American High Commissioner in Austria. Devers was chief of the Army Field Forces at Fort Monroe, Virginia, and training troops. Gerow was to be the commandant of the Army War College. Eisenhower, who would soon leave for Washington to succeed Marshall as Army Chief of Staff, asked Patton to stay in Germany at least three months after his departure, and Patton tentatively agreed out of his loyalty to his boss. He really wanted Devers's training command or Gerow's War College post so that he could transmit his lessons of warfare, his methods of fighting, his accumulated experience to the next generation of warriors. But he, the real hero of the war, had been miserably edged out by the others; he had no specific place in the coming scheme of things. Was he too good? Was his name too big? Had he been "too d— military"?

Newspapers, particularly the liberal press, criticized the occupation. Nazis in Germany, the New York *Times* reported, still had the best jobs in commerce and industry and still lived in the best houses. The military government was apparently more concerned with efficiency than with fulfilling the objectives of the war.

At a press conference on September 22, immediately after the normal weekly briefing on Saturday morning, Patton was questioned on whether the denazification program was proceeding as fast as possible. There were only eleven reporters present, a trifle compared to the numbers during the war, and Patton was irritable and in a hurry, his mind elsewhere. No known Nazis, Patton responded flatly, held public office in his area. Then he put his foot into his mouth. If the United States had lost the war and the conquerors removed all political officials, he said, they would exclude all the Republicans and Democrats from their jobs. Turning out the efficient people in Germany would create administrative turmoil and cause innocent people to starve and to freeze. It was more essential, Patton said, to revive the German economy.

Some observers felt the journalists were baiting Patton, egging him on to make sensational statements for the headlines. Patton felt that the reporters were expressing hostility not against him personally but against the Army in general. "There is," he recorded, "a very apparent Semitic influence in the press." The sentiment was helping Communism instead of building up Germany as a buffer state against Russia. Aching to fight "the Mongols" with skilled German veterans as his allies, he wrote in his diary, "I have never had any animus against the professional soldiers who fought against me." He was espousing a medieval notion. The military, like the knights in western Europe, were members of an international brotherhood or sacred guild, who re-formed the ranks of fraternity upon the close of a war. That was what he wished to see in 1945.

The *Times* seized upon Patton's press statement and quoted him as having said, "The Nazi thing is just like a Democrat-Republican election fight." The news spread sensationally. Editorials around the country questioned not only Patton's understanding of the moral basis of the war but also the Army's ability to supervise the occupation.

The stories and editorial comments disturbed Eisenhower, who questioned Patton. He said he was misquoted. Would he then hold another conference and set the record straight? Patton agreed. He had a paper typed, and he read it to the reporters. But he strayed from his written remarks to explain what he meant and in the course of it he repeated himself. A very large percentage of German tradespeople, small businessmen, and professionals, he said, gave the Nazi party the lip service that permitted them to keep their jobs. That was all there was to it. Dismissing them from office or denying them work would retard the economic recovery of Bavaria.

The press featured his statements and further dismayed Eisenhower. "I am again at one of those critical periods," Patton noted, "when I may be sent home in a hurry at any moment." For "the Devil and Moses [have] gotten together to plan for an early and certain resumption of hostilities." His son George, he wrote Bea, "need not worry about missing a war. The next is on the way." As he saw it, "The noise against me is only the means by which the Jews and Communists are attempting and with good success to implement a further dismemberment of Germany." Clearly, he had become delusional.

Eisenhower summoned him to Frankfurt and suggested Patton's transfer to the Fifteenth Army, a headquarters that was compiling and writing the lessons of the war. Having had enough of governing eastern Bavaria and truly interested in extracting from the records, preserving in the archives, and disseminating to the Army successful methods of combat, Patton agreed. But he hated to give up his Third Army.

Truscott came to succeed him, and on October 7, a dreary, rainy day reflecting the mood at the headquarters, the change-of-command ceremony took place. The assembled officers and men were sad or uncomfortable. Patton spoke, saying, "All good things must come to an end. The best thing that has ever come to me thus far is the honor and privilege of having commanded the Third Army. The great successes we have achieved together have been due primarily to the fighting heart of America." Truscott was emotional in his remarks— "very much perturbed," Patton thought. After cocktails and lunch, Patton was accompanied by Truscott to the railroad station and sent off on the Third Army train to his new assignment.

"I feel that the Third Army has died," Weyland wrote him a few weeks later. "To me, the Third Army meant Patton. When you left it, it ceased to be a thing alive." Patton tended to agree. Divisions, corps, and armies, he was sure, had souls. He found it unfortunate that Marshall and Eisenhower, who were essentially staff officers, had been at the top of the Army.

They had practically never exercised command, and they thought of units as "animated tables of organization rather than as living entities."

In Bad Nauheim on the following morning, responding to questions from a reporter, Patton said, "If a man has done his best, what the hell [more] is there? I consider that I have always done my best. . . . [My] conscience is clear." Only a goddam fool, he added, believed there would be no future war. Beyond that, he refused to discuss American-Soviet relations.

With everyone in his new headquarters working hard, Patton began to enjoy himself, although he grumbled in his diary and in his letters to Beatrice. Eisenhower had no backbone, no moral fortitude, mainly because he already aspired to the presidency. "The whole damned world is going Communist." He was seriously thinking of retiring or resigning from the Army in outrage and protest. "I realy shudder for the future of our country."

He traveled to Paris, Rennes, Chartres, and other cities, where he "collected ten Citizen of Honor certificates, two plaques, and a tremendous case of indigestion." In Brussels, where the King of the Belgians decorated him, he caught a bad cold. In Metz, Reims, Luxembourg, Verdun, and elsewhere, there were honors and ceremonies galore. He went to Copenhagen, then to Stockholm, where he met the surviving members of the Swedish team in the Olympic Games of 1912. He spent a good part of November writing his "Notes on Combat," composing ten single-spaced typed pages. It was almost like old times.

On his sixtieth birthday, he felt fine. Everyone told him how good he looked. He was tickled to learn what former soldiers of the Third Army now back in the United States were saying about him. When asked about Patton, they invariably replied in much the same vein: "Goddam that old son of a bitch. Wasn't he swell!" He was beaming, his old gracious self.

But he had been in a slight automobile accident, and again wondered if his life was running out. His vehicle had suffered only a bent fender, but the close call made him think of the Spitfire plane firing at him and the oxcart pole narrowly missing him. Was this latest brush with death another sign?

When Eisenhower left for Washington, Patton, as the senior American officer, commanded the theater, going to Frankfurt "about three times a week mostly to sign court-martial sentences." Early in December, Joseph McNarney arrived to take

October 7: Patton hands over his beloved Third Army to Lieutenant General Lucian Truscott at Bad Tolz, Germany.

over. At the luncheon welcoming McNarney, Patton could hardly hold his bitterness in check. "I have rarely seen assembled a greater bunch of sons-of-bitches," he wrote to Bea. He no longer felt himself to be part of the establishment, part of the gang. Almost everyone, he was certain, resented his victories.

Patton intended to go home for Christmas and not to return to Europe. What he would do then he would first discuss with Beatrice. If he was offered a good job, he would probably stay in the Army. Otherwise he would retire.

He was scheduled to fly to the United States on Monday, December 10. Two days earlier, Geoff Keyes, one of his best friends, drove over, and spent Saturday evening and night with him. On Sunday morning Keyes said goodbye and wished him well. An hour or so thereafter, having nothing to do, Patton and Gay set out in Patton's chauffeured limousine, accompanied by a jeep carrying a hunting dog, to hunt pheasant near Mannheim. On the way, they stopped to tramp around some ruins on a hill. Continuing, they were proceeding at a relatively low rate of speed when their car collided with an Army truck. The crash and the sudden stop sent Patton, who was in the backseat, hurtling through the air. The top of his head grazed the diamond-shaped interior light on the roof, and a protruding corner ripped off the skin of his skull, which hung down like a flap. His face smashed into the driver's partition. The impact broke his nose and his neck. The damaged vertebrae paralyzed him from the neck down. No one else in this freak accident was so much as scratched.

Taken to a hospital in Heidelberg, he tried to joke about his injuries. "Relax, gentlemen, I'm in no condition to be a terror now." A few minutes later, he said, "Jesus Christ, what a way to start a leave."

The physicians easily taped and stitched back the skin on top of his head and repaired his nose, but the fracture-dislocation of his third and fourth cervical vertebrae, affecting his spinal cord, was serious. They placed him in traction and hoped for the best. An Army plane brought a noted neurosurgeon from Oxford University to treat him, but there was nothing the surgeon could do.

Informed of what had happened to her husband, Beatrice wanted to go to him. Eisenhower placed an airplane at her disposal. Together with a leading American specialist, R. Glen Spurling, who had recently been separated from the service, she flew to Heidelberg. A few days afterward, her brother, Fred Ayer, came by commercial air.

Patton was reasonably comfortable and, except for the drag of the traction exerted by large hooks inserted under his cheekbones, in no pain. His condition was unchanged. He was cheerful, happy to see Beatrice, apparently unworried and calm.

But he wanted to know the truth. Alone with Spurling for a few minutes, he asked what chance he had to ride a horse again.

Spurling was direct. "None," he said.

"In other words," Patton responded, "the best I could hope for would be semi-invalidism."

Spurling was again direct. "Yes."

Patton gravely thanked him for being honest. As he thought about Spurling's words, he became depressed. During the nights, when only his nurse was on duty there, he was discouraged and morose. All he wanted to do, he said, was to sleep. As a well-bred gentleman, he tried to be jovial with the few visitors he was allowed, keeping up appearances.

Many reporters came to Heidelberg to check on Patton's progress, and their stories pushed the Nuremberg trials of the top Nazi figures off the front pages. The hospital staff distributed periodic press releases, but some correspondents endeavored to disguise themselves as medical attendants or to bribe personnel in order to gain entry to his room. The papers and radio broadcasts were full of reports of him, and get-well messages from friends—Eisenhower and President Harry S Truman among them—and strangers and organizations such as the Jewish War Veterans and a leading Negro journal poured in. Beatrice answered them all.

Immobile and helpless, Patton lingered for thirteen days, his hardy constitution keeping him alive.

Bea spent most of the afternoon of December 21 reading to him. He dozed off at 4:00 P.M. His breathing was irregular, and she continued to sit at his bedside. An hour and a half later, when his respiration was better, she and Spurling went to dinner at the hospital mess. Twenty-five minutes afterward, a messenger asked them to come at once. When they reached his room, they found him dead. He had slipped away. He expired from "pulmonary edema and congestive heart failure."

According to Spurling, "Patton died as he had lived—bravely." He never expressed a word of complaint. He treated

Patton died in Heidelberg on December 21. Here the devoted Willie waits by his master's baggage for shipment back to America.

everyone at the hospital "with the kindest consideration." He took and followed orders "without question." As a matter of fact, "He was a model patient."

For a Friday evening, Heidelberg was uncommonly silent. The stillness persisted throughout the weekend. The service clubs for the troops were closed, flags were at half-mast, a spirit of sorrow pervaded. A soldier on duty in the city wrote to his parents that he was "in mourning" for "one of the greatest men that ever lived. . . . The rest of the world thinks of him as just another guy with stars on his shoulders. The men that served under him know him as a soldier's leader. I am proud to say that I have served under him in the Third Army. . . . We are making every Heinie that passes stop and take off his hat. They can't understand our feelings for him. I don't know whether or not you can understand them either."

In a general order announcing Patton's death, Keyes added a few words of tribute. A "great friend, a gallant warrior, and inspiring leader," Patton was "the ablest American field commander faced by the German Army on any front." He "deserves more than a lion's share of the credit for the victories of our arms in the bitter European struggle just ended."

It was true. A German senior officer captured in March revealed: "The greatest threat . . . was the whereabouts of the feared U.S. Third Army. General Patton is always the main topic of military discussion. Where is he? When will he attack? Where . . . ? How? With what? . . . General Patton is the most feared general on all fronts. The successes of the U.S. Third Army are still overshadowing all other events of the war, including the campaign in Russia. . . . The tactics of General Patton are daring and unpredictable. . . . He is the most modern general and the best commander of armored and infantry troops combined." Even Joseph Stalin had expressed admiration for Patton and the Third Army's sweep across France. Gerd von Rundstedt, one of the distinguished German field marshals, when questioned after the war, said simply, "Patton was your best."

On Saturday, December 22, the day after his death, Patton's body was placed in state in a villa nearby. Many persons came to view his remains, to pay their respects, and to say goodbye. On Sunday the casket was closed and, escorted by cavalry and the pallbearers, taken to the Heidelberg Protestant Church, which was banked with flowers. After the Episcopal service, the coffin was taken to the railroad station and put on a train.

The cars left for Luxembourg and the American military cemetery in the suburb of Hamm.

Across the German border in France, between 7:00 and 11:00 P.M., the train stopped six times at stations where honor guards were in formation, waiting to place wreaths on the casket. Beatrice descended to the platform each time, inspected the troops, received with dignity the brief words of sympathy offered, and responded in her flawless French.

It was raining in Luxembourg on the following morning as the cortege proceeded through city streets lined with solemn civilians and soldiers. An hour and a half later at the cemetery there were religious services and military ceremonies. Overhead in the overcast sky, his former corps commander, Walton Walker, flying from Texas to the funeral, was unable to land, and his circling plane provided a far-off murmur of regret.

Patton was buried under a white marker no different from the others, in the midst of the rows of crosses and stars of David. Three years later, so many people had come to visit his grave that the American Battle Monuments Commission moved his body to the front of the burial ground. There, just below the low wall overlooking the cemetery, he reposes at the head of his combat dead.

Between Patton's accident and death, in the space of two weeks, the American people revised their judgment of him. Had he died at once, he would probably have vanished from the public consciousness. He might have been remembered as a peculiar, an eccentric, an unbelievable and exaggerated caricature. Instead, as he fought for his life, the news media had a chance to recall at length his triumphs and featured his successes. His swashbuckling and color, his flamboyance and profanity were no longer deemed extraneous to his accomplishments. They were all part of his image, and his image in large part was responsible for his victories. As an enthralled public followed his last struggle in the hospital with sympathy, they came to appreciate his impact on the war, to be grateful for his results, to admire what he had done—his troop training in the United States, his landings near Casablanca, his triumphs in Tunisia, his victories in Sicily, his astonishing breakout and pursuit across France, his sparkling performance at Bastogne and in the Battle of the Bulge, his leap across the Rhine. Who else could have done all that? Only Patton, who had thereby shortened the war. The understanding and applause, together

Mrs. Patton leaving church in Heidelberg after the funeral. Behind her is Patton's old comrade in arms, Lieutenant General Geoffrey Keyes.

With Master Sergeant William Meeks, Patton's orderly for eight years, at the head of the escort, Patton's coffin leaves Heidelberg appropriately—on a Third Army half-track.

with the profound grief at his death, transformed him almost at once into a folk hero, a man who was already a legend.

An infinite number of tributes attested to his place in history. "He was the greatest soldier of them all," the "greatest general American has known," the "greatest soldier of this terrible war." He was "more firmly fixed in our minds than any other military commander," said a letter from London. "I did love him as a leader," said a soldier who had lost a leg. He "will be a source of strength for the rest of my life," said a captain. It was, said a perceptive writer, "a shame that death should have been necessary to clarify his true value and virtue."

With his pistols and scowling face, he seemed to have stepped out of the movies as a cowboy hero of the West, never old, the essence of youth in spirit and action, a winner. And like the American cowboy, he did not outlive his era. He died at just the right time, while his triumphs in the war remained fresh, before he could destroy his reputation by absurd ravings. Had he lived, he would no doubt have felt himself to be outside the mainstream of American life. He would have turned into an anachronism.

For he had been truly a man of his times. Although nurtured on the notions of antiquity, the chivalric feudal age, and the Romantic tradition, he was altogether a product of the early twentieth century. His cherished beliefs were simplistic, and they sprang from an American culture not yet urbanized, an ethnicity not yet diluted, a society not yet unsettled by technology, social upheaval, and new political realities. Holding tenaciously to the tenets of his upbringing, he was no proponent of change, no rebel. However much he squirmed inwardly under the restrictions of the military, he was a conformist. In public he exhibited a perfect obedience to the chain of command. To him, the aim of war was to gain military victory, and that had motivated all his efforts.

Behind his profanity, underneath his tough exterior, was an emotional, volatile, capricious being. His sense of authority was stark, and his arrogance bordered on contempt. His twinkling eyes could change instantly into pools of blazing anger. He jumped from vulgarity to scholarship as nimbly as a cat. He breathed vitality until the last months of his life.

Sensitive, gentle, and charming in private, Patton was always on guard, alert to correct any slips that might betray his pose. His cousin and boyhood companion Arvin Brown noted "the depth of your feeling and understanding that you so often try to conceal by a studied pretense of being something other than your own great self."

His prose showed how alive he was to beauty, how immersed he was in history, how keen he was in observation, how subtle his wit. His descriptions of the colors in the desert, of the Roman ruins in Tunisia, of the Greek temples in Sicily were sensitive and knowledgeable. A chateau near Briquebec in Normandy drew his attention because the tower was in "transition between a square keep and a round keep, having 11 sides." Malta fascinated him, for the forts "in the great siege of 1528 are different from any I have ever seen. They are pre-Vauban . . . with walls up to 16 feet thick and very high. All built by slave labor, Saracen slaves."

Writing to Beatrice of southern Germany, he said, "It is the prettiest country . . . with snow mountains, forests of all shades of green, and green fields . . . full of pretty girls, all of whom say they are Czechs." Of France: "I did not remember the lovely colors of the trees in the fall here. They are not as brilliant as ours at home but are very effective." To Nita, "I saw so many dead Germans that it actually made me sick."

Asked to write a prayer for inclusion in a book for soldiers and sailors, Patton set down the items for which he asked Divine assistance. "God of our Fathers," he wrote, "who by land and sea has ever led us on to victory, please continue your inspiring guidance in this the greatest of our conflicts. Strengthen my soul so that the weakening instinct of self-preservation, which besets all of us in battle, shall not blind me to my duty to my own manhood, to the glory of my calling, and to my responsibility to my fellow soldiers. Grant to our armed forces that disciplined valor and mutual confidence which insures success in war. Let me not mourn for the men who have died fighting, but rather let me be glad that such heroes have lived. If it be my lot to die, let me do so with courage and honor in a manner which will bring the greatest harm to the enemy, and please, oh Lord, protect and guide those I shall leave behind. Give us the victory, Lord."

To Beatrice in 1917: "This is the last letter I shall write you from Mexico. I have learned a lot about my profession and a lot how much I love you. The first was necessary the second was not." In another letter: "I cannot send you any kisses this evening because we had onions for dinner." Flying in a light plane over the battlefield in the Cotentin, he noted, "The

Patton's grave in the American Army Cemetery at Hamm, Luxembourg.

whole countryside is covered with enormously distended cows, which . . . smell to high heaven, or at least to 300 feet high, as that was my altitude."

After the Sicilian campaign: "The other day I had tea with a very fat princess with a black beard which she shaves. . . . She has a girl friend who should be a wrestler but is a famous pianist. All she can play are etudes and movements, but she does that with utter abandon and great power. I have never seen such forearms. I made a hit by not talking during the playing—you taught me that—so now she thinks I love music and threatens to have a musical evening where we will just play, not eat or drink. Certainly an inexpensive system if the piano stands up."

To his brother-in-law Fred Ayer: "We have an officer of quite high rank here who is very pompous. . . . One of his current hobbies is sanitation. Recently, on inspecting a company he noticed that every man had a fork in his left-hand shirt pocket. The General asked the reason for this. The soldier questioned replied that in order to carry out the General's wishes as to sanitation, they never passed the bread by hand, but if anyone wanted a piece of bread he stuck his fork in it and took it. The General said that that was excellent and complimented the men. On going outdoors he noticed that every soldier had a string hanging out of the lower part of his fly. He asked why the string and was informed that the string was for the purpose of getting the penis out without touching it with the hand, again complying with the General's idea of sanitation. The General was much pleased and complimented the soldier again. But suddenly an idea struck him and he said, 'That is all right, but how do you get it back?' The soldier replied, 'I don't know what the others do, but for myself, I use my fork.'"

Patton made caustic remarks privately about his contemporaries, Eisenhower, Bradley, Clark, Bedell Smith, Montgomery. No one, according to Patton, was as good as he. They were all mediocre or tired or clerks or unimaginative or afraid or cautious or just plain old dumb. It was a real compliment when he said of his old friend Courtney Hodges, "He is not so dumb as I thought he was."

Like those who are unsure of their abilities, he needed continual reassurance, recognition, praise. He received less than he expected, less than he needed, less than he thought he deserved. He sought it relentlessly, from Bea especially, and from others.

Jean Gordon returned to the United States in November 1945. Upon Patton's death, a Clubmobile girl telephoned to extend sympathy. Jean was calm. She said she thought it better for Uncle Georgie. "There is no place for him anymore," she said, "and he would have been unhappy with nothing to do." Two weeks later, in her apartment in New York, Jean put her head into her gas oven and committed suicide. According to her friends, she was inconsolable after the young married man whom she loved returned home to his wife. According to family gossip, when two aunts went to identify Jean's body, now resting on her bed, one of them reached into Jean's bodice and fished out a note, which read, "I will be with Uncle Georgie in heaven and have him all to myself before Beatrice arrives."

Whatever Jean meant to Patton, no one could replace Beatrice. She accepted her husband's frailties, put up with his peccadilloes, tirelessly nourished his self-esteem, tried to turn his doubts into certainties, protected and soothed him as she accompanied him in his quest for greatness, which she believed in more than he. Extraordinary in her ability to charm strangers, she devoted herself fiercely to his career. His parents and Aunt Nannie had implanted the seeds of his ambition, but without Beatrice he probably would never have reached his goal.

She was riding with her brother Fred at Green Meadows in 1953 when she toppled from her horse, dead of an aneurysm before she struck the ground. Her body was cremated and the ashes were buried in a rolling meadow on the property. According to rumor, her wish to be with her husband in death was carried out. Some of her ashes were transported to Hamm, it is said, and secretly interred with Patton's remains.

"Leadership," said Patton, "is the thing that wins battles. I have it—but I'll be damned if I can define it. Probably it consists in knowing what you want to do and doing it and getting mad if any one steps in the way. Self-confidence and leadership are twin brothers." The sublime irony is that Patton's self-confidence was an act, forced and assumed, put on, riveted to his exterior. Yet his leadership was real and inspiring, almost palpable. It worked.

The seeming confidence of his actions and the supreme rightness of his decisions emerged, paradoxically, from his own sense of dyslexic inadequacy. Succeeding in his endeavors at terrible cost to himself, Patton sought perfection and was never satisfied with his performance. He was always apprehensive of being found wanting, not quite up to the standards he imposed on himself. He feared that he lacked the traits to reach the goal he dreamed of gaining, and he worked extremely hard to make up for the lack. What made it possible for George Patton to achieve his ardent wish was not only his driving willpower; it was also his great good fortune that his life required the qualities essential to brilliant leadership.

A throwback to the Teutonic knight, the Saracen, the Crusader, George Patton was one of America's greatest soldiers, one of the world's great captains. Some mystery will ever remain around his genius for the art of war, but that too is part of the legend.

SELECTED BIBLIOGRAPHY

Robert S. Allen. *Lucky Forward.* 1964.
Fred Ayer, Jr. *Before the Colors Fade.* 1964.
Martin Blumenson. *The Patton Papers, 1885–1940.* 1972.
——. *The Patton Papers, 1940–1945.* 1974.
Charles R. Codman. *Drive.* 1957.
H. Essame. *Patton: A Study in Command.* 1974.
Ladislas Farago. *Patton: Ordeal and Triumph.* 1963.
——. *The Last Days of Patton.* 1981.
Alden Hatch. *George Patton, General in Spurs.* 1950.
William Bancroft Mellor. *Patton, Fighting Man.* 1946.
George S. Patton, Jr. *War As I Knew It.* 1947.
Jack Pearl. *Blood and Guts Patton.* 1961.
Harry H. Semmes. *Portrait of Patton.* 1955.

NOTE: George C. Scott's role as the general in the film *Patton* is a remarkably accurate portrayal of the public figure.

INDEX